Genocide and the Global Village

Genocide and the Global Village

KENNETH J. CAMPBELL

palgrave

First published 2001 by
PALGRAVE™
175 Fifth Avenue, New York, NY 10010 and
Houndmills, Basingstoke, Hampshire, England RG21 6XS.
Companies and representatives throughout the world.

Palgrave is the new global publishing imprint of St Martin's Press LLC
Scholarly and Reference Division and Palgrave Publishers Ltd (formerly
Macmillan Press Ltd).

ISBN 0-312-21890-7 (cloth)
ISBN 0-312-29325-9 (paper)

Library of Congress Cataloging-in-Publication Data
Campbell, Kenneth J.
Genocide and the global village / Kenneth J. Campbell.
    p.   cm.
    Includes bibliographical references and index.
    ISBN 0-312-21890-7 — ISBN 0-312-29325-9 (pbk.)
    1. Genocide—Government policy.   2. Genocide—Prevention.   3.
International relations.   4. International cooperation.   I. Title.

HV6322.7.C35   2001
304.6′63—dc21

                                        2001021892

A catalogue record for this book is available from the British Library.

Design by Letra Libre.

First Edition: September 2001
10 9 8 7 6 5 4 3 2 1

Printed in the United States of America.

Contents

Preface

I am not a genocide scholar, nor am I an international lawyer, a human rights specialist, an ethnic conflict specialist, or a moral philosopher. However, I do know a bit about the proper use of military force, which is the critical point of breakdown in the international community's response to contemporary genocide. The international community failed, tragically and ignominiously, to use decisive force to prevent or suppress post–Cold War genocide in Bosnia, Rwanda, and Kosovo. This is despite the fact that international leaders possessed timely knowledge of the crimes and more than adequate military capacity to stop them. Explaining this failure is the purpose of this book.

While the use of force problem served as my "point of entry"[1] into this deeply disturbing dilemma, I have tried to learn much about, and integrate knowledge of, international law, human rights, ethnic conflict, complex humanitarian emergencies, ethics and morality, forced migration, and genocide and crimes against humanity. The challenge posed to the international community by contemporary forms of genocide is a complex and difficult one, far more so than even I had anticipated when I first began researching contemporary genocide in early 1996.[2] At times I have gotten myself tied up in conceptual knots trying to solve this academic and policy puzzle. I think I now have it figured out, but the reader must be the final judge of that.

My analysis of the global problem of genocide focuses much on the United States. In my view, this is as it should be. For at this point in world history, the United States is not just any nation; it is far and away the most powerful actor in the international community. Thus, for better or worse, American leadership is crucial to resolving this problem. America, alone, cannot stop every genocide in the world, but genocide will continue to go either unchecked or will finally be stopped after long, painful, and costly delay, unless America plays a leading role in a global effort to prevent genocide.

I have tried to avoid prejudgments about the responsibility for contemporary genocide. Instead, I have attempted to be a fair and honest umpire and to "call them as I see them." But I hope the reader will keep in mind that, despite my very best efforts, I am just as human and liable to imperfection as the subjects I have placed under my analytical lens. I must, however, admit up front to one intractable bias toward the problem of genocide: *I am against it!* This bias tends to make me partial *toward* the victims of genocide and *against* its perpetrators. For this bias in favor of humanity, I make no apologies.

In point of fact, I have a personal motive for taking up this topic. As a young artillery forward observer with a marine "grunt" company in Vietnam in 1968/69, I gained intimate knowledge of war, atrocities, and the reality of quick, random, and ugly death.[3] This traumatic experience drove me to learn more about the legal, moral, and political aspects of the proper—and at times *improper*—uses of military force. My near decade of research (1986–1995) on the U.S. military's lessons of Vietnam— institutionalized in the Weinberger Doctrine—and the American military's application of these lessons throughout the 1980s and 1990s eventually brought me to the problem of genocide.[4] Why was there insufficient international political will to employ decisive military force to stop genocide in Bosnia, Rwanda, and Kosovo? How can the political will be built to suppress future genocide? What will the twenty-first century look like if we fail to halt genocide? My long and often frustrating search for the answers to these critically important questions has finally produced the work the reader is about to begin. I hope the answers I offer are useful.

I have asked for and received much help and encouragement while struggling with this project over the past several years. In particular, I want to thank Helen Fein, Richard Falk, Christopher Joyner, Joel Rosenthal, Morton Winston, Frank Chalk, Samantha Power, Caroline Kennedy-Pipes, Roger Winter, James Smith, James Turner Johnson, Jacques Semelin, Karen Mingst, James Rosenau, Richard Haass, Bernard Hamilton, James Arbuckle, David Cortright, Israel Charney, David Forsythe, and Steven Jacobs.

I also want to express my deep appreciation to the University of Delaware's Office of Vice-Provost for Research for providing me with a General University Research Grant so that I might see this project to fruition. Additionally, I wish to thank my colleagues in the "IR Group" at the Department of Political Science and International Relations at the University of Delaware—James K. Oliver, Robert Denemark, Kurt Burch, and William Meyer—for their scholarly support. I must also thank the University Honors Program for its consistent support of my research agenda. I want to give particular thanks to three of my recent graduate students—Joann Kingsley, Rob DiPrizio, and Eric Leonard—for their most welcome help and valuable insights. I also benefited greatly from my undergraduate research assistants: Violetta Zein, Lirija Luigju-raj-Henry, Erastus Bogonko Mong-are, Christopher Dolotosky, Patrick Finnegan, Gil Avin, Sharon Lee, and Chris Celio. A very warm thanks go to the wonderful students in my senior honors seminar: Genocide and the New World Order, particularly Gil Avin, Jacquie Brandner, Nate Heller, Carlos Pla, Evan Rosen, and Jennifer Gartner. So too to Rachel Gordon, Jason Kroll, and Katie Heck for their thoughtfulness and moral support.

Finally, I want to express my deep love and gratitude to my wife, Cathleen, and my daughter, Meagan, for putting up with me while I struggled long and hard with the dark demons of this problem, as well as with those deep within myself.

Abbreviations

EU	European Union
FAR	Forces Armee Rwandaises
FEWER	Forum on Early Warning and Early Response
G-8	Group of Eight
ICB	International Commission on the Balkans
ICC	International Criminal Court
ICJ	International Court of Justice
ICRC	International Committee of the Red Cross
ICT	International Criminal Tribunals
ICTY	International Criminal Tribunal for the former Yugoslavia
IDP	internally displaced person
IGO	intergovernmental organization
IISS	International Institute for Strategic Studies
IMF	International Monetary Fund
IPEP	International Panel of Eminent Personalities
JNA	Yugoslav People's Army
KLA	Kosovo Liberation Army
MAD	mutually assured destruction
MNC	multinational corporation
MRND(D)	Mouvement Revolutionnaire National pour le Developpement (et la Democratie)
MSF	Medecins Sans Frontiers
NGO	nongovernmental organization
OAU	Organization of African Unity
OSCE	Organization for Security and Cooperation in Europe
RPF	Rwandan Patriotic Front
SANU	Serbian Academy of Science and Art
TMC	Times Mirror Center (for People and Press)
UN	United Nations
UNAMIR	United Nations Assistance Mission for Rwanda
UNHCHR	UN High Commissioner for Human Rights
UNHCR	UN High Commissioner for Refugees
USAID	U.S. Agency for International Development
USCR	U.S. Committee for Refugees
WTO	World Trade Organization

*All of us are capable of great cruelty,
but only some of us choose to engage in it.*

INTRODUCTION

Return of an "Odious Scourge"

The disease of criminality, if left unchecked, is contagious.

—Raphael Lemkin[1]

T he reemergence of genocide has posed the greatest threat to international order during the past decade of post–Cold War
"uncertainty." Between 1992 and 1995, more than two hundred
thousand people were killed by "ethnic cleansing" in Bosnia and several
million more were made refugees. In Rwanda, during the spring of 1994,
approximately eight hundred thousand people were butchered in a "ma-
chete genocide" that lasted just ten short weeks—a rate of killing that
was five times faster than the Nazis' industrial methods during World
War II. Yet, the international community failed to stop this genocide,
and it remains in a quandary today over how to respond to this "odious
scourge" to humanity.

Initial theories tried to explain the cause of this new round of genocide as the product of new "zones of turmoil," "global turbulence,"
"clashes of civilizations," or "coming anarchy," about which international
leaders could do little. However, these pessimistic approaches were not
helpful to policymakers looking for ways to respond to such grave and
unsettling crises.[2] In fact, the "gloom and doom" theories were recipes for
policy paralysis, and political leaders increasingly straining under intense
domestic and international pressure to "do something" could not sustain
a passive strategy toward genocide.[3] A different, more proactive approach
to genocide was required.

Unfortunately, the challenge of contemporary genocide turned out to be a far more complex and difficult problem than most first thought. After years of analyzing the phenomenon of contemporary genocide and struggling with the unfolding cases of this crime, most scholars, analysts, and decisionmakers have yet to devise an effective strategy for stopping genocide. International leaders have made rhetorical commitments to stop future genocide, but there are few signs of concrete preparations for responding robustly, if and when it happens again. Stopping genocide has not been designated a "vital interest," no clear criteria have been developed for distinguishing between genocide and other lesser humanitarian emergencies, and no forces have been designated to "stand by" for a rapid response to a sudden genocidal threat. The sad fact remains that the international community is politically and logistically little more prepared to deal with genocide today than it was in 1992 or 1994 or 1998.

There are some analysts who see significant progress in political leaders' enforcement of international norms that place humanitarian rescue above national sovereignty.[4] However, whatever modest "progress" may have been made, it has come as the result of a *reactive* process of "muddling through"— with great reluctance and at great cost in precious time, lives, resources, and credibility—each time international leaders have been faced with another genocidal crisis. This, of course, does not bode well for the international community's response the next time genocide rears its ugly head.

Other analysts, scholars, and decisionmakers see a promising solution to the challenge of contemporary genocide in improved early warning and prevention systems, or in the establishment of a new legal framework for humanitarian intervention. Others see it in improved methods of peacekeeping, or in the growing power of international criminal law to punish perpetrators and deter would-be *genocidaires*.[5]

While all of these approaches can help at the edges of the problem, the basic riddle remains unresolved: How can the international community successfully stop genocide? For the fact of the matter is that there was plenty of advanced warning of the impending genocides of the 1990s, but the international community still failed to prevent them. A new legal framework for intervening to stop genocide is not necessary since this legal framework has existed for more than fifty years in the form of the Nuremberg Principles and the Genocide Convention. The legal framework notwithstanding, the international community has not been inclined to stop genocide. As Timothy Garton Ash has pointed out:

> The Western liberal societies that care most about stopping gross violations of human rights in other countries also have the most difficulty in willing the means best suited to achieve that end.[6]

UN peacekeeping coordination and support can be improved significantly, but the strategy of peacekeeping is fundamentally alien to the nature of genocide and cannot effectively stop it. Finally, improving judicial punishment of responsible individuals is important in avoiding blaming an entire nation and facilitating reconciliation, but without the credible threat of force to suppress ongoing genocide and to arrest its leading perpetrators, punishment will never be more than partially effective.[7]

A few analysts and scholars have recognized that, despite some recent gains, the problem of genocide remains largely unresolved.[8] However, none so far have come forth with a strategic approach that accurately identifies the fundamental nature of genocide as a core threat to the international system. Nor has anyone yet properly located genocide, and the critical imperative to stop it, within the larger geostrategic context of a rapidly globalizing, post–Cold War period of world-order transition. For it is true that continued *ad hoc* approaches are not sufficiently effective and continued failure to stop genocide is unacceptable. No viable solution can be devised for the terrible problem of genocide without taking such a strategic approach to it.

Michael Howard defines the strategic approach to international relations as "one which takes account of the part which is played by force, or the threat of force, in the international system."[9] Since genocide is a profoundly improper use of force, and stopping genocide requires the quick and decisive use of force, a strategic approach to genocide seems indicated. However, a strategic approach is precisely what has been lacking in the international community's approach to contemporary genocide. Therefore, it is the central task of the present work to fill this important analytical gap in the study of contemporary genocide.

Genocide is, in fact, the *worst* crime under international criminal law, equal to or greater than the crime of aggression. Consequently, the leaders of the international community are bound by solemn legal and moral commitments made a half century ago to prevent, suppress, and punish this "odious scourge" to humanity. However, international leaders in this post–Cold War era have largely failed to do this. The upshot is that humanity has suffered catastrophic losses, the integrity of critical international institutions has been undermined, and the moral leadership of the most powerful nation has been questioned. In point of fact, unchecked genocide has damaged the very fabric of our present liberal international society.

My thesis is that the principal reason for the international community's failure to stop contemporary genocide was U.S. policymakers' misunderstanding of the strategic nature of genocide, and their subsequent failure to treat the prevention of genocide as a vital national interest.

This strategic failure then led U.S. policymakers to misuse military force, employing inappropriate force—or no force at all—to stop genocide. U.S. policymakers also misread domestic public opinion, incorrectly assuming that there was little chance the public would support a decisive use of force to stop genocide.

No member of the international community is immune from at least some responsibility when the entire community fails in its moral and legal duty to stop genocide. Yet, the responsibility cannot be spread evenly. Some states have more power than others, and therefore bear a greater obligation to preserve the fundamental integrity of the international system. This is the international systemic equivalent of the Nuremberg principle of "command responsibility" (see Appendix A). Some states, because of their superior power, benefit more than others do from the stable, peaceful functioning of the international system. Therefore, these states have a greater objective stake in defending the integrity of the international system from grave threats, for it is precisely these states that stand to lose the most if the system collapses in chaos and violence.[10]

One state in particular—the United States—is so powerful in this post–Cold War era that its global leadership responsibilities are disproportionately far greater than any other state's. It is, therefore, to U.S. policy that one must devote especially close scrutiny when trying to understand and explain international failure to stop contemporary genocide. This, of course, does not absolve other, less powerful states from their responsibilities for this ignominious failure; it merely puts the problem into its proper political, legal, and moral context.

A brief word of caution to the reader: We might be wise, when trying to apportion blame for the humiliating failure to stop genocide in the 1990s, to remember that the world has changed much in a very short period of time, and that *no one* accurately predicted that the Cold War would end when it did, the way it did—dismantled from the top, without global nuclear war or bloody internal upheaval. It may, therefore, behoove us to embrace a modicum of modesty when considering the culpability of our political leaders in this great failure. In fact, we might do well to reconsider the words of Roger Hilsman, a foreign policy expert in the Kennedy administration and, hence, no stranger to the pressures and confusion in the corridors of power at times of great crisis:

> When knowledge is inadequate, when problems are complex, and especially when they are also new—presenting a challenge with which there has been no experience—there is in such circumstances room to spare for disagreement, conflict, and turmoil![11]

The theoretical framework for this study is a hybrid of realism, neoliberal institutionalism, and social constructivism. My theoretical approach recognizes the centrality of power and the primacy of the state in this historical period, but it defines power as including the intangible element of morality, it emphasizes the rapidly growing importance of non-state actors, and it accepts the possibility that institutional learning can affect policy and produce civilizational progress.[12] The methodological approach employed is a hybrid of traditional critical and empirical analysis, integrating and weighing the best evidence from the best scholarly and policy literature drawn from disparate specializations in an effort to obtain a comprehensive and accurate understanding of the stated problem. These specializations include international law, international organization, international security, human rights, peacekeeping, humanitarian intervention, military studies, refugees and forced migration, international political economy, area studies (that is, the Balkans and Central Africa), public opinion, U.S. foreign policy, and genocide studies.

The organization of the book is the following: *Chapter 1* lays out the "grand strategic context" of this great crime, that is, the framework of a rapidly globalizing, increasingly interdependent, international system within which this transsovereign threat takes place.[13] *Chapter 2* analyzes the nature of genocide as a complex systemic threat to the viability of the present international order. It posits that the correct identification of genocide's fundamental nature requires that the task of stopping it is designated a vital national interest. *Chapter 3* examines the controversy over the Pentagon's "Weinberger-Powell Doctrine" on the proper use of force and its relevance to the strategic approach to genocide. *Chapter 4* analyzes the "zero-casualty" syndrome allegedly plaguing public opinion regarding distant, bloody, ambiguous interventions, and the syndrome's potential relevance to recent efforts to stop contemporary genocide.

Chapters 5, 6, and *7* examine three cases of contemporary genocide and international failure in the 1990s: Bosnia, Rwanda, and Kosovo. These chapters try to demonstrate with concrete examples how international leaders failed to identify genocide as the principal characteristic of the conflict, how this initial mistake led them to misuse force, and how they were eventually pressured into addressing genocide—though very late and at much greater cost—by the same domestic public they had initially dismissed as unwilling to do so. *Chapter 8* proposes a strategic remedy for stopping genocide that focuses specifically upon the need to employ the expertise of genocide scholars in the education of political leaders, the construction of a viable international antigenocide regime, and consolidation of a global normative consensus for the prevention of genocide.

The arguments and proposals that follow are far from perfect; they will undoubtedly require further research and continued revision. However, I believe these arguments represent significant improvement on existing scholarly analyses, which have tended to miss the strategic dimension of genocide or at best treat it superficially.[14] For this reason, and because unchecked genocide puts *all* of humanity at great risk, I believe this analysis warrants serious consideration by the reader.

CHAPTER I

The Grand Strategic Context

No political society, national or international, can exist unless people submit to certain rules of conduct.

—E. H. Carr[1]

In an ever more interdependent world the need for control mechanisms outstrips the capacity or readiness of national governments to provide them . . . not only have states lost some of their earlier dominance of the governance system, but also the lessening of their ability to evoke compliance and govern effectively is in part due to the growing relevance and potential of control mechanisms sustained by transnational and subnational systems of rule.

—James Rosenau[2]

The paradox and novelty of the globalization of violence today is that national security has become a multilateral affair. . . . [It] can now be protected only if nation-states come together and pool resources, technology, intelligence, and sovereignty.

—David Held, et al.[3]

In today's increasingly interdependent world, the process of globalization—open societies, open technologies, and open markets—is producing effects that are both good and bad; globalization is giving us both progress and problems.[4] Globalization itself is not new. As a historical process, it has been occurring for a long time. However, in this age of information technology, globalization is proceeding at an unprecedented speed, which is in turn changing the very nature of world politics by increasing the vulnerability of states and peoples to distant threats.[5]

Although we enjoy many positive effects of globalization, its negative effects have outstripped the ability of sovereign states and intergovernmental organizations (IGOs), such as the United Nations, to manage them adequately. These transnational (or "transsovereign") threats spill over from one global function to another—economic, military, social, environmental, and the like—increasing in speed and intensity.[6] Consequently, a fundamental contradiction has emerged between the growth of transnational problems and the decline of sovereign state power in managing these problems. This has created a global "governance gap" regarding transnational threats.[7] As Raimo Vayrynen explains:

> There is in the present international society an enforcement gap that needs to be filled if global governance is to be effective at all. Norms of security, democracy, and human rights cannot be upheld in the absence of international institutions and other capabilities by which to address the problem of compliance. The United Nations obviously has done better than many of its critics acknowledge in coping with security and monetary relations and international public "bads." Yet, the United Nations as an institution is only a partial answer to the contemporary challenge of global governance.[8]

GLOBAL GOVERNANCE

Global governance is a political process intended to address the gap created by globalization between the proliferation of transsovereign threats and the relative decline of state power. As Karen Mingst explains:

> The first (troublesome dilemma) is the increasing demand for policy to address global problems versus the recognized weakness of contemporary international organizations and states. . . . Adherents of global governance generally acknowledge that the need for governance emerges out of the globalization process.[9]

Global governance is defined here as a complex process of global cooperative management intended to maximize the advantages of globalization and minimize its threats, especially threats to the fundamental integrity of the global system.[10] Global governance is based upon shared values, principles, rules, and institutions. It includes states, IGOs, nongovernmental organizations (NGOs), multinational corporations (MNCs), communities of scientific experts ("epistemic communities"), the global mass media, and prominent individuals. It is a relatively new development, which seeks to go beyond reliance upon state-dominated international regimes, which are proving increasingly inadequate, and build a complex, dense web of international networks to govern an emerging global civil society.[11] Global governance is but the latest chapter in the development of international organization and, if mismanaged, may permit or produce global catastrophe, as the failure of earlier international organizational schemes has done.[12]

HISTORICAL CYCLES OF LEARNING-BY-CATASTROPHE

For the Westphalian system of nation-states, innovation in the maintenance of international order has always come in the wake of catastrophic war. In every case, the collapse of the prevailing international order brought on general war so devastating to all parties that even the "winners" suffered catastrophic losses. After each of these general wars, the victorious nation-states attempted to construct a new international order that improved their chances of preventing a repetition of catastrophic war while continuing to maintain an essentially decentralized system of independent states. It was a fine line to walk.

The catastrophe of the Thirty Years' War produced the Westphalian classical European balance-of-power system, resting on the Adam Smith-like assumption that competing national interests would somehow produce a natural balance that would ensure peace and stability. The collapse of this classical balance-of-power system brought the catastrophe of the Napoleonic Wars, which was then followed by the Concert of Europe. The collapse of the Concert of Europe triggered the catastrophe of World War I and produced the League of Nations. The failure of the League brought the catastrophe of World War II and produced the United Nations. In each new cycle of breakdown, catastrophic war, and new international order, institutional learning driven by trauma produced innovations in international organization that were intended to avoid a repeat of the previous catastrophe. However, once implemented, these innovations in international organization were eventually outstripped by accelerating change. The result was a "governance gap" that permitted the emergence of new challengers, eventual systemic breakdown, and greater catastrophe.

In the seventeenth and eighteenth centuries, it was the classical, laissez-faire balance-of-power system that eventually proved inadequate and permitted the rise of Napoleon. In the nineteenth century it was an *ad hoc* system of conferences and conventions that eventually proved inadequate and permitted the outbreak of the Great War. In the twentieth century "interwar" period, it was a halfhearted collective security system that quickly proved inadequate, thus permitting the outbreak of World War II. During the Cold War, it was a more sophisticated collective security system that attempted to prevent World War III. As Inis Claude has explained:

> The collapse of world order [in 1939] produced not so much a sense of futility and hopelessness of international organization as a vivid awareness of the need for a resolute determination to achieve an improved system of international organization. It became clear that the modern world had developed the habit of responding to catastrophe by intensifying its quest for effective organization.[13]

However, the United Nations' collective security system quickly proved inadequate. Its efforts to preserve peace and security were frozen by a fifty-year Cold War between the two superpowers, the United States and the Soviet Union.

The post–World War II international system was not in reality the collective security system envisioned by the founders of the United Nations, but a bipolar, nuclear "balance-of-terror" system. Both East and West blocs in the ideologically divided international system formally subscribed to the basic principles of the Westphalian state system: national sovereignty, territorial integrity, legal equality, and political independence. Both endorsed the Nuremberg criminalization of aggression and genocide. However, each subscribed to a radically different political and socioeconomic vision of world order that they promulgated within their own bloc. Given the nuclear arms race and the development of the doctrine of mutual assured destruction (MAD), neither dared commit blatant aggression against the other's bloc, and both presented a credible deterrent against intrabloc aggression or genocide. The one quasi exception was the *politicide*—not technically genocide because the victims constituted a political and socioeconomic class—in Cambodia in the mid-1970s. This was a contested area between three global powers playing a game of triangular diplomacy, where the U.S. was exhausted (from the Vietnam debacle), the Chinese supported the Khmer Rouge killers, and the Soviets supported the Vietnamese invaders who suppressed this great crime. This Cold War paralysis of the UN collective security system ended with the collapse of the Soviet bloc in the 1989–1991 period.

THE UNICYCLE MOMENT

The Cold War came to a sudden end a decade ago and the current post–Cold War era seems to have many decisionmakers, policy analysts, and scholars confused and uncertain. However, in this period of great turbulence and complexity, we should be clear about one large, simple, but critically important fact: this transition era is completely *unique* in the historical cycles of rising and falling international orders. In two critical respects this is so: first, this transition is occurring (so far) *without* the general catastrophe typically associated with such periods.[14] Second, in no previous transition era did the prevailing powers charged with creating an improved international order possess the scientific and technical capacity—as the leading powers now do—to destroy the entire international system along with everyone in it. This is the first time in the cyclical creation of new international orders that the great powers possess the power to end the "great game" for all players, for all time! In no previous transition period from one international order to another has this been the case. In this sense, the present cycle is truly singular.

These two critical peculiarities should give pause to the architects of our new emerging global order. For the above factors seem to indicate that our leaders maximize their efforts to break with this cycle of "learning-by-catastrophe" and make a leap in institutional learning *without* waiting for a breakdown of the international order and a systemic catastrophe from which none of us might recover. The unique characteristics of this critical transition period seem to place a premium on state cooperation at least regarding those core problems which, if not managed or mitigated, threaten to unravel the entire international order. The main task in this period of transition, in the midst of globalization, is to consolidate, reinforce, and extend the present, post—Cold War liberal international order.[15] At the heart of this effort at global governance must be the prevention of genocide and crimes against humanity.[16]

CONTEMPORARY GENOCIDE
AS A TRANSSOVEREIGN THREAT

Genocide is a transsovereign problem facing the international community. Indeed, it is the worst problem. Although the practice of genocide is not new, the contemporary process of globalization has rendered it a transnational threat that outstrips the ability of states, and state-based international governmental organizations, to prevent, suppress, or punish this crime.[17] The harm that genocide causes cannot remain within sovereign boundaries, nor can this grave human rights problem keep from spilling over into regional functions such as traditional security, political stability, and economic prosperity. The impact of genocide is global and multidimensional, dense and complex. Hence, in an era of rapid globalization, state foreign policies based upon narrowly defined "national" interests are conceptually obsolete and structurally inadequate to the task of stopping the transsovereign threat of genocide.

The unprecedented violence of the twentieth century has produced three great global prohibitions: first, the prohibition of aggression; second, the prohibition of genocide; and third, the prohibition of nuclear war. If not enforced, they threaten to bring the entire international system crashing down around us all. The international community has been largely successful in prohibiting aggression and nuclear war over the last half-decade, but it has been very unsuccessful in prohibiting genocide during the post–Cold War era. Unless this failure is remedied, unchecked genocide could destroy the very fabric that holds together our present international system.

GREAT POWER RESPONSIBILITIES

No international order can long exist without the most powerful state within that order defending and preserving it. In fact, every international order that has existed since the emergence of the Westphalian state system in 1648 has been the product largely of one leading state, whether it was France during the seventeenth and early eighteenth centuries, Britain during the late eighteenth and nineteenth centuries, or America during the twentieth and early twenty-first centuries. The international order promulgated by the leading state is an extension of the national values, power, and interests of that state. Consequently, a condition of strategic interdependence naturally develops between the leading state and the larger international order it has constructed. As Inis Claude has explained:

> The idea of international responsibility is generally associated, primarily if not exclusively, with great powers. Indeed, it might be argued that a great power or a world power is by definition a state that has interests and responsibilities beyond both its own boundaries and its immediate neighborhood. . . . Great powers are singled out, because it is presumed that their capability, unlike that of lesser states, is not likely to be exhausted by the requirements of national interest; they are expected to have a surplus of resources that can be devoted to the needs of the system at large. . . . [W]e take it as axiomatic that great powers are fundamentally responsible for the international system as a whole. . . . It is their task to protect the weak and to feed the poor. The prospects of political freedom, human rights, and social justice—indeed, the future of human civilization—depend largely upon what they do and refrain from doing.[18]

The critical implications of this strategic reality are that the leading state must assume the structural obligation to defend and extend the prevailing international order, and it must redefine its own national interests to include the core interests of the international system. If the leading state fails to do this—if it fails to *lead*—then it invites relative or absolute decline and the disintegration and collapse of the prevailing international order from which it has benefited disproportionately. This is the situation we face at the cusp of a new millennium.

In the early twenty-first century, the United States is far and away the most powerful state in the international system. In a recent article in *Foreign Affairs*, W. Bowman Cutter, Joan Spero, and Laura Tyson wrote: "As a power of unrivaled dominance, prosperity, and security, [the U.S.] must now lead the peaceful evolution of this system through an era of significant changes."[19] Evidence of U.S. globalism is ubiquitous. For instance, 30 percent of the growth experienced by the United States over the last six years came from expanding global markets, while Americans represent 40 percent of all international travelers.[20]

How important, though, is it for the U.S. to contribute its own military power to stop genocide in a distant foreign land? In point of fact, it is *critically* important! The United States is the "indispensable nation" in any significant global military intervention. As Brown and Rosecrance explain.

> The United States is particularly key: it alone has the firepower, transport, command and control, communications, intelligence, logistics, and power projection capabilities needed for large-scale operations.[21]

What, then, should a wise global leader have done when faced with contemporary genocide? First, wise leadership should have accurately and publicly *framed* the issue as genocide, citing the overwhelming evidence gathered by the competent UN organs. Second, the global leader should have pressed the UN Security Council to determine genocide to be a *core threat* to the peace and security of the international system and therefore absolutely *vital* to halt! Third, the global leader should have urged the Security Council to define *clear objectives* for UN forces, such as defeating the perpetrators, rescuing the victims, and detaining the leaders of this great crime for possible trial and punishment. Fourth, the global leader should have urged that UN forces be properly sized and mandated for *war-fighting*, not peacekeeping, with ground troops given primacy in a robust "AirLand" campaign against the *genocidaires*. Fifth, the global leader should have rallied *domestic political support* for the risks and potential sacrifices—in blood and treasure—inherent in such a decisive use of force. Finally, the global leader should have urged the Security Council to issue a *diplomatic warning* to the perpetrators of genocide to cease immediately their criminal actions or face the application of overwhelming force. *Simultaneously*, they should have been preparing those military forces for use "with all deliberate speed," thereby reinforcing the credibility of the diplomatic warning.

When actually faced with the horror of contemporary genocide, however, the global system's predominant power—the United States—not only failed to provide enlightened leadership, it actively *blocked* others from doing so! In all three cases of contemporary genocide—Bosnia, Rwanda, and Kosovo—the United States refused to consider using its own ground troops to prevent or suppress ongoing genocide, and prevented others in NATO and the UN from doing so. This inaction and obstruction regarding the suppression of contemporary genocide—a core threat to the viability of the international system—was the greatest failure of international leadership since Munich, 1938.

CHAPTER 2

Misunderstanding Genocide

The first, the supreme, the most far-reaching act of judgment that the statesman and commander have to make is to establish . . . the kind of war on which they are embarking; neither mistaking it for, nor trying to turn it into, something that is alien to its nature. This is the first of all strategic questions and the most comprehensive.

—Carl von Clausewitz[1]

De quoi s'agit-il? (What is it all about?)

—Marshall Ferdinand Foch[2]

Regardless of where or on how small a scale it begins, the crime of genocide is the complete ideological repudiation of, and a direct murderous assault upon, the prevailing liberal international order. Genocide is fundamentally incompatible with, and destructive of, an open, tolerant, democratic, free market international order. As genocide scholar Herbert Hirsch has explained:

> The unwillingness of the world community to take action to end genocide and political massacres is not only immoral but also impractical . . . [W]ithout some semblance of stability, commerce, travel, and the international and intranational interchange of goods and information are subjected to severe disruptions.[3]

Where genocide is permitted to proliferate, the liberal international order cannot long survive. No group will be safe; every group will wonder when they will be next. Left unchecked, genocide threatens to destroy whatever security, democracy, and prosperity exists in the present international system. As Roger Smith notes:

> Even the most powerful nations—those armed with nuclear weapons—may end up in struggles that will lead (accidentally, intentionally, insanely) to the ultimate genocide in which they destroy not only each other, but mankind itself, sewing the fate of the earth forever with a final genocidal effort.[4]

In this sense, genocide is a grave threat to the very fabric of the international system and must be stopped, even at some risk to lives and treasure.

The preservation and growth of the present liberal international order is a *vital* interest for all of its members—states as well as non-states—whether or not those members recognize and accept the reality of that objective interest.[5] Nation-states, as the principal members of the present international order, are the only authoritative holders of violent enforcement powers. Non-state actors, though increasing in power relative to states, still do not possess the military force, or the democratic authority, to use military force, which is necessary to stop determined perpetrators of mass murder. Consequently, nation-states have a special responsibility to prevent, suppress, and punish all malicious assaults on the fundamental integrity of the prevailing international order.

The most powerful nation-state in the international system, as possessor of the greatest capabilities and the chief beneficiary of the system's privileges, also bears the *primary* responsibility for defending the integrity of the international system against criminal threats to destroy it. For the leading nation-state, this obligation is both a vital *national* and *international* interest that demands the use of decisive military force. If the leading nation-state either fails to recognize the true nature of this threat, or recognizing the threat, shies away from using decisive force to defeat this threat, then the leading nation-state jeopardizes the fundamental integrity of the liberal international order, as well as its own privileged position within that order. This is the essence of the crisis now facing the international community regarding the grave challenge of contemporary genocide.

HISTORICAL BACKGROUND

Genocide long predates the Holocaust of the twentieth century. Though Raphael Lemkin did not coin the term "genocide" until 1944,[6] the destruction of a people because of their identity occurred with some fre-

quency in premodern history.[7] Ancient, medieval, and early modern societies developed rules and customs limiting the use of force against ad-
versaries from within one's own civilization, but the wholesale slaughter
of "heathens" from "barbarian" lands was accepted as "moral" and "just."[8]
By the twentieth century, however, the international system was becoming truly global and interdependent, and the concept of "civilization" was
increasingly being applied to all humanity. Yet, a few retrograde states
continued to embrace mass extermination as an acceptable method of
destroying a people they considered less than human.

Early in the twentieth century, the Turks attempted, in an organized
and systematic way, to destroy the Armenians in eastern Anatolia. Turkish forces, beginning in April 1915, exterminated approximately one million Turkish Armenians, a Christian minority in a Muslim country. Some
were executed, while many others were deported to the deserts of Syria
and Mesopotamia, where they died of starvation or exposure.[9]

The German Nazis' destruction of the European Jews, Gypsies, and
other "undesirables," however, was unprecedented in human history in
both its scope and intensity. The Nazi genocide was an extreme process,
consisting of the premeditated, organized, systematic annihilation of an
unarmed, defenseless people by a state determined to defy conventional
norms of morality and civilization. It was a deeply pernicious process designed to destroy the political, economic, social, cultural, religious, and
moral institutions of the Jewish people as a whole, as well as to destroy
the liberty, security, health, dignity, and the very life of individual Jews.[10]

The destruction of the Jews was in fact a *central war aim* of the Nazis,
one that they continued to pursue even when it was clear to their leaders
that the war against the Allies had been lost. For the Nazis, achieving the
elimination from Europe of all Jews was a victory in itself. Thus, Raphael
Lemkin argued:

> Because the imposition of this policy of genocide is more destructive for a
> people than injuries suffered in actual fighting, the German people will be
> stronger than the subjected peoples after the war even if the German army
> is defeated. In this respect genocide is a new technique of occupation
> aimed at winning the peace even though the war itself is lost.[11]

The stages in this destruction process were: *definition* of the targeted
people as subhuman, *expropriation* of their possessions, *concentration* into a
ghetto, *deportation* from the ghetto, and finally *annihilation* in death camps.
At first, the annihilation stage was carried out via mobile killing units
sent east behind advancing German troops. But the imperatives of speed
and efficiency soon led the Germans to construct killing centers, the

most infamous being the Auschwitz-Birkenau complex in Poland.[12] In the end, upwards of six million Jews were murdered, as well as two million Gypsies (Roma and Sinti) and others identified as "undesirables" by the Nazis.[13]

As the Allies received more and more credible intelligence about the Nazis' mass-murder operations, they considered taking action to stop or at least interdict and disrupt the extermination process. However, in the end, the Allies decided to limit their actions to public condemnations and dire warnings about the justice awaiting the perpetrators of such criminal deeds.[14]

When the death camps were discovered and the enormity of the horror became apparent, the world was shocked and revolted. Upon liberating the Nazi concentration camp at Ohrdruf, General Eisenhower, supreme allied commander in Europe, ordered all available U.S. military units to walk through the death camp. Eisenhower wanted American troops to see for themselves the Nazi barbarity and thereby understand the full importance of their war effort, which is the moral imperative for defeating the Nazis.[15]

Immediately following the end of World War II, the victorious Allies established the United Nations as a universal IGO, embracing collective security as a way of preventing another catastrophic world war. According to the charter of the United Nations, the chief threat to international peace and security was aggression. Aggression against any one state was to be viewed as aggression against all states. In this way the sovereign rights of states were to be protected. But the United Nations also viewed genocide as a core threat to the integrity of the international system. In reaction to the undeniable evidence of Nazi aggression, war crimes, and genocide, world leaders pledged that justice and the rule of law would prevail in the coming era. As President Harry Truman wrote at the time:

> One of the most important long-range achievements of the General Assembly's First Session was the adoption of resolutions introduced by the United States on the codification and development of international law.
>
> The General Assembly unanimously directed its committee on codification to give first attention to the charter and the decision of the Nuremberg Tribunal, under which aggressive war is a crime against humanity for which individuals as well as states must be punished. The Assembly also agreed that genocide—the deliberate policy of extermination of a race or class or any other human group—was a crime under international law. These developments toward the application of international law to individuals as well as to states are of profound significance to the states. We cannot have lasting peace unless a genuine rule of world law is established and enforced.[16]

The Allies paid particular attention to atrocities committed by the Nazis against noncombatants, especially their so-called "final solution." Consequently, the Allies decided to punish crimes against humanity, as well as war crimes and aggression, at the Nuremberg Trial of 1946.[17] In his opening address to the International Military Tribunal at Nuremberg, U.S. chief prosecutor, Justice Robert H. Jackson, spoke to the higher aims of the Allied Powers in trying the Nazi leaders:

> Civilization can afford no compromise with the social forces which would gain renewed strength if we deal ambiguously or indecisively with the men in whom those forces now precariously survive.[18]

The venerable Colonel Henry Stimson, in an article on the Nuremberg Trial in *Foreign Affairs*, wrote:

> The defendants at Nuremberg were leaders of the most highly organized and extensive wickedness in history. . . . A standard has been raised to which Americans, at least, must repair: for it is only as this standard is accepted, supported and enforced that we can move onward to a world of law and peace.[19]

Though the UN Charter did not explicitly provide for an enforcement process for the prohibition of genocide, on 11 December 1946 the UN General Assembly declared genocide to be a crime punishable under international law (see Appendix B). The General Assembly then referred the matter to the Economic and Social Council (ECOSOC) with the charge of drawing up a draft convention. Working with the secretary general's office and "experts in the fields of international and criminal law," the council set up an *ad hoc* committee to draw up a draft convention. With the input of member states, as well as the Commission on Human Rights, the council submitted this draft in August 1948. On 9 December 1948, the General Assembly unanimously approved the text of the Convention on the Prevention and Punishment of the Crime of Genocide (see Appendix C).[20] This universal prohibition against genocide was intended to institutionalize the lessons of the Holocaust, and to serve as a central moral and legal pillar in the foundation of a post-1945 world order.[21]

U.S. PRIMACY

The United States emerged from World War II as the most powerful nation-state in the international system. The U.S. became the driving force behind the creation of the United Nations and accepted a special responsibility to guarantee the peace and security of the post–World War II order by preventing future aggression and genocide. However, while world leaders (and international relations scholars) gave the task of halting aggression the highest priority, genocide was all but ignored.[22] As William Schabas, has explained:

> The law and politics of genocide stagnated for several decades following the adoption of the convention in 1948. The thinking and writing about its scope since 1948 have been meager and sometimes superficial, with a few notable exceptions. When the horrors of ethnic conflict became the scourge of the last decade, the convention was, so to speak, hauled off the shelf and dusted off.[23]

Nevertheless, the American public absorbed the lessons of World War II: that both aggression *and* genocide (initially subsumed under "crimes against humanity") must be prohibited! Historian Bradley F. Smith explained the great impact of the Nuremberg Trial on the public:

> What the trial did . . . was to implant certain concepts, including aggressive war and crimes against humanity, into the public mind with such force that they became integral elements in the thinking of late twentieth century man.[24]

COLD WAR PARALYSIS

During the Cold War, the UN Security Council was ideologically prevented from enforcing the prohibitions against aggression and genocide (even if political leaders had continued to give attention to genocide). With each side in the East-West conflict possessing a veto in the Security Council, this collective security enforcement mechanism was effectively paralyzed. During this bipolar, nuclear "balance of terror," a number of genocide-like crimes against humanity were perpetrated with impunity, for example, in East Pakistan (1971), in Cambodia (1975–1978), and in Uganda (1979).[25]

With the end of the Cold War, the international community faced for the first time the real possibility of legitimately and effectively stopping aggression and genocide. An opportunity to address blatant aggression presented itself in August 1990, when Iraqi military forces invaded, conquered, and absorbed the sovereign and independent nation-state of Kuwait. Over the next eight months, the United States, with the unprecedented authorization of the UN Security Council, led an international coalition of military forces in the defeat of the Iraqi military, the liberation of Kuwait, and the restoration of its status as a sovereign state.[26]

Opportunities to stop genocide presented themselves in Bosnia between 1992 and 1995, in Rwanda in the spring of 1994, and in Kosovo in 1998/99. However, the international community failed to prevent, suppress, or punish, adequately, these crimes, which threatened the very fabric of an emerging global society.

DEFINITION

There seems to be more than a little confusion in the scholarly community about the proper definition of genocide. Some scholars use a very broad definition of the crime, including economic, political, social, and/or environmental groups.[27] Others insist on using a narrower definition. However, regardless of how many varying and conflicting academic opinions there may be on the "best" definition of genocide, there is only one universally accepted *legal* definition of genocide upon which effective international prevention, suppression, and punishment can be authoritatively based. We find that definition in Article II of the UN's Convention on the Prevention and Punishment of the Crime of Genocide:

> In the present Convention, genocide means any of the following acts committed with intent to destroy, in whole or in part, a national, ethnical, racial or religious group, as such:
>   a. Killing members of the group;
>   b. Causing serious bodily or mental harm to members of the group;
>   c. Deliberately inflicting on the group conditions of life calculated to bring about its physical destruction in whole or in part;
>   d. Imposing measures intended to prevent births within the group;
>   f. Forcibly transferring children of the group to another group.[28]

During the UN debates preceding the adoption of the Genocide Convention, some nations proposed that political and economic groups be included in the legal definition of genocide. However, the Soviet Union, fearing its leaders might some day become the targets of criminal prosecution for their liquidation of the kulaks (large landowners) and other "nonproletarian" elements, blocked these proposals. The above legal definition is therefore the product of political compromise, as well as justice and morality.[29]

Besides being the only legally acceptable definition of genocide, the definition found in the Convention is the only *practical, workable* definition of genocide, if the international community is ever to have any hope of cooperating in halting genocide. International law offers the one authoritative source for legitimate collective action, as it represents the highest level of political unity among nation-states on a difficult issue at this time in world history. The task of motivating nation-states to enforce the present legal definition of genocide has proven politically difficult in recent years. Hence, any attempt at broadening the definition, without first demonstrating a willingness to enforce the present definition, would make multilateral action to stop genocide *less* likely rather than more.

The political reality is that the international community is not prepared at this time to reopen the debate and amend the Genocide Convention by broadening the current definition of genocide. The chances of persuading leaders of the international community to enforce the present narrow legal definition of genocide are significantly greater, in my estimation, than are the chances of broadening *and then enforcing* the legal definition of genocide. As Professor William Schabas explains:

> The [legal] definition has stood the test of time, despite arguments that it omits political and social groups, and fails to contemplate persecution based on gender. At least on an international level, the 1948 convention's definition has become a kind of international law boilerplate, appearing in the statutes of the ad hoc tribunals for the former Yugoslavia and for Rwanda, and in the recently adopted text of the International Criminal Court.[30]

Can the crime truly be genocide if the goal is not the *total* destruction of the group, but its *partial* destruction, that is, killing, beating, and raping some, and deporting the rest? Again, we must refer to the wording of the Genocide Convention. The language of the Convention is quite clear on this point: "intent to destroy, in whole or in part." The intention of the perpetrators does not have to be the *total* extermination of the group for the crime to qualify as genocide. The *partial* destruction of a group is genocide as well, even if the number killed is relatively small. As William Schabas explains:

> The actual quantity killed or injured remains a relevant material fact, but what is really germane to the debate is whether the author of the crime *intended* to destroy the group "in whole or in part."[31]

The international community does not have to sit around and wait for the number of victims to reach a certain threshold before it determines that genocide has occurred. The answer, instead, lies in recognizing a *process.* If the crime being committed involves the beating, raping, robbing, abusing, deporting, and killing of a people because of their national, ethnic, racial, or religious identification, with the intention of destroying the group in whole or in part, it is genocide, regardless of the number of victims. Therefore, when the Nazis perpetrated their "final solution," it was genocide at six million, at six hundred thousand, at sixty thousand, and at the first six thousand, for it was the intentional *process* that made it genocide, not finally reaching some arbitrary number.

According to Helen Fein, executive director of the Institute for the Study of Genocide and founder of the Association of Genocide Scholars, perpetrators of genocide are repeat offenders. If not confronted by credible counterforce, they will continue to commit genocide, again and again.[32] Therefore, if the international community allows genocide to go unchecked in one place (as in, Bosnia), we should not be surprised if the same perpetrators repeat it somewhere else (as in, Kosovo).

How does one objectively and authoritatively determine that genocide has occurred? Genocide is a bit of an orphan in contemporary international law. No subfield of international law seems willing to admit principal responsibility for monitoring compliance with the Genocide Convention. At first glance, one might assume genocide falls under the laws of war, or what in modern parlance is called *international humanitarian law.* However, because genocide is not a war crime, the International Committee of the Red Cross (ICRC), the world's official guardian of international humanitarian law, does not consider the genocide to be part of its normal area of responsibility. If, for instance, one were to click onto the ICRC's web page and view its list of treaties, from 1864 to 1997, that make up international humanitarian law, one would find no sign of the Genocide Convention.[33]

So is genocide part of *human rights law?* Technically it is, but the Office of the UN High Commissioner for Human Rights (UNHCHR), which has created permanent treaty bodies (special commissions, special rapporteurs, and the like.) for all its human rights treaties, has not created any treaty body—temporary or permanent—to monitor compliance with the Genocide Convention. Instead, the UNHCHR leaves monitoring and reporting of violations of the Genocide Convention to an *ad hoc* process of reporting by international nongovernmental organizations (NGOs) in the fields of human rights, humanitarian assistance, refugees, and development.[34]

Perhaps, since it is an international crime, genocide should fit more comfortably under *international criminal law.* However, international criminal law seems to be more comfortable dealing with crimes committed by nonstate actors that police forces, not military forces, need international coordination to suppress, such as drug trafficking, hijacking, organized crime, piracy, and terrorism. Genocide, a crime committed by leaders of nation-states, is simply too overwhelming for the present international criminal justice system to do much about without significant military assistance from the UN Security Council, something for which the permanent members on the Security Council have shown little stomach.[35]

Where does the primary responsibility for compliance with the Genocide Convention rest? What legally authoritative, permanent, international body is chiefly responsible for monitoring compliance with the Genocide Convention, and petitioning the international community to respond rapidly, collectively, and forcefully to cases of genocide? The answer is *none!* According to Markus Schmidt, legal expert for the Office of the UNHCHR, "There is no authoritative international body which would monitor, on an early warning basis, developments that might lead to genocidal acts."[36]

How did the international community determine that genocide occurred in Bosnia and Rwanda? How might the UN still determine that genocide was indeed perpetrated in Kosovo? In point of fact, the entire international response to genocide in the 1990s has been an *ad hoc,* seat-of-the-pants affair, a sort of embryonic *global governance* regime. The scattered, uncoordinated, often unofficial reports from field-workers with NGOs, the UN High Commissioner for Refugees (UNHCR), and the UNHCHR regarding genocide in Bosnia and Rwanda eventually persuaded the UN secretary-general to approach the Security Council for emergency help. After debating the issue and the preliminary evidence of genocide, the Security Council created special Commissions of Experts to investigate and report back to the secretary general. After the secretary general appointed international experts in law, criminal justice, and forensic evidence and supported them with military engineers (for exhumation of mass graves), these commissions traveled to the areas in question, conducted their investigations, and submitted their reports. Upon receiving the reports from these commissions indicating that, in their view, there was ample evidence, based on the legal definition of genocide, to conclude that this heinous crime had been perpetrated, the secretary-general petitioned the Security Council for a response. The Security Council then responded to these preliminary determinations of genocide by condemning the crime and setting up *ad hoc* International Criminal Tribunals (ICT) to indict, and if they are ever apprehended, try, convict, and punish individual perpetrators of genocide. Once set up and running, the Office of the Prosecution for the International Criminal Tribunals issued indictments of individuals for committing the crime of genocide.[37]

This process, unfortunately, took far too much time in a genocidal situation where speed and decisiveness were essential; this "wheel" had to be "reinvented" for each new case of genocide. Roger Winter, executive director of the U.S. Committee for Refugees (USCR), spoke to this problem:

[W]hat the international community can and must do is to put into place processes to prevent and suppress genocide, which can be activated immediately. When genocide is in motion, time is your enemy. These mechanisms must be decided on now, so they are available the next time there's another Rwanda on the horizon. We need to establish trip wires and benchmarks to abort the lengthy deliberation process and allow the world community to respond quickly. We need the ability to make decisions quickly, so that these mechanisms can be brought on line as soon as we need them. We need to be able to take steps against a government engaged in genocide—whether it's quick arrest of leaders of genocide, sanctions, use of military force or somewhere in between.[38]

THE WORST CRIME

There is no doubt that this is . . . the greatest and most horrible single crime ever committed in the whole history of the world.
—Winston S. Churchill (1944)[39]

Genocide is the supreme crime! It is arguably the worst crime that can be committed in the present global system of nation-states and peoples. Genocide is equal to or worse than the crime of aggression.[40] Genocide attacks civilization itself. Contemporary civilization is based upon certain fundamental shared moral values, one of which is the principle that groups of people have the right to exist as a distinct nationality, race, ethnicity, and religion. The International Court of Justice (ICJ) spoke to this point in an Advisory Opinion on the Genocide Convention in 1951:

The Convention was manifestly adopted for a purely humanitarian and civilizing purpose . . . its object on the one hand is to safeguard the very existence of certain human groups and on the other to confirm and endorse the most elementary principles of morality.

In such a convention the contracting states do not have any interests of their own; they merely have, one and all, a common interest, namely, the accomplishment of those high purposes.[41]

If left unchecked, genocide eats away like a cancer at the structure of global society, eventually undermining and destroying just those international institutions designed to foster global cooperation, mitigate global conflict, and avoid global catastrophe such as the world experienced in the 1930s and 1940s.

Most scholars, political analysts, and policymakers, unfortunately, treat genocide as a mere humanitarian concern, having little to do with the traditional interests of nation-states. They too often fail to see genocide as a threat to *strategic global* interests, such as political stability, economic prosperity, peace, and security. Genocide, in fact, occupies *a unique area of overlap* between humanitarian concerns and more traditional state interests to the degree that international peace and security are indivisible in a world of rapidly increasing globalization. For globalization not only speeds up the positive effects of open markets, open technologies, and open societies, it increases the spread of pathological behavior such as genocide.[42]

A CORE THREAT

Contemporary genocide is a core systemic threat that increasingly challenges the ability of states, and IGOs such as the United Nations, to prevent, suppress, and punish this crime properly. While states and IGOs face greater difficulties in trying to address these transnational problems with state-based resources, the process of globalization has increased the ability of domestic publics and non-state actors around the world to learn of these problems in "real time," and increased their democratic access to both states and IGOs to demand that "something" be done! In the words of James Rosenau:

> It is not a long step from being aghast over scenes in Oklahoma City, Rwanda, Bosnia, and many other remote places pervaded by disaster, to a sense of vulnerability as a human, a feeling that the well-being—perhaps even the fate—of the species is at stake and that some kind of action has to be taken.[43]

Genocide is a first-order threat to today's embryonic "global village" because it attacks multiple functional levels of global society—social, political, military, economic, cultural, legal, and moral—on an increasingly blurred interactional scope—state, regional, and global. Genocide causes social fragmentation, political destabilization, military conflict, economic disruption, cultural destruction, general lawlessness, and moral collapse. As Tony Judt, director of the Remarque Institute at New York University, has argued, genocide is not only immoral, it is "deeply disruptive of international relations, and thus a threat to everyone's interests, however selfishly conceived."[44]

Left unchecked, this systemic pernicious behavior will intensify, accelerate, and proliferate from the local to the state to the regional and eventually to the global level of human relations. Permitted to proliferate, genocide will soon threaten the unity and integrity of essential regional and international institutions: the UN, the North Atlantic Treaty Organization (NATO), the Group of Eight leading industrial powers (G-8), the European Union (EU), the World Trade Organization (WTO), and so forth. In a world filled with weapons of mass destruction, such global fragmentation and disintegration could well invite global catastrophe.

Some critics of humanitarian intervention to suppress genocide have argued that the Westphalian legal principles of territorial integrity, political independence, and nonintervention prohibit any outside interference in the internal affairs of a sovereign nation-state, even if genocide is being perpetrated. Some go as far as to assert that Article 2 (7) of the UN Charter prohibits *the UN itself* from intervening in the affairs of a sovereign state for the purpose of suppressing genocide. For instance, Michael Glennon argues that the UN Charter allows for international intervention only in response to traditional aggression.[45] However, this is a seriously flawed interpretation of international law, according to most international legal scholars. The renowned international scholar and creator of the word "genocide," Raphael Lemkin, wrote in 1947:

> By declaring genocide a crime under international law and by making it a problem of international concern, the right of intervention on behalf of minorities slated for destruction has been established.[46]

Richard Lillich argues that traditional international law has long recognized humanitarian intervention, specifically forceful outside intervention in response to state mistreatment of its own nationals in a manner that "shocks the conscience of mankind."[47] Hilaire McCoubrey and Nigel White also make this point:

> The only possible breach of international law which may justify military intervention, apart from self-defense, is when another peremptory rule of international law has been broken. . . . Such an argument can be raised only in support of the alleged right of humanitarian intervention. This assumes that the abuse of the human rights of the *population has reached the level of genocide* [emphasis added].[48]

A "peremptory rule," or *jus cogens,* is a norm

> accepted and recognized by the international community of States as a whole as a norm from which no derogation is permitted and which can be

modified only by a subsequent norm of general international law having the same character.[49]

The prohibition of genocide is just such a peremptory norm, and as such it "trumps" state sovereignty and permits multilateral military intervention to suppress genocide.[50] McCoubrey and White further argue that "it could be argued that when the abuse of human rights reaches such an atrocious level, the ban on force no longer operates."[51]

Further evidence that genocide should be treated as a catastrophic crime threatening international peace and security is to be found in the United Nations 1998 Rome Statute for the International Criminal Court (ICC). Referring to the Rome Statute, UN Secretary General Kofi Annan said:

> There can be no global justice unless the worst of crimes—crimes against humanity—are subject to the law. In this age more than ever we recognize that the crime of genocide against one people truly is an assault on us all—a crime against humanity.[52]

Professor Lori Fisler Damrosch of Columbia University School of Law writes:

> No doubt, the Security Council does have authority to adopt measures of military protection of endangered populations, under both Chapter VII of the UN Charter and Article VIII of the Genocide Convention.[53]

Rein Mullerson and David Scheffer write:

> In those situations in which the humanitarian crisis arises from an act of genocide, the right of forcible humanitarian intervention can be derived from the Genocide Convention.[54]

Finally, the International Criminal Tribunals for the Former Yugoslavia and Rwanda were created at the request of the UN Security Council and have their legal basis in Chapter VII of the UN Charter, which authorizes the Security Council to take whatever measures necessary to restore international peace and security.[55]

When we add to this the language of the Genocide Convention authorizing the "competent organs" of the United Nations to take whatever action they "consider appropriate for the prevention and suppression of genocide," it seems reasonably clear that the UN already possesses the legal authority—if not the solemn responsibility—to employ collective force to suppress ongoing genocide.

There are also clear moral imperatives to halt genocide. Despite significant international variation in human values, and legitimate debate over the "universal" applicability of human rights standards, there is little or no disagreement over the moral status of genocide. Genocide is rejected by *all* nation-states as a behavior not of civil society but of barbarism, and states that engage in genocide invariably deny their guilt, thereby paying homage to the principle. The prohibition against genocide is, therefore, *universal!* No nation dares stand before the world and declare its "cultural right" to commit genocide.

Michael Walzer argues that "humanitarian intervention comes much closer than any other kind of intervention to what we commonly regard, in domestic society, as law enforcement and police work." He recognizes that this is ruled out unless the intervening nations are authorized by "the society of nations." Walzer also argues that:

> Humanitarian intervention is justified when it is a response (with reasonable expectations of success) to acts "that shock the moral conscience of mankind." The old-fashioned language seems to me exactly right. It is not the conscience of political leaders that one refers to in such cases. They have other things to worry about and may well be required to repress their normal feelings of indignation and outrage. The reference is to the moral convictions of ordinary men and women, acquired in the course of their everyday activities.[56]

Walzer also speaks to the debate over the cultural relativity of moral values when he writes that morality is dualistic, with minimal, general, universal characteristics that are few and simple, and maximal, particular, local characteristics that are many and complex. Further, the negative aspect of justice, which rejects brutality, is, according to Walzer, universal and intense, and not rendered relative by local custom. Rather, this form of morality is major, emotional, and "close to the bone."[57] He also argues that all other states, especially great powers, have a vested interest in stopping this core threat to international order:

> [A]ll states have an interest in global stability and even in global humanity, and in the case of wealthy and powerful states like [the U.S.], this interest is seconded by obligation. . . . Active opposition to massacre and massive deportation is morally necessary; its risks must be accepted.[58]

The moral philosopher Father J. Bryan Hehir writes:

> The Westphalian legacy made nonintervention virtually absolute in status; only the case of genocide provided an exception to the rule.[59]

Stanley Hoffmann also contends that collective intervention is ethically justified when massive violations of human rights occur, such as genocide, or "deliberate policies of barbarism." In fact, according to Hoffmann, not to intervene in such cases would be "politically nefarious and ethically scandalous."[60] David J. Scheffer writes of genocide and other mass atrocities:

> These crimes involve issues of morality, national reconciliation, the rule of both domestic and international law, and the deterrence of future atrocities. Lingering on the horizon are rogue horsemen seemingly liberated from the rule of international law. Individuals acting with impunity, sometimes shielded by governments that embrace violations of international humanitarian law, are threats to the peace and security of their own peoples and, inevitably, to the international community.[61]

Genocide is also bad for business.[62] Currently, the travel and tourism industry is the world's largest, in terms of numbers of people employed. To do well, this industry must offer its customers two essential conditions: safety and comfort. However, these are the *last* conditions one is likely to find in regions of unchecked genocide.[63] Genocide scares away foreign direct investment, as well as international economic institutions such as the IMF and the World Bank. These outside lenders are not likely to return for a very long time, especially if the perpetrators of genocide are still at large in the region. It is a sad truth that unchecked genocide creates an economic black hole for its "hosts." And although some analysts tend to marginalize Africa as not of great strategic interest, Andrew Natsios, former director of the U.S. Agency for International Development (USAID), writes:

> This is a dangerous mistake. Many unstable African countries are richly endowed with natural resources that are now being diverted by warlords to advance their internal political and military objectives. Even now these warlords sell raw materials they control—like the diamond mines in Angola and Sierra Leone—to multinational corporations to fund their war efforts. Their activities now concentrate on survival in chaos, but a consolidation of power could shortly change their focus to even more deadly behavior.[64]

Genocide generates sudden, massive, desperate refugee flows that place heavy economic burdens, severe social strains, and great political instability upon neighboring nation-states.[65] If genocide continues unchecked, it invites unauthorized, unilateral, crosscutting foreign interventions to rescue endangered minorities or to stop the massive flow of refugees at its source.[66] Such interventions greatly increase the danger of spreading conflict throughout the region.

Unchecked genocide also threatens the unity and integrity of regional and international security organizations ostensibly committed to the defense of universal human rights standards, as well as supporters of the legal and moral prohibition against genocide. Failure to defend the basic values upon which these organizations were built undermines their credibility and integrity. As the worst possible human rights abuse, indeed a catastrophic abuse of human rights, the international crime of genocide therefore constitutes a unique area of overlap between human rights and international security.

Unchecked genocide threatens not just the political stability of government in whose jurisdiction the crime is perpetrated; it threatens the political stability of the whole region. Public shock and outrage at the slaughter tends to put intense pressure upon governments of the region to do something to stop the slaughter, rescue endangered minorities, stem the flow of refugees, and punish the perpetrators. Political destabilization as a result of unchecked genocide also occurs on the international level. World public opinion tends to demand a stop be put to this worst of all crimes against humanity. The governments of the leading nations of the world become the targets of this political firestorm, which in turn creates enormous political tension in the international political organization most concerned with matters of peace and security, the UN Security Council.[67] Natsios asks:

> Can the last remaining superpower be morally neutral and politically paralyzed in the face of massive losses of human life in . . . a genocide without it affecting America's image as a world leader? . . . The application of an exclusively geostrategic approach to a genocide . . . is difficult to defend with the U.S. public, international opinion, and the moral imperative that must be considered in any decision.[68]

According to David Mitrany's theory of international functionalism, one can achieve *positive* spillover of cooperation from nonsecurity functions, such as economic and social policy, into security functions, that is, problems of war and peace.[69] But the *reverse* is also true. One can achieve *negative* spillover of conflict, from security issues into nonsecurity functional areas. This is in fact what occurred in the 1930s and 1940s, as the disunity and disintegration within the collective security organization, the League of Nations, spilled into the international economic system and spawned free-for-all protectionism. The end result was global economic depression and catastrophic general war.[70] It is quite possible, therefore, that in the present period proliferating cases of unchecked genocide could so strain international relations as to jeopardize the basic integrity of key international economic institutions such as the International Monetary Fund (IMF), the WTO, and the World Bank.

Because the crime of genocide is a *complex systemic threat*—just as serious as the crime of aggression, if not more so—to the fundamental integrity of the international system, it requires a speedy and robust response from the international community. Treating genocide as merely a "humanitarian" problem and giving it the lowest level of priority on the international use-of-force scale is a grave and dangerous strategic mistake that could significantly contribute to the erosion and collapse of our highly interdependent global system on which all states depend for peace and prosperity. Such a dark scenario is in no nation's long-term interest, especially the international system's most powerful member, the United States. As the greatest beneficiary of a properly functioning global system—economically, politically, militarily, and socially—the U.S. stands to lose the most if this system malfunctions and collapses into economic depression, chaos, genocide, and war. W. Bowman Cutter, Joan Spero, and Laura Tyson write:

> The painful experiences of many transition economies and the unexpected financial crises of the 1990s have reminded the world that to work well, markets require a strong commitment to the rule of law.[71]

The interconnectedness of contemporary global prosperity, global security, and global order is a fragile relationship that can be damaged or destroyed fairly easily, according to Robert Keohane and Joseph Nye:

> Such trends can be set back, perhaps even reversed, by cataclysmic events, as happened in earlier phases of globalization.[72]

Cataclysms such as those that occurred in the 1930s could occur again in the twenty-first century unless the international community learns how to prevent, suppress, and punish the worst international crimes. Genocide, therefore, requires an authoritative, multilateral, robust response. The global community, in addressing this problem, must take a sound *strategic* approach that correctly identifies the nature of the threat and adopts the proper goals and means to deal with it.

MISUNDERSTANDING GENOCIDE

Genocide is not just another human rights abuse. While genocide clearly violates the most fundamental human rights of its victims, it is much worse than all other human rights violations. So catastrophic is genocide's insidious impact on humanity that it amounts to a barbarous assault on civilization itself. As such, genocide is defined by the international community as a "grave threat to international peace and security," a level of severity that most other human rights violations—except perhaps crimes against humanity—do not meet.[73] Therefore, it is a mistake to lump genocide in with other human rights abuses, such as suppressing a private newspaper or arresting a pro-democracy demonstrator.[74]

Genocide is not just another humanitarian emergency either. Although humanitarian emergencies were on the rise in the 1990s, one must make a careful distinction between an accidental disaster, natural or man-made, and a maliciously organized campaign of mass murder. Earthquakes, floods, or widespread starvation as an unintended by-product of civil war (as in, Bangladesh, Somalia, and Ethiopia) are not as threatening to international peace and security as is genocide (as in, Bosnia, Rwanda, and Kosovo).[75] The two phenomena require different tactical approaches as well. In the case of unintended human disasters, international *impartiality* is appropriate, even essential. In the case of genocide, international impartiality toward both the victims and the perpetrators is profoundly wrong and objectively abets the crime.

Genocide is not just another civil war, ethnic conflict, or failed state. To label it in such neutral terminology is to obscure its true criminal nature.[76] Many civil wars and ethnic conflicts have occurred in the world in recent years, but rarely have they included genocide. According to Charles Kegley and Eugene Wittkopf, 103 civil wars occurred between 1989 and 1997, but only two of these involved genocide. Of the 57 cases of ethnic conflict identified in 1993 by Ted Gurr and Barbara Harff, only two included genocide.[77] The International Panel of Eminent Personalities addressed the importance of distinguishing between ethnic atrocities and genocide in their report to the Organization of African Unity on Rwanda:

> The culture of violence that characterized so much of the colonial rule and its aftermath and that operated with such complete impunity for so long, is relevant to the story of Rwanda. But we must draw a vital distinction here: Genocide is of a different nature, a different order of magnitude, than even the unspeakable horrors we have so far been discussing. The world has known an unending torrent of violence, repression, slaughter, carnage, massacres, and pogroms. . . . Terrible as they all are, none is on par with genocide.[78]

Failed states involve "civil strife, political corruption, economic collapse, societal degradation, domestic chaos, human rights abuse, crumbling state infrastructure, and government failure."[79] Somalia in the 1990s is a good example of a failed state.[80] However, the genocide in Bosnia, Rwanda, and Kosovo was not of this chaotic and anarchical type; instead it was, in all three cases, premeditated and systematically organized by powerful criminal political elites.[81]

It must be emphasized that genocide is not, strictly speaking, a war crime. Unfortunately, many policymakers fail to understand the important distinction between war crimes and genocide, often using the terms interchangeably, thereby increasing confusion and encouraging moral equivalence. According to the Principles of International Law Recognized in the Charter of the Nuremberg Tribunal and Judgment of the Tribunal, war crimes are:

> [v]iolations of the laws or customs of war which include, but are not limited to, murder, ill-treatment of prisoners of war or persons on the seas, killing of hostages, plunder of public or private property, wanton destruction of cities, towns, or villages, or devastation not justified by military necessity.[82]

War crimes are often spontaneous acts, committed in the heat of battle, the result of individual combat stress, retribution for similar acts by the enemy, or the actions of renegade military units. They are often unauthorized, unsystematic, undirected, isolated incidents of aberrant criminal behavior. They tend to be the exception rather than the norm in combat, though they occur to some degree in virtually all wars.[83]

Genocide, on the other hand, is *not* a spontaneous crime of passion or an isolated incident. As explained above, genocide is a premeditated criminal campaign intended to destroy, in whole or in part, a population based solely upon its national, racial, religious or ethnic identity. Genocide is a premeditated, calculated, systematic, *malicious* crime, authorized by a state's political leaders.

What if genocide occurs during a conflict that was initially a civil war or ethnic conflict? Genocide is so great a crime that it can never be a secondary aspect of any conflict. If genocide occurs during a conflict, regardless of the conflict's original nature, genocide immediately becomes the principal aspect of the conflict and its essential nature. This point cannot be stressed enough, for it is a point on which much misunderstanding and failure has been concentrated regarding the proper approach to the conflicts in the post–Cold War period. Once genocide was threatened or perpetrated, regardless of how these conflicts began, their fundamental nature was *transmogrified* from civil war or ethnic conflict to genocide! At that critical point of change, the international community should have identified these conflicts clearly and openly as genocide and adopted a strategy and tactics appropriate for this great crime.

With any genocide, the first objective of international forces must be the quick and decisive suppression of the crime and the rescue of the victims, rather than a cease-fire and negotiations between "warring factions." In a case of genocide, the perpetrators and their targets are not "warring factions," but victims and their executioners. Those victims who occasionally take up arms against their tormentors are no more a "warring faction" in a civil war than were the Jewish fighters in the Warsaw ghetto resisting the Nazis' "final solution" in 1943.[84] With ongoing genocide (or with spree killing, in a domestic analogy), quick and forceful crime suppression must, in the short run, take precedence over the longer-run objective of peace and reconciliation. A "peace" imposed by *genocidaires* makes a mockery of justice and makes accomplices of those international leaders disreputable enough to have aided in its negotiation.

All this means that stopping genocide is a vital national interest for *all* nation-states, since genocide poses a threat to international peace and security, as well being a shocking assault on our moral values.[85] It also means that the international community, and especially its most powerful and capable members, must be prepared to use force to stop this most pernicious of international crimes.

CHAPTER 3

Misusing Force

The soldier, be he friend or foe, is charged with the protection of the weak and unarmed. It is the very essence and reason for his being. When he violates this sacred trust, he not only profanes his entire cult but threatens the very fabric of international society. The traditions of fighting men are long and honorable. They are based upon the noblest of human traits—sacrifice.

—U.S. General Douglas MacArthur, Tokyo, 1946[1]

Perpetrators of genocide, just like perpetrators of aggression, respect little short of coercive force. For the leaders of such massive and malicious crimes, diplomatic warnings mean little unless they are backed by the credible threat of force. Nor do political and economic sanctions have much effect on the behavior of *genocidaires,* as the speed with which genocidal killing is perpetrated makes slow, gradual, non-lethal remedies irrelevant. Quick suppression via substantial and decisive military force is the *key* to stopping genocide; it fills the gap between prevention and punishment and maximizes their effectiveness.

Yet a fear of sustaining military casualties in a distant quagmire—the so-called "Vietnam-Beirut-Mogadishu syndrome"—has so far prevented leading states from employing the ground forces necessary to halt genocide. The refusal of states, especially the most powerful state in the international system, the U.S., to use decisive force to stop genocide either on their own or through the United Nations has rendered prevention incredible and punishment partial, at best. Brian Urquhart, former undersecretary-general of the UN, expressed the frustration of many over this difficult dilemma:

> What is to be done when hundreds of thousands of people in a hitherto little-known region of the world are hounded from their homes, massacred, or starved to death in a brutal civil war, or even in a deliberate act of genocide? . . . As the new century dawns, one of the biggest problems for international organizations and their member governments is to learn how to react to the great human emergencies that still seem to occur regularly in many parts of the world.[2]

For the successful prohibition of genocide, the international community must be prepared to employ decisive military force, including ground combat troops, to prevent, suppress, and punish this crime. However, the international community seemed to lack the political will to adopt such a robust policy because international leaders did not believe stopping genocide warranted the decisive use of force. Given this approach to the problem, they feared that if they employed decisive force to stop a less-than-vital interest, they would suffer domestic political backlash once casualties among their own troops began to rise. This intense concern with the potential political impact of military casualties on public opinion can only be understood in the context of the debate over the lessons of Vietnam.[3]

VIETNAM AND THE PROPER USE OF FORCE

The use of military force is the most important—and the most controversial—public policy question any democratic nation can consider, for it is a question of war and peace, life and death.[4] Philip Everts, director of the Institute for International Studies at Leiden University, underscored this point recently when he wrote:

> [W]ar has been democratized both passively and actively, and this has made the relationship between war and democracy, between the use of military force and public support for such use, into a problem of the first order of magnitude.[5]

For the United States, no other public policy question during the last fifty years was more controversial and traumatic than the use of American military force in Vietnam.[6] The humiliation of a superpower losing a war to a small, fifth-rate power in a remote corner of the world drove American strategists to search for the most important lessons of that debacle, so that future Vietnams could be avoided. "No more Vietnams!"

became the prevailing sentiment for theorists, analysts, and policymakers striving to learn when and how to commit American forces successfully to combat abroad in the post-Vietnam period.[7]

One of the early influential critiques of America's war in Vietnam was Telford Taylor's *Nuremberg and Vietnam: An American Tragedy* (1970).[8] Taylor, who was a U.S. prosecutor at the 1946 Nuremberg Trial, argued that the U.S. war in Vietnam might well be illegal and immoral. He pointed to the My Lai massacre and other alleged American atrocities as evidence that U.S. military forces were employing disproportionate and indiscriminate force in Vietnam. He concluded that "The sad story of America's venture in Vietnam is that the military means rapidly submerged the political ends" and that "Somehow we failed ourselves to learn the lessons we undertook to teach at Nuremberg, and that failure is today's American tragedy."[9]

A second influential analysis was Bernard Brodie's *War and Politics* (1973).[10] In his penetrating work, Brodie, the dean of American strategic thinkers, relied upon the theories of Carl von Clausewitz in identifying *purpose* as the central element in any strategy for taking a nation to war. Quoting Marshall Ferdinand Foch, Brodie asked: *"De quoi s'agit-il?"* What is it all about?[11] War takes place within a particular milieu, which gives war all its purposes. "[T]he question of *why* we fight must dominate any consideration of means."[12] In Vietnam, according to Brodie, U.S. leaders failed to develop and maintain clarity of purpose. They relied, instead, upon clichés about "Munich" and "dominoes," "prestige" and "credibility."[13] In the absence of clear purpose, then, political and military leaders tended to let means—more and more force—dominate their strategy in an ultimately irrational and self-defeating policy. "We had to destroy the town in order to save it!" became typical of dysfunctional U.S. policy in Vietnam.[14] Brodie concluded that this fundamental strategic mistake of not establishing and maintaining the clarity and primacy of purpose undercut popular support and raised serious doubts about the wisdom and morality of the war. He wrote:

[I]n any war marked by something well short of full and unified commitment of the people, the considerations that guide the military commanders and the top political leadership of the country will be tested not only against individual private self-interest but also against various sensibilities of the community, including what in a few will be moral sensibilities. This is one of the lessons that have already emerged out of Vietnam. In such a situation, axioms and cliches derived from old patterns of *Realpolitik,* already out of harmony with modern times, sound doubly hollow.[15]

A third important analysis was John Mueller's *War, Presidents and Public Opinion* (1973)[16] in which Mueller demonstrated with polling data that in more limited, more ambiguous wars, there was an inverse relationship between casualties and public support. According to Mueller, in post–World War II wars—Korea and Vietnam—where "the enemy is less 'evil,' and the purpose is less clear," the empirical evidence suggested that "in wars like these public support declines as the length and the costs of the war grow." The lesson seemed to be that the American public had little tolerance for ambiguous interventions that were expensive in terms of U.S. military casualties.[17]

A fourth important analysis of the war in Vietnam was Michael Walzer's *Just and Unjust Wars* (1977).[18] In his book, Walzer determined that the American war in Vietnam was immoral both as an unjustified intervention and because it was promulgated in an unnecessarily brutal manner. Walzer argued that America's South Vietnamese ally never gained legitimacy in the eyes of its own people, and that U.S. tactics such as "free-fire zones," "body count," and "search and destroy" too often indiscriminately targeted noncombatant Vietnamese.[19]

A fifth important analysis was Leslie Gelb and Richard Betts's *The Irony of Vietnam*, published by the Brookings Institution (1978).[20] In their analysis, Gelb and Betts argued that public support was *key* in any attempt to take a democratic nation to war. According to Gelb and Betts: "The war could be lost only if the American public turned sour on it. American public opinion was the essential domino."[21] If this "essential domino" of public support collapsed, the war policy would inevitably become unsustainable. Hence, it was the responsibility of political leaders to convince their domestic public to support a potentially costly war if their use-of-force policy was to have any hope of succeeding.

Finally, Colonel. Harry Summers's *On Strategy* (1982/1984) was generated by the U.S. Army's search for lessons from Vietnam.[22] Of all the institutions in American society affected by the catastrophe of Vietnam, the army suffered the most. Because of Vietnam, the army came close to complete disintegration and breakdown. During the latter years of Vietnam, the army suffered an organizational equivalent of a near-death experience. It was wracked by drug abuse, racial conflict, combat avoidance, mutiny, fragging, organized political resistance, draft evasion, desertion, decreased reenlistment, expelled ROTC units, and deep cuts in its budgets.[23] The search for learning was the army's way of healing and trying to avoid a repetition in the future, one they might not survive.

In his work, Colonel Summers criticized the lack of clear purpose, the use of ambiguous and contradictory political and military objectives, and the reliance upon insufficient force and gradual escalation. However, Summers argued that the primary failure of American leaders—both civilian and military—was *moral* rather than material. As Summers pointed out:

By any statistical measure, the United States could not lose in Vietnam. But as Napoleon said, there is more to war than can be counted. In Vietnam the failure was moral, not material.[24]

Summers insisted that political leaders failed in their moral responsibility to be honest with the American people about the true nature of the U.S. commitment in Vietnam (it was a real war, not a "conflict") and that military leaders failed in their responsibility to be honest about the bleak prospects for victory in Vietnam.[25] He argued, instead, for the inclusion of the American people and their representatives in Congress as a crucial part of Clausewitz's "remarkable trinity"—the people, the government, and the army—in any strategy for taking the nation to war.[26] Summers's theory of a special relationship between the public and the military was best expressed in a 1976 speech by Army Chief of Staff General Fred C. Weyand:

Vietnam was a reaffirmation of the peculiar relationship between the American Army and the American people. The American Army really is a people's Army in the sense that it belongs to the American people who take a jealous and proprietary interest in its involvement. When the Army is committed the American people are committed, when the American people lose their commitment it is futile to try to keep the Army committed. In the final analysis, the American Army is not so much an arm of the Executive Branch as it is an arm of the American people. The Army, therefore, cannot be committed lightly.[27]

Summers's work became especially influential within the national security community because the U.S. Army adopted it as its official lessons of Vietnam and sent copies to its entire general officer corps. Additionally, all of the military services adopted *On Strategy* for use in their service academies and war colleges, and Summers's book quickly proliferated within the executive branch and the Congress as well.[28]

Another of the military's important post-Vietnam revisions concerned their doctrine on war-fighting. In August 1981, the army issued Field Manual (FM) 100-1, *The Army*, which became the source book for strategic doctrine. It gave particular attention to the coordination and air and ground forces in warfare, and the primacy of ground forces in that relationship. It stated:

[T]he fundamental truth is that only ground forces possess the power to exercise direct, continuing and comprehensive control over land, its resources, and its people. . . . [L]andpower can make permanent the otherwise transitory advantages achieved by air and naval forces.[29]

A June 1986 revision of FM 100-1 further states:

> The Army is the decisive component of military force by virtue of its ability to control the land areas essential to people and nations. People live on land. Ultimately, the control of land determines the destiny of peoples and nations.[30]

The AirLand Battle Doctrine was devised by the army and endorsed by the air force.[31]

THE WEINBERGER-POWELL DOCTRINE

At about the same time that the U.S. Army was institutionalizing Colonel Summers's On Strategy and teaching the AirLand Battle Doctrine, the Reagan administration was seriously considering direct military intervention in Central America to contain and roll back Soviet and Cuban-supported Marxist forces. The Sandinistas had seized state power in Nicaragua a few years earlier from the U.S.-backed Somoza regime. In El Salvador, the FMLN guerrillas were trying to topple the U.S.-backed Duarte government. Secretary of State Alexander Haig and others on the National Security Council staff wanted the United States to use military force—ground troops if necessary—to halt what they saw as Soviet-Cuban aggression in the Western Hemisphere. However, the Pentagon, citing a distinct lack of American public support for such a potential costly adventure, actively obstructed and frustrated these plans. Eventually, the military chiefs prevailed and no direct U.S. military intervention occurred.[32]

In October 1983, after becoming an active participant in a many-sided civil war in Beirut, 241 U.S. Marine "peacekeepers" were killed by a truck-bomb while sleeping in their barracks. The military chiefs, never enthusiastic about this ambiguous intervention in the first place, successfully prevailed on President Reagan to withdraw the remainder of the U.S. forces in Lebanon. A year later, virtually on the anniversary of the Beirut truck-bombing, Secretary of State George Shultz gave a speech in New York calling for more latitude in the use of military force. Urging an end to "self-doubt," "self-flagellation" and "paralysis," he said:

> [W]e cannot allow ourselves to become the Hamlet of nations, worrying endlessly over whether and how to respond. A great nation with global responsibilities cannot afford to be hamstrung by confusion and indecisiveness. . . . The public must understand before the fact that occasions will come when their government must act before each and every fact is known-and decisions cannot be tied to the opinion polls.[33]

Shultz's speech was in fact the first public airing of what had been a private, behind-the-scenes feud between the Pentagon and hawkish Reagan administration officials in the State Department, CIA, and the White House, who ridiculed the military chiefs as "wimps-in-uniform," so traumatized by their experiences in Vietnam that they were afraid to use the massive military power at their disposal.[34] As Shultz later explained in his memoirs:

> The argument turned into a battle royal between Cap Weinberger and me over the use of force. To Weinberger, as I heard him, our forces were to be constantly built up but not used. . . . Only if and when the population, by some open measure, agreed in advance would American armed forces be employed, and even then, only if we were assured of winning swiftly and at minimal cost. This was the Vietnam syndrome in spades, carried to an absurd level, and a complete abdication of the duties of leadership.[35]

Not surprisingly, Shultz's public criticism provoked a response from the Pentagon. One month later, on 28 November 1984, Secretary of Defense Caspar Weinberger gave a speech to the National Press Club in Washington, D.C., called "The Uses of Military Power."[36] The significance of this speech, which quickly became known as the "Weinberger Doctrine," indicates a lengthy excerpt:

> Of the many policies our citizens deserve—and need—to understand, none is so important as those related to our topic today—the uses of military power. . . . National power has many components, some tangible—like economic wealth, technical pre-eminence. Other components are intangible—such as moral force, or strong national will. Military forces, when they are strong, ready and modern, are a credible—and tangible—addition to a nation's power. When both the intangible national will and those forces are forged into one instrument, national power becomes effective. . . . Unless we are certain that force is essential, we run the risk of inadequate national will to apply the resources needed . . .
>
> [S]ome theorists argue that military force can be brought to bear in any crisis. Some of these proponents of force are eager to advocate its use even in limited amounts simply because they believe that if there are American forces of any size present they will somehow solve the problem. . . . [E]mploying our forces almost indiscriminately and as a regular and customary part of our diplomatic efforts-would surely plunge us headlong into the sort of domestic turmoil we experienced during the Vietnam War . . .
>
> Policies formed without a clear understanding of what we hope to achieve would also earn us the scorn of our troops, who would have an understandable opposition to being used—in every sense of the word—casually and without intent to support them fully . . .

I have developed six major tests to be applied when we are weighing the use of U.S. combat forces abroad. Let me now share them with you:

1. First, the United States should not commit forces to combat overseas unless the particular engagement or occasion is deemed vital to our national interest or that of our allies . . .

2. Second, if we decide it is necessary to put combat troops into a given situation, we should do so wholeheartedly, and with the clear intention of winning . . .

3. Third, if we do decide to commit forces to combat overseas, we should have clearly defined political and military objectives . . .

4. Fourth, the relationship between our objectives and the forces we have committed—their size, composition and disposition—must be continually reassessed and adjusted if necessary . . .

5. Fifth, before the U.S. commits combat forces abroad, there must be some reasonable assurance we will have the support of the American people and their elected representatives in Congress . . .

6. Finally, the commitment of U.S. forces to combat should be a last resort . . .

These tests I have mentioned have been phrased negatively for a purpose—they are intended to sound a note of caution—caution that we must observe prior to committing forces to combat overseas. When we ask our military forces to risk their very lives in such situations, a note of caution is not only prudent, it is morally required.[37]

General Colin Powell, in his memoirs, discussed the significance of the Weinberger Doctrine:

Weinberger's antagonist, George Shultz, was dismissive of Cap's approach. I had watched the irony of their squabbling for months. The Secretary of State was often ready to commit America's military might, even in a no-man's land like Lebanon. What was the point of maintaining a military force if you did not whack somebody occasionally to demonstrate your power? On the other side was the man responsible for the forces that have to do the bleeding and dying, arguing against anything but crucial commitments. . . . In short, is the national interest at stake? If the answer is yes, go in, and go in to win. Otherwise, stay out.

Clausewitz would have applauded. And in the future, when it became my responsibility to advise Presidents on committing our forces to combat, Weinberger's rules turned out to be a practical guide.[38]

Powell later added the need for a clear "exit strategy," a reemphasis of the need for clear political and military objectives, which earned him a place next to Weinberger—whether or not he wanted it—as the author of the doctrine.[39]

After prevailing over an initial challenge by Secretary of State Shultz, the Weinberger-Powell Doctrine was promulgated throughout the military services, the executive branch, and Congress over the next several years. Nothing increases the credibility of a controversial policy like success, and increasingly successful applications of the Weinberger-Powell Doctrine brought it hegemony—though not universal consensus—within the U.S. foreign policy community.

The Weinberger-Powell Doctrine was applied as policy with success in Libya in 1986, in the reflagging of the Kuwaiti oil tankers in 1987, in suppressing the coup attempt against President Corazon Aquino of the Philippines in 1989, and in the invasion of Panama in 1989.[40] The greatest successful application of the Weinberger-Powell Doctrine was Operation Desert Shield/Desert Storm in 1990/91. In the war against Iraq, the tenets of the Weinberger-Powell Doctrine were applied chiefly by Chairman of the Joint Chiefs of Staff Colin Powell, who actually had little trouble convincing President Bush of the wisdom of most of Weinberger's tests.

The Allied forces also applied the AirLand Battle Doctrine, which stressed the primacy of ground troops, as a blueprint for victory in the Gulf War.[41] Though it appeared to many casual observers, watching on their television screens the neat videos of precision-guided munitions striking their targets, that the air war defeated the Iraqi forces and the ground campaign merely mopped up, the truth was somewhat different. Iraq's substantial, well-dug-in ground forces did not begin to leave Kuwait until *after* the Allied ground campaign commenced on 24 February 1991. On that day, Iraq's best forces in Kuwait, seven Republican Guard divisions, still retained 57 percent of their tanks, 76 percent of their armored vehicles, and 80 percent of their artillery.[42] It was the mission of these elite units to ride out the bombing campaign, hold onto Kuwait, and lead the counterattack against an advancing Allied ground force. Defeating the Republic Guard divisions received high priority in the battle plan of the Allied coalition.[43] Their success in doing so validated for the U.S. military their post-Vietnam doctrines on the proper use of force—the Weinberger-Powell Doctrine and the AirLand Battle Doctrine—and actually entrenched it deeper.[44] The 1990s, however, presented the Weinberger-Powell Doctrine with perhaps its most difficult challenges.

Post–Cold War conflicts in Bosnia, Somalia, Rwanda, Haiti, and Kosovo reignited the bitter debate of the proper use of military force. On 21 September 1993, chairman of the House Armed Services Committee, Les Aspin, made a speech in Washington, D.C., on the "Use and Usefulness of Military Forces in the Post–Cold War, Post-Soviet World." In his speech, Aspin identified two powerful schools of thought on the use of force. First, the "all-or-nothing" school, represented by Colin Powell, wants to use overwhelming force or stay out altogether. The second, the "limited-objectives" school, sees compellence through air power and precision-guided weapons as an alternative approach. Aspin explained:

> What this means is that we have the technology which has improved our ability to make air strikes with little, if any, loss of U.S. lives and with a minimum of collateral damage and loss of civilian lives on the other side. This is a big, big change.[45]

Aspin aligned himself with this latter approach, which set the stage for confrontation with the military when Aspin was appointed by President Clinton to be Secretary of Defense the following year.

The showdown over the use-of-force doctrine came in Mogadishu in October 1993, when "mission creep," a gradual, almost imperceptible, expansion of the objective of the Somalia operation from humanitarian assistance to "nation-building" again made U.S. forces, over the objections of the Pentagon, a biased player in a many-sided civil war. The tragic result was the deaths of eighteen U.S. servicemen on a dusty, downtown street in Mogadishu, as well as the deaths of hundreds of unarmed Somali civilians and massive collateral damage.[46] Subsequent results of this failed use of force were the resignation of Aspin and the promulgation of Presidential Decision Directive 25 (PDD 25) seven months later. PDD 25 was the Clinton administration's reluctant acceptance of the Weinberger-Powell Doctrine and its application to UN peace operations. It contained all the original elements of Weinberger's six tests and stipulated that these conditions be applied to U.S. participation in any UN Chapter VII (collective security) response to a significant threat to international peace and security.[47] Thus, the Weinberger-Powell Doctrine not only prevailed, it had now gone global.

GENOCIDE AND IMPROPER STRATEGY

The Weinberger-Powell Doctrine dictated that the first step in any attempt to halt contemporary genocide be the accurate identification of the conflict's genocidal nature. The Weinberger-Powell Doctrine also required that the defeat and arrest of the perpetrators and the rescue of the victims be the clear objectives. It also demanded that war-fighting forces be employed—including ground combat troops—rather than lightly armed peacekeeping troops. Air power alone is insufficient for compelling perpetrators to stop committing genocide. "Jointness" is required if the mission is to succeed.[48] Finally, the dominant Weinberger-Powell Doctrine demanded that the public and Congress be won over to the policy in order to insure its sustainability in the longer run. In this the political leaders failed miserably, identifying the conflicts instead as "civil wars," "ethnic conflicts," or "failed states," and applying an inappropriate peacekeeping strategy that was thoroughly alien to the genocidal nature of these conflicts. Political leaders, assuming that genocide was a secondary or tertiary aspect of what were primarily civil wars or ethnic conflicts, applied a peacekeeping strategy that proved profoundly inappropriate to a core criminal threat to global order. The tragic result of this profound failure of political leadership was that genocide was perpetrated with impunity. But despite the fact that the fault for this failure lay with the political leaders, the military leaders continued to be blamed for their "Vietnam syndrome."[49]

The initial failure to identify, correctly, the nature of the conflict not only led to the misuse of force, but it led political leaders to underestimate the willingness of the public to support a policy of stopping genocide, even at the risk of military casualties. Therefore, political leaders avoided taking their case for preventing genocide directly to the people, a failure that only delayed the decision to use decisive force and increased the costs when it was finally and reluctantly taken.

Misreading the Public

Ms. Marvin said she was uncertain what course the United States should follow, because she did not know the alternatives. All she can be sure of, she said, is "I'm very against genocide."

—New York Times, April 1999[1]

Public opinion is centrally important in the process of taking a democratic nation to war. However, in this uncertain and tumultuous post–Cold War period where internal conflicts are the norm, how does the "lone superpower" walk that fine line between neoisolationist indifference and "globocop"? According to Catherine Kelleher, at the heart of the debate over the use of force is the question:

> [How] do we now choose between what some portray as our moral responsibility to intervene to prevent further atrocities and protect the innocent, and what others argue should be our principled avoidance of an involvement in an uncertain quagmire?[2]

The quagmire concern seemed to loom large for American policymakers confronting multiple humanitarian emergencies in the 1990s. The shadow first of Vietnam and later Somalia loomed large over them all.[3] Policymakers assumed that a new general phenomenon was at work: the "body-bag syndrome," a tendency for public opinion to turn against interventions that threaten to generate troops casualties. This "casualty hypothesis," according to Philip Everts, contends that:

[P]ublic support for the use of military force in high-risk operations in circumstances other than direct threats to the country's security will not be
forthcoming, and that initial support in such cases will dwindle as soon as
casualties are incurred.[4]

Political leaders fear being politically whipsawed by first the "CNN effect" and then the "Dover factor." They fear that televised scenes of humanitarian suffering will produce a public outcry to "Do something!"
only to be followed by angry demands of "Bring our troops home!" once
the flag-draped coffins begin arriving to Dover Air Force Base. Consequently, decisionmakers have sought to avoid political risk by keeping
consideration of U.S. combat troops in complex humanitarian emergencies—including cases of genocide—"off the table." As Mendlovitz and
Fousek have explained:

> The rather gruesome and tragic image of the body bag conveys perhaps the
> greatest obstacle to effective UN actions to halt the recent killings in both
> the former Yugoslavia and Rwanda. That is to say, the major states of the
> world—the United States, Britain, France, and perhaps Russia—had the
> capacity to intervene in these situations and could have done so in a man-
> ner that would have saved countless lives. But these powerful states failed
> to act because their chief executives were fearful of an irate domestic back-
> lash should any of their military personnel be killed in carrying out hu-
> manitarian intervention.[5]

This assumption that "the political traffic [public opinion] will not
bear" a policy of using U.S. troops to suppress genocide in Bosnia,
Rwanda, or Kosovo seemed to have solid evidence.[6] For instance, an
ABC poll conducted in the fall and winter of 1992/93 found that 58 percent of Americans were firmly opposed to using U.S. ground troops
under any circumstances in the war in Bosnia.[7] In early 1993, the Times
Mirror Center for the People and the Press found that 55 percent of
Americans opposed the use of military force to stop the fighting in
Bosnia. In September 1993, according to an NBC poll, 59 percent opposed the use of U.S. troops in Bosnia, even as peacekeepers. By December 1993, a New York Times poll showed that 65 percent of Americans
opposed U.S. military involvement in Bosnia. It seemed that, across the
board, Americans believed that Bosnia was not an American fight.[8]

Regarding Rwanda, after the debacle just five months earlier in
downtown Mogadishu in which eighteen U.S. soldiers died—and the
firestorm of criticism that followed it—U.S. officials assumed that another U.S. intervention in the heart of Africa was politically out of the
question.[9] In three consecutive polls during the Kosovo conflict, a small

majority of Americans, an average of 53 percent, agreed it would not "be worth the loss of some American soldiers' lives to help bring peace to Kosovo."[10]

This evidence, however, is not as solid and compelling as it may first appear. The polling figures cited above are based upon *ambiguous characterizations* of the conflicts as "civil wars" or "ancient feuds," for which "peace" or "conflict resolution" are the stated objectives. These polls neglected to use the more accurate description of "genocide" when characterizing the situations in Bosnia, Rwanda, and Kosovo, and therefore miss the important point that the public has not applied its Vietnam reluctance to core goals such as genocide.[11] When the survey questions are more accurately framed as "genocide," a *radically different* response is obtained.

For example, a 1994 poll conducted by the Program on International Policy Attitudes (PIPA) at the Center for International and Security Studies at the University of Maryland found that 65 percent of Americans believed that the U.S. should intervene to stop genocide. When asked what should be done if the UN determined that genocide was occurring in Bosnia and Rwanda, *80 percent* of the respondents said they favored military intervention.[12] The moral conviction that genocide must be stopped was also strong in the focus groups run by PIPA. For instance, one man from Kalamazoo said:

> I think any reason for deciding whether someone lives or dies because of culture or race . . . or religion is wrong. If Bosnia was an issue of . . . territory, then maybe you should just let them fight it out. But . . . genocide is wrong and when that is occurring, something needs to be done to stop it.[13]

In subsequent polls conducted by Steven Kull and his associates of four congressional districts for which U.S. representatives were particularly unsupportive of UN operations, the results showed that an "overwhelming" 79 to 80 percent agreed with the argument that the United States should be involved in UN peacekeeping because "if we allow things like genocide or the mass killing of civilians to go unaddressed . . . eventually our interests would be affected."[14] PIPA'S October 1999 poll showed continuing support for a U.S.-led multilateral force to stop genocide. Kull and Clay Ramsey pointed out that:

> UN peacekeeping in principle garners strong majority support from the public, while counterarguments (based on cost or lack of connection to U.S. national security) do poorly in polls. Support derives both from peacekeeping's potential for burden-sharing and from humanitarian and moral concerns, especially in situations in which genocide is a factor.[15]

Regarding Kosovo, in a poll conducted between 13 and 17 May 1999, Steven Kull found that 60 percent of Americans supported intervention with ground troops if NATO decides it is the only way to stop ethnic cleansing. His evidence showed that support for involvement derived largely (69 percent) from the belief that genocide was occurring in Kosovo. The argument that U.S. interests were not at stake in Kosovo, and therefore American lives should not be put at risk, received the *lowest* level of support (41 percent). Only a small minority (21 percent) wanted the U.S. to pull out of Kosovo if American troops were killed in a ground invasion.[16]

Kull and his associates at PIPA explored the reasons why policymakers underestimated the public's opposition to genocide by interviewing a number of them on Capitol Hill and in the executive branch. They reported that:

> In the interviews with policy practitioners we asked how they arrived at their conclusions about the public. These interviews reveal two key dynamics that could well contribute to policymakers misreading the public: a failure to seek out information about the public and a tendency to assume that the vocal public is representative of the general public.[17]

One former high-ranking executive branch official responded in an interview to the question about how he gathered information on public opinion by saying:

> Haphazardly . . . a great deal of it is anecdotal. I mean there would be a poll here or a poll there . . . or a congressman would call in and say, my constituents are writing five to one about this . . . but it's largely anecdotal. And how you respond depends on what your philosophy is.[18]

Philip Everts argues that policymakers' false assumptions tend to have an insidious effect on public support:

> [O]ne is struck by the facile way in which the body bag argument is used by politicians and the media. There is a tendency to parrot one another and to anticipate situations, which may indeed be caused by such talk.
>   The frequent—and somewhat patronizing—statements of politicians and observers about a to-be-expected body bag effect on public support may turn out to be self-fulfilling prophesies . . . Thus the lack of public support may turn out to be the consequence and not the cause of governmental inaction and moral failure.[19]

This political *mis*leading by policymakers seems to explain much of the early absence of public support for ground intervention to stop genocide in Bosnia and Rwanda. Some of this *mis*leading was probably the result of complexity, confusion, and honest ignorance. However, once leaders responsible for framing the issue accurately learned that it *was* a case of genocide, they intentionally avoided describing the situation in those terms, and instructed others to do the same, in order to avoid the nation's legal obligations to intervene under Article VIII of the Genocide Convention, and to minimize their own political risk.[20]

Empirical evidence of U.S. policymakers' systematic avoidance of the "g" word was obtained through an electronic search of White House documents covering the period of 1 January 1993 to 1 January 1998. The search produced 1,292 White House documents that mentioned "Bosnia" but only twenty-one of them also mentioned "genocide," and *only three* of them (0.2 percent) actually *admitted* that genocide occurred in Bosnia! A similar search for "Rwanda" produced 173 documents of which only six also contained the word "genocide," and *only five* (2.9 percent) *admitted* that genocide occurred in Rwanda.[21]

This evidence, of course, raises serious questions about the democratic content of U.S. foreign policy regarding genocide. A policy supposedly based upon "the informed consent of the people" can hardly be considered "democratic" when the public is intentionally *mis*informed, confused, and deceived by their leaders about the true nature of the crisis in question. The general ambiguity that results from such conscious obfuscation breeds precisely the public reluctance to risk troops that the leaders predict. Only when a pollster finally frames the question as "genocide" does the fog of ambiguity lift and the latent, strong, and stable public support for ground troops to stop genocide—despite casualties—become clear.

Other failures to follow the lessons of both the Holocaust and Vietnam—not developing clear antigenocide objectives, not configuring and arming forces to fight genocide, not mobilizing forces quickly—flowed from these fundamental strategic mistakes of not treating genocide as a vital interest, not using ground troops, and underestimating public opinion. The impact of these strategic failures can be seen and appreciated better by examining more closely the individual cases of genocide in Bosnia, Rwanda, and Kosovo.

CHAPTER 5

Genocide in Bosnia

The evil represented in this museum is incontestable. But as we are its witness, so must we remain its adversary in the world in which we live, so we must stop the fabricators of history and the bullies as well. Left unchallenged, they would prey upon the powerless; and we must not permit that to happen again.

—President Bill Clinton,
U.S. Holocaust Memorial Museum, 1993[1]

The U.S. Government has been of the opinion since 1993 that genocide occurred in Bosnia and Herzegovina.

—Ambassador for War Crimes David J. Scheffer,
U.S. Holocaust Memorial Museum, 1998[2]

President Clinton refused to engage our troops in a ground war in Bosnia . . . To do so would have risked a Vietnam-like quagmire.

—National Security Adviser Tony Lake,
George Washington University, 1996[3]

Genocide was perpetrated in Bosnia between 1992 and 1995, despite the presence of armed representatives of the United Nations. The international community possessed full knowledge of the crime and more than sufficient military power to stop the perpetrators in their tracks. However, Western nations—particularly the United States—lacked the political will to do more than supply the victims with humanitarian assistance. Western political leaders failed because they misunderstood the true nature of genocide in Bosnia, misunderstood how to use force properly in Bosnia, and misread the latent public support for stopping genocide in Bosnia. Because of their "ignominious failure,"[4] a genocide that could have been prevented completely or stopped early was allowed to drag on for three years. To those who knew better, the paralysis of the West in the face of genocide was bitterly exasperating. The journalist David Rieff perhaps expressed this feeling best when he wrote:

> To utter words like "Never again," as Clinton did at the opening of the Holocaust Museum, was to take vacuity over the border into obscenity as long as genocide was going on and Clinton was doing nothing to stop it. His words were bitterly meaningless. For if there was to be no intervention to stop a genocide that was taking place, then the phrase "Never again" meant nothing more than: Never again would Germans kill Jews in Europe in the 1940s.[5]

HISTORICAL BACKGROUND

Before war and genocide was visited upon the people of Bosnia, the population was made up of three major communities: 44 percent were Muslims, 31 percent were Serbs, and 17 percent were Croats.[6] The three groups lived together fairly peacefully for centuries, frequently intermarrying. Bosnia's Muslims became the most secularized and assimilated Muslims in all of Europe. The couple of times that major violence did occur between the groups, it was in the context of the two world wars of the twentieth century and had its origins beyond Bosnia's borders.[7]

In the mid-1980s, following the death of Tito, and coinciding with the general collapse of communism throughout Eastern Europe, Serbian communist apparatchik Slobodan Milosevic seized the chance to fill the power vacuum. Demonstrating a capacity for political opportunism, Milosevic transformed himself in the late 1980s from a staunch communist into a born-again Serbian ultranationalist in order to seize the leadership of Serbia's League of Communists. He exploited cultural and religious differences and animosities, and fanned the flames of ethnic and nationalist hatred, in order to enhance his personal political power. He embraced the political program of the most ultranationalists Serbs— a fringe faction that was never permitted to promote their neofascist ideology under Tito—and adopted their strategic objective of a Greater Serbia, "cleansed" of all non-Serbs.[8]

THE CRIME

Milosevic first seized control of the Serbian-dominated Yugoslav People's Army (JNA). Then he co-opted the Serbian intellectuals' nationalist program to consolidate his power and expand the territorial borders of Serbia. This program was most explicitly expressed in the 1986 Memorandum of the Serbian Academy of Sciences and Arts, which stated that the Serbs were the most oppressed people in Yugoslavia and must therefore all live together in one Greater Serbia or perish.[9] The Memorandum defined the Muslim as alien, neoprimitive, warlike barbarians, seeking to destroy all Serbs and establish an Islamic state in the heart of Europe. Milosevic and his ultranationalist allies promised to "liberate" Serbs throughout the former Yugoslavia and bring them all together in an expanded Greater Serbia through a process of "ethnic cleansing," a euphemism for the destruction and/or deportation of all non-Serbs, particularly Muslims. Regularly using state-controlled radio and television, Milosevic spread hatred of the Muslims by arguing that the very survival of the Serbs as a nation depended on such an extreme campaign of ethnic cleansing.[10]

In March 1989, Milosevic abolished the autonomy of Kosovo and Vojvodina, two provinces of Serbia, and began a campaign of violent repression against the ethnic Albanians of Kosovo, who made up 90 percent of the province's population. This sent a clear message to all non-Serbs throughout Yugoslavia that they too were in danger from violent Serbian nationalism. The disintegration of Yugoslavia thus became virtually inevitable. The response from non-Serbs was not long in coming. On 25 June 1991, the Yugoslav republics of Slovenia and Croatia declared independence. War quickly followed. With the Bosnian declaration of sovereign independence on 15 October 1991, the war spread to Bosnia. The greatest of the contemporary catastrophes in the Balkans (to date) was then begun.[11]

Between 1992 and 1995, Serbian forces in Bosnia used mass killings, beatings, torture, systematic rape, castration, starvation, and forced deportation against hundreds of thousands of Bosnian Muslim civilians, simply because of their national, ethnic, and religious identity. Paramilitary forces controlled by Milosevic were used to promulgate some of the worst atrocities against Bosnian Muslims. Ultranationalist Serbs burned Muslim homes, destroyed their religious, intellectual, historical, and cultural institutions, and seized whatever valuables the Bosnian Muslims possessed. In every town, Bosnia's Muslim elites—judges, doctors, teachers, business leaders—were "disappeared." The Serbs drove out the Bosnian Muslims they did not kill, creating the greatest wave of refugees

Europe had seen in fifty years. By late 1993, the Muslim population of Bosnia had been reduced from 350,000 to 40,000.[12]

The Serbs' standard operating procedure was to attack Bosnian Muslim towns and villages with tanks, artillery, and mortars, then enter the town or village and eliminate any remaining resistance. Serb forces often used loudspeakers to terrorize Muslims into fleeing. In some cases, houses were color-coded to indicate the owner's ethnic group and then Muslim houses were systematically destroyed. Sometimes, Muslim residents were forced to sign over their property.[13] Serb forces also systematically destroyed most of the Muslim mosques, historical monuments, and libraries in Bosnia, often by demolishing them with explosives and bulldozing the rubble. They even deleted all Muslim place-names in the areas they seized. The destruction of all signs or symbols of Islamic or Ottoman culture was an important war aim for the Serbs, as they sought to purify and cleanse their expanded society of all non-Serb references.[14] A United Nations Commission on Human Rights report described:

> mass killing, torture, disappearances, rape, and other sexual abuses against women and children, use of civilians as mine clearers, arbitrary executions, destruction of houses, religious objects and cultural and historical heritage, forced and illegal evictions, detentions, arbitrary searches and other acts of violence.[15]

Hundreds of thousands of Muslim civilians were forced by Serb troops to flee their towns and villages for Muslim-controlled areas of Bosnia or for neighboring nations. Some were deported to Macedonia. Others were sent by train to the Hungarian border, but Hungary refused to admit them. They were then placed in concentration camps just inside Bosnia. Thousands of Muslims were deported from northwestern Bosnia in sealed freight cars—without food, water, fresh air, or toilets—to a Muslim enclave in central Bosnia.[16]

Serb forces set up concentration camps in Bosnia for Muslim detainees, and reports soon appeared of inhuman, Nazi-like conditions, including beating, torture, sexual mutilation, and summary execution.[17] Peter Maass described this brutality in one such camp, Omarska:

> Every imaginable degradation had been played out at Omarska during the previous months. It was not a death camp on the order of Auschwitz. There was no gas chamber to which the prisoners were marched off every day. What happened at Omarska was dirtier, messier. The death toll never approached Nazi levels but the brutality was comparable or in some cases, superior, if that word can be used. The Nazis were interested in killing as

many Jews as possible. The Serbs, however, wanted to . . . have sadistic fun by torturing [their prisoners] in the cruelest of ways and then kill them with whatever implement was most convenient.[18]

Serb forces also established camps for Muslim women in which detainees were systematically and repeatedly raped by Serb troops, paramilitary forces, and police. Rape was used by the Serbs as a weapon of war to destroy the Muslim people of Bosnia, the objective being to give birth to Serb babies. The European Council estimated that more than twenty thousand Muslim women and girls were raped in the first year of the war.[19]

To a far lesser extent, Croat forces in Bosnia used similar tactics against Muslims in a drive to absorb Croat-dominated portions of Bosnia into a Greater Croatia. At various times and places during the conflict, all three sides committed some atrocities against one or both of the other parties, often in retaliation for early atrocities committed against their own people. Nevertheless, Serb forces were responsible for the overwhelming majority of the atrocities committed in Bosnia, and only the Serbs committed atrocities on a massive scale, in a systematic way, and with the orders coming from the top.[20]

After the initial waves of expropriation, deportation, summary execution, rape, torture, and destruction, the Serbs began to feel the political heat from an outraged international public (due in large part to a Western media that refused to remain morally "neutral" in the face of genocide.)[21] Milosevic and his ultranationalist allies then switched to a strategy of protracted siege and starvation. This stage of the war dragged on until the summer of 1995, when Serb forces overran the town of Srebrenica, separated the civilian men from the women and children, deported the latter and summarily executed the former. Upwards of eight thousand unarmed, defenseless Muslim men between the ages of sixteen and sixty were brutally murdered by Serb forces and buried in mass graves just outside Srebrenica.

When the Serbs first began to close on the town, NATO air strikes were launched to punish the Serb forces and prevent them from taking Srebrenica. However, the Serbs threatened to kill captured Dutch peacekeepers and shell civilians indiscriminately. The Dutch government and the UN representative then cancelled the air strikes, and the Serbs were permitted to finish their "ethnic cleansing" of Srebrenica. This great horror—the largest atrocity committed in Europe since World War II—finally provoked substantial and decisive international military intervention, with the result that all parties signed on to the Dayton accords later that year.[22]

INTERNATIONAL FAILURE

The characterization of the international community's response to genocide in Bosnia as a "failure" must be somewhat qualified. Not *all* of the international community failed; many non-state members of the international community—IGOs, NGOs, epistemic communities, the media, eminent individuals—acted honorably. For instance, in July 1992, the Institute for the Study of Genocide, a nongovernmental organization based in New York, warned the United Nations and the United States of their suspicion that genocide was being perpetrated Bosnia.[23] Media commentators, human rights representatives, members of the U.S. Congress, Jewish advocacy groups, Muslim advocacy groups, and others pressured the Bush administration in 1992 to declare Serb atrocities as "genocide."[24] From mid-1992 to mid-1993 Roy Gutman, a reporter for *Newsday*, wrote detailed dispatches describing the genocide in Bosnia, for which he won the 1993 Pulitzer Prize.[25] Finally, those elements of the United Nations system that were least liable to control by the great powers identified genocide in Bosnia early on and called for immediate international action to halt it.

For example, on 18 December 1992, the UN General Assembly passed a resolution describing Serbia's "ethnic cleansing" of Bosnia's Muslim population "a form of genocide" and condemning it. On 8 April 1993, the International Court of Justice, after examining considerable evidence, issued a unanimous order to Serbia to do all in its power to abide by the Genocide Convention. On 15 June 1993, the United Nation's World Conference on Human Rights appealed to the UN Security Council to take the measures necessary to end genocide in Bosnia.[26]

However, the UN Security Council, dominated as it is by the five permanent members—and especially the United States—reacted with ambivalence. The Security Council seemed to make a promising beginning in October 1992 when, responding to mounting complaints from states, nongovernmental organizations, news media, and international public opinion, it created a Commission of Experts to investigate alleged atrocities in Bosnia. This Commission was made up of leading international legal experts from five different nations: Canada, Egypt, the Netherlands, Norway, and Senegal. From 1993 to 1995, it sought evidence from nation-states, international governmental and nongovernmental organizations and conducted its own on-site investigations, using a team of sixty-five criminal investigators, forensic scientists, and military engineers for mass-grave exhumations.[27]

The Commission examined more than sixty-four thousand pages of documents, three hundred hours of videotaped testimony, and intelli-

gence data from satellite photo reconnaissance, intercepted radio trans-
missions and cell phone conversations. In a series of reports beginning
1993 and culminating in its *Final Report* of 1995, the Commission concluded that there was ample evidence that all three sides were committing at least some war crimes. However, the Commission pointed out
that the Serbs seemed to be responsible for the overwhelming majority
of war crimes, and that *only* the Serbs were engaging in a calculated campaign of genocide. The Commission's *Report* stated in part:

> There is sufficient evidence to conclude that the practices of "ethnic
> cleansing" were not coincidental, sporadic or carried out by disorga-
> nized groups or bands of civilians who could not be controlled by the
> Bosnian-Serb leadership. Indeed, the patterns of conduct, the manner
> in which these acts were carried out, the length of time over which they
> took place and the areas in which they occurred combine to reveal a
> purpose, systematicity and some planning and coordination from higher
> authorities. Furthermore, these practices are carried out by persons
> from all segments of the Serbian population in the areas described:
> members of the army, militias, special forces, the police and civilians . . .
>   Similar practices were also, on occasion, carried out by Croats against
> Muslims in Bosnia and Herzegovina. But, the Croatian authorities have
> publicly deplored these practices and sought to stop them, thereby indi-
> cating that it is not part of the Government's policy.
>   Bosnian Government forces have also committed the same type of
> grave breaches of the Geneva Conventions against Serbs and Croats, but
> not as part of a policy of "ethnic cleansing." The number of these viola-
> tions, as reported, is significantly less than the reported violations allegedly
> committed by other warring factions.
>   The Commission is unable to determine the amount of harm and the
> exact number of violations committed by each of the warring factions.
> Nevertheless, it is clear that there is no factual basis for arguing that there
> is a "moral equivalence" between the warring factions.
>   . . . The Commission emphasizes that in addition to the individual
> criminal responsibility of perpetrators who commit violations, the military
> and political leaders who participate in the making, execution and carry-
> ing out of this policy are also susceptible to charges of genocide and crimes
> against humanity, in addition to grave breaches of the Geneva Convention
> and other violations of international humanitarian law.[28]

Based on the Commission's reports, the UN Security Council voted to
create the International Criminal Tribunal for the former Yugoslavia.
The Commission of Experts then turned over all its evidence to the
prosecutor for the new International Criminal Tribunal, Judge Richard
Goldstone.[29] On 24 July 1995, having examined all the evidence provided

by the Commission of Experts, as well as new evidence provided by states and human rights NGOs, Judge Goldstone issued indictments charging war crimes, crimes against humanity, and genocide. Members of all three warring factions were indicted for war crimes, but only the Serbs, including Bosnian Serb political leader Radovan Karadzic and Bosnian Serb military commander General Ratko Mladic, as well as other Serb leaders, were indicted for crimes against humanity and genocide.[30]

In a separate case, the government of Bosnia brought suit against the government of Serbia in the International Court of Justice at the Hague for failure to enforce the Genocide Convention, to which both were signatories. After reviewing all the evidence presented and hearing all the arguments presented by both sides, the fourteen-judge panel of the ICJ *unanimously* issued an order on 8 April 1993 directing the government of Serbia to comply with the Genocide Convention. The order read in part:

> The Government of the Federal Republic of Yugoslavia (Serbia and Montenegro) should immediately, in pursuance of its undertaking in the Convention of the Prevention and Punishment of the Crime of Genocide of 9 December 1948, take all measures . . . within its power to prevent commission of the crime of genocide.[31]

Finally, the United Nations' World Conference on Human Rights, referring to the Serbs in Bosnia, condemned genocide and ethnic cleansing in its final declaration:

> The World Conference on Human Rights expresses its dismay at massive violations of human rights, especially in the form of genocide, "ethnic cleansing," and systematic rape of women in war situations, creating mass exodus of refugees and displaced persons.[32]

Unfortunately, the leading members of the Security Council undercut the efforts of the ICT by failing to provide adequate enforcement of the Judge Goldstone's indictments. The Security Council left the responsibility of arresting the indicted up to the member states of the UN if and when these suspects happened to fall into their hands. Military forces of some NATO states occupying zones of Bosnia eventually carried out arrests of several important suspects. However, the highest-ranking suspects—Mladic and Karadzic—have been allowed to remain at large, thereby endangering long-term peace and reconciliation.[33]

More importantly, the Western states on the Security Council, particularly the U.S., failed to do what was needed to stop *ongoing* genocide in Bosnia. Under the watchful eyes of UN forces, "ethnic cleansing and other war crimes continued virtually unabated."[34] Instead of treating genocide as a core threat to the international system, Western leaders narrowly viewed genocide as a moral, less-than-vital threat, not liable to the use of decisive force, especially *American ground troops*. In fact, some Western nations refused to admit publicly that genocide was actually occurring in Bosnia, despite the determinations of the competent legal bodies of the UN. The United States, for instance, consistently denied between 1992 and 1995 that genocide was occurring in Bosnia, despite having concluded *internally* as early as 1993 that genocide had been perpetrated in Bosnia.[35]

American political leaders feared that a ground combat intervention to halt mass atrocities in Bosnia would produce a Vietnam-like quagmire and troop casualties that would not be supported by domestic public opinion.[36] Richard Holbrooke labeled this fear the "Vietmalia syndrome," after the trauma created by the twin foreign policy debacles of Vietnam and Somalia.[37] However, U.S. military power was absolutely *central* to any successful international effort to halt genocide in Bosnia. All other Western powers were far less capable than the U.S., militarily, and none of them were politically likely to risk their troops to stop genocide in Europe if the most powerful state in NATO—and in the world—refused to do so.[38] And since the U.S. was paying 40 percent of NATO's bills and U.S. participation was critical to NATO's command, control, communications, intelligence, airlift, and sea lift capabilities, the use of NATO to stop Serb genocide was also out of the question.[39] As David Callahan has explained:

> It was naïve to imagine that the Europeans were ready to handle a major security challenge on their own. . . . NATO was the only institution in Europe capable of organizing a decisive Western response, and the use of this body required the leadership, or at least the active participation, of the United States.[40]

James Gow, in his careful study of Western diplomatic maneuvering on Bosnia, also came to the conclusion that Washington's refusal to commit U.S. combat troops was the decisive variable in the paralysis of international policy in Bosnia. He wrote: "In the final analysis, the critical factor in the failure of the Western countries to intervene was the refusal of the U.S. to put ground troops into the ring."[41] Ironically, the "indispensable nation" had become the "immovable obstruction" standing in the way of using decisive force to stop genocide in Bosnia. The immense frustration that this caused many in the human rights and humanitarian assistance communities was expressed by international human rights expert Aryeh Neier. He wrote:

Time and again, it appeared that international outrage had boiled over and might push the Security Council to employ substantial military force against the Serbs to make them stop bombarding civilian communities, wantonly destroying ancient cultural monuments, and forcibly deporting and interning noncombatants in detention camps, and to put an end to torture, rape, summary executions, and the massacres euphemized as "ethnic cleansing." But each time, until August 1995, the major powers that ran the Security Council backed away from significant armed intervention.[42]

NOT A "VITAL INTEREST"?

In May 1993, President Clinton dedicated the U.S. Holocaust Memorial Museum. Yet, that same month U.S. Secretary of State Warren Christopher framed the situation in Bosnia as "a humanitarian crisis a long way from home, in the middle of another continent." Some thought they heard the echo of Neville Chamberlain's 1938 description of Czechoslovakia: "a quarrel in a far-away country between people of whom we know nothing!"[43]

In fact, U.S. policymakers were remarkably deceptive in their characterization of the conflict in Bosnia between 1992 and 1995. U.S. political leaders made no effort to rally their domestic publics to support a robust campaign to suppress genocide. Rather they sought to avoid the word "genocide" altogether in their public statements, as the evidence from the electronic search of White House documents, presented in the previous chapter, demonstrates. Of course, in private, Western policymakers would defend this apparent contradiction as a necessity of "realism," given the apparent lack of public support for committing U.S. troops to the conflict in Bosnia.[44]

Clear evidence of the U.S. government's *structural* failure to treat genocide as a threat equal to aggression and a vital interest requiring decisive force can be found in official policy statements on national security priorities and the use of force. For example, in 1993 then-U.S. Ambassador to the United Nations Madeleine Albright explained the "four overarching goals" in American foreign policy. First was strengthening major market democracies; second, helping emerging democracies; third, isolating rogue states; fourth and last were "humanitarian concerns"—presumably encompassing the halting of genocide, although genocide was not explicitly mentioned.[45]

President Clinton's first national security adviser, Anthony Lake, also indicated the low U.S. priority for humanitarian concerns in a 1996 speech at George Washington University:

I would cite seven circumstances, which, taken in some combination or even alone, may call for the use of force or military forces: To defend against direct attacks on the United States, its citizens, and its allies; To counter aggression; To defend our key economic interests, which is where most Americans see their most immediate stake in our international engagement; To preserve, promote and defend democracy, which enhances our security and the spread of our values; To prevent the spread of weapons of mass destruction, terrorism, international crime and drug trafficking; To maintain our reliability, because when our partnerships are strong and confidence in our leadership is high, it is easier to get others to work with us. And for humanitarian purposes, to combat famines, natural disasters and gross abuses of human rights.[46]

Presumably, genocide can be included under this last (and lowest) priority of "gross abuses of human rights," although, again, there is not explicit mention of genocide in the document.

In May 1997, the White House published *National Security Strategy for a New Century,* listing three categories of threats to vital U.S. interests: (1.) regional or state-centered threats, (2.) transnational threats, and (3.) threats from weapons of mass destruction. "Aggression" was identified under the first category, while "internal conflicts," "failed states," and "uncontrolled refugee migrations" were mentioned under the second. Perhaps the authors of the document assumed genocide was covered by the second category, "transnational threats" (which, of course, it is), but again there was no explicit reference to either genocide or catastrophic human rights abuses. Under the subsection "Military Activities," using force is described as appropriate to "promote regional stability, deter aggression and coercion, prevent and reduce conflicts and threats," but again there is no mention of stopping genocide or other crimes against humanity.[47] Three years after the horror of Rwanda, genocide had not yet appeared on the "radar screens" of U.S. national security decisionmakers.

The U.S. government also consistently denied between 1992 and 1995 that the problem in Bosnia was a vital interest of the United States. In June 1993, Secretary of State Christopher said that Bosnia "involves our humanitarian concerns, but it does not involve our vital interests."[48]

Tony Lake's speech also, then, revealed the mistake of U.S. and other Western leaders in developing inappropriate political and military objectives for international forces in Bosnia. Their primary political objective was not to stop genocide, but to return "peace" to the region. Their primary military objective was not to rescue the victims of genocide but to deliver humanitarian assistance to the victims while they waited to be slaughtered. International leaders did not size and mandate their forces to fight a war against *genocidaires,* but to be "neutral" and "impartial" peacekeepers in the midst of genocide.[49] U.S. and Western leaders gave their military forces a UN Chapter "Six-and-a-Half" mandate—more than peacekeeping but less than war fighting—to *muddle through* an ambiguously defined humanitarian crisis, to avoid interfering with genocide, and protect themselves only. Their mandate was to protect international humanitarian personnel, to feed and clothe refugees but not protect them, and to protect themselves. Hence, UN troops in Bosnia were given the nickname "UN *Self-*Protection Force.[50]

This tactic of using UN peacekeepers to feed the intended victims, but not to protect them from the perpetrators of genocide, was profoundly inappropriate and bound to lead to the unnecessary slaughter of the victims and the humiliation of the UN forces. Indeed, in May 1995, the Serbs seized more than three hundred UN peacekeepers and held them hostage against possible NATO bombing.[51] Consequently, genocide continued unchecked in Bosnia until November 1995.[52]

FAILURE REVERSED?

The stalemate in Bosnia was finally broken by the international public outrage over the Serb massacre of seven thousand unarmed Bosnian Muslim men in the summer of 1995. This outrage triggered the Europeans to prepare to withdraw their peacekeeping forces and seriously undermined NATO's unity and fundamental integrity.[53] French president Chirac viewed the Srebrenica massacre as similar to World War II atrocities and urged the Clinton administration to provide U.S. helicopters to transport French ground troops to Bosnia to defend the remaining "safe haven."[54] The British and other European powers were also putting intense pressure on Washington to reconsider its flat ban on U.S. ground troops. Bosnia had brought U.S.-Western European relations to its worst point since the Suez Crisis of 1956.[55] Early in the post–Cold War era, the very survival of NATO was suddenly at stake, as the Atlantic alliance seemed to be coming apart at the seams over genocide in Bosnia.[56]

This crisis posed an agonizing political dilemma for U.S. policymakers: commit U.S. ground combat troops to a bloody conflict they believed the American public would not support, or allow NATO to disintegrate? As early as 1992 the U.S. military had warned of the fallacy of relying upon air power alone in Bosnia and privately expressed a preference for a sizable ground force to defeat the Serbs and stop the slaughter.[57]

The U.S. solved its dilemma in a creative and deceptive way. "Decisive and substantial force" was finally used to stop Serb genocide, but without having to commit American ground forces. Instead, a proxy army was used to defeat the Bosnian Serbs on the ground, while NATO provided the air power. Retired high-ranking U.S. military professionals, working for a private Washington, D.C.-area firm called Military Professional Resources Incorporated, trained the Croatian army in AirLand Battle Doctrine under a State Department license.[58] This Croatian army then proceeded to "cleanse" the Krajina region of Croatia of 150,000 Croatian Serbs, many who had lived there for generations.[59] The Croatian army then joined forces with the much weaker and poorly equipped Bosnian army to attack and defeat the Bosnian Serbs in the Bihac pocket of western Bosnia. Richard Holbrooke actually gave the game away in his book on Bosnia when he described a note that Bob Frasure had passed to him at a meeting with Croatian president Tudjman in Zagreb in August 1995:

> Dick: We "hired" these guys to be our junkyard dogs because we were desperate. We need to try to "control" them. But this is no time to get squeamish about things. This is the first time the Serb wave has been reversed. That is essential for us to get stability, so we can get out.[60]

Consequently, the popular impression that NATO air power, alone, was responsible for ending "ethnic cleansing" in Bosnia is a false and misleading one (and may have contributed to a similar miscalculation about the efficacy of air power four years later in Kosovo). The Bosnian Serbs capitulated not because of the air strikes, but because the Croatian army changed the situation on the ground by reducing in a matter of days Serb-held territory in Bosnia from 70 percent to 49 percent—*and dropping fast.*[61] As Timothy Garton Ash was to explain five years later, in the wake of another NATO air campaign that failed, on its own, to stop Serb "ethnic cleansing":

> Western leaders trying to prevent "another Bosnia," learned a wrong lesson from Bosnia. They thought Milosevic had been bombed into accepting the Dayton agreement in 1995. They forgot that it had first required a large ground offensive—by Croatian troops![62]

Only at that point was the West able to cut the deal at Dayton, cynically casting Milosevic as a great "peacemaker!" Some evidence suggests that Milosevic's price for playing this role at Dayton was the West's withholding from the ICTY evidence of his leading role in perpetrating genocide in Bosnia, a Faustian deal that seemed to backfire in Kosovo three years later.[63]

A United Nations report on its failure at Srebrenica indicated that the UN's greatest mistake was the strategic failure to recognize that the essential nature of the Bosnian conflict was genocide, which led to the ineffective use of peacekeeping tactics not forceful enough to stop genocide.[64] Michael Ignatieff wrote that the international community's failure to stop genocide in Bosnia

> resulted in the death of 200,000 people and the deportation of several million inhabitants. This was a shame . . . embarrassment at the palpable failing of leadership . . . Bosnia made it perfectly plain that there were substantial costs to a presidential reputation if a commander-in-chief stood by while massacre occurred.[65]

SOME TOUGH QUESTIONS

Was Serb "ethnic cleansing" of Muslims in Bosnia really genocide? The well-respected NGO—and recipient of the Nobel Peace Prize—Medecins Sans Frontiers (Doctors Without Borders) has taken the position that, unlike Rwanda, Bosnia was *not* a case of genocide.[66] Others argue that if genocide occurred in Bosnia, all three sides—Croats, Muslims, and Serbs—are responsible.[67] However, as explained above, the most authoritative and competent international legal bodies—the UN Commission of Experts, the ICJ, the ICTY, the UN Human Rights Commission—have determined, after careful review of the enormous quantity of evidence, that while all sides committed at least some atrocities, only the Serb side perpetrated a conscious policy of premeditated, organized, systematic genocide in Bosnia. And while MSF is an excellent international humanitarian organization of physicians and other health-care workers, it is not more legally competent or authoritative than the highest international legal bodies in interpreting the Genocide Convention. Indeed, if the "shoe were on the other foot," MSF would most certainly—as they should—raise serious questions about the *medical* competency of an international humanitarian organization of *lawyers,* if they stubbornly insisted that the HIV virus did not cause AIDS!

Was not the Pentagon extremely reluctant to use force in Bosnia? Did not the military chiefs, suffering from "Vietnam syndrome," also block the use of U.S. combat troops in Bosnia? Indeed, analysts and political pundits have often asserted this. For example, policy analyst David Callahan wrote:

> Within the American military there was particular hesitancy about using limited force as part of a strategy of preventive action. The so-called Powell doctrine—based on the lessons of Vietnam and, more recently, Lebanon—held that force should be used only when it could be applied decisively with a near guarantee of success. . . . A central lesson from the Yugoslav episode is that clear-cut standards of the Powell doctrine are incompatible with the demands of preventive action, at least as applied to ethnic conflicts.[68]

However, this criticism is not accurate. The military chiefs were not re-luctant to use ground combat forces because they were dealing with eth-nic conflict, they opposed the commitment of ground forces because the *political* leaders had neither clarified the nature of the conflict, framed it as a vital interest, or convinced the American people that it was worth taking casualties. So long as the political leaders insisted on prolonging the ambiguous character of the Bosnian situation, the military leaders had little choice but to oppose the use of ground troops. General Powell, no fan of calling the use-of-force doctrine the "Powell Doctrine,"[69] tried to explain this in his autobiography:

> My own views on Bosnia had not shifted from the previous administra-tion. . . . Our choices ranged from limited air strikes around Sarajevo to heavy bombing of the Serbs throughout the theater. I emphasized that none of these actions was guaranteed to change Serb behavior. Only troops on the ground could do that. . . . My constant, unwelcome message at all the meetings on Bosnia was simply that we should not commit military forces until we had a clear political objective. . . . The debate exploded at one session when Madeleine Albright, our ambassador to the UN, asked me in frustration, "What's the point of having this superb military that you're always talking about if we can't use it?" I thought I would have an aneurysm. American GIs were not toy soldiers to be moved around on some sort of global game board. . . . The West has wrung its hands over Bosnia, but has not been able to find its vital interests or matching com-mitment. No American President could defend to the American people the heavy sacrifice in lives it would cost to resolve this baffling conflict.[70]

But what if an American president had used the "g" word and accurately framed the Bosnian situation as genocide? What if an American presi-dent had the political courage to define stopping genocide as a vital American interest? What if an American president tapped into the la-tent public support for stopping genocide that was built up by fifty years of remembering the lessons of the Holocaust? What if an American president asked the people to support the use of U.S. combat troops as part of a larger international force to be sent to Bosnia to stop genocide? Would the military chiefs have been less resistant to sending ground troops to Bosnia? In all probability, yes!

What about the Russians, though? Would they have not supported their Slavic "brothers," the Serbs, if such a bold antigenocide policy were attempted? Would not the Russians wield their veto power to stop UN authorization of such an intervention? On political grounds, the Rus-sians would not have wanted to be closely associated with Serb leaders indicted for genocide by an organization—the ICTY—that they, the

Russians, helped create. In strictly military terms, the Russians were in no position to do in Bosnia what they could not do in Chechnya—use military force effectively. As the report of the International Commission on the Balkans (ICB) explained:

> From Russia there was rhetorical support for Serbia. . . . But ever since the failed coup in Moscow in August 1991, there has been no chance whatsoever of direct Russian support for Belgrade.[71]

Though there was some controversy over whether or not what occurred in Bosnia was really genocide, there is little doubt about it in the case of Rwanda. There the failure of the international community to stop genocide was ever greater.

CHAPTER 6

Genocide in Rwanda

Genocides are a modern phenomenon—they require organization—and they are likely to become more frequent in the future.

—Gerard Prunier[1]

If there is anything worse than the genocide itself, it is the knowledge that it did not have to happen.

—International Panel of Eminent Personalities[2]

A fundamental misunderstanding of the nature of the conflict contributed to false political assumptions and military assessments.

—UN Department of Peacekeeping Operations[3]

HISTORICAL BACKGROUND

Prior to independence from European colonialism, there existed little violence between the Tutsi, the Hutu, and the Twa (or pigmies), the three ethnic groups inhabiting the region.[4] Although a caste system developed in Rwanda about four hundred years ago, with cattle-owning Tutsi establishing a patron-client relationship with the farming Hutus, the two largest ethnic groups nevertheless shared a common language, culture, and religion. As Tutsi from the central kingdom of Rwanda gradually conquered peripheral Tutsi and Hutu principalities, Rwanda became increasingly consolidated. The two groups were not entirely antagonistic toward each other; Tutsi and Hutus frequently intermarried and a modicum of social mobility was possible.[5]

When wars did occur in the region, *Rwandans* waged them: Tutsi, Hutu, and Twa fighting *together* against their non-Rwandan neighbors.[6] However, with the arrival of first the Germans, and then the Belgians, European colonizers employed nineteenth-century, social-Darwinist theories of racial superiority to treat the taller, slimmer, lighter-skinned Tutsi as superior to the shorter, thicker, darker Hutu. This systematic social prejudice and preferential treatment created over the long term a deep and bitter resentment among the Hutu toward their Tutsi overlords.[7]

German colonization of Rwanda (1885–1916) was implemented with a relatively small number of German colonizers who relied on the assistance of various Tutsi leaders to carry out their rule. In 1916, the Belgians seized Rwanda from the Germans and following the defeat of Germany in World War I, the League of Nations awarded to Belgium the mandate to rule Rwanda, which it did until 1962. During this time, the Belgian colonialists ruled Rwanda indirectly, through Tutsi administrators. The Belgians purged Hutu leaders from positions of influence and power and awarded the minority Tutsi the dominant positions in Rwanda society, in education, employment, and the like, thus closing off any Hutu social mobility. This severe discriminatory practice deepened Hutu bitterness and resentment toward the Belgians and their Tutsi clients and increased ethnic polarization between the Hutu and Tutsi.[8] According to Edmond Keller, director of the Center for African Studies at University of California-Los Angeles,

> [T]he historical memory of the Hutus of Rwanda can be traced back to recollection of Tutsi collaboration with Belgian colonialists, brutal administrative practices, and systematic discrimination throughout the colonial era.[9]

In 1962, when the Hutu-led guerrilla movement won independence from Belgium for Rwanda, the Hutus purged the Tutsi from their government and military positions and systematically discriminated against them, in a game of turnaround-is-fair-play. However, the Tutsi did not go quietly and soon a cycle of violence engulfed the new nation-state as the two ethnic groups competed for power. Pressure of overpopulation and poverty also contributed to ethnic tensions. Ethnic massacres occurred in 1963, 1966, and 1973. Many Tutsi fled Hutu discrimination and violence and became refugees in nearby nations, particularly in Uganda.[10]

Postcolonial Hutu rule of Rwanda initially produced a democracy, but this was short-lived as President Gregoire Kayibanda soon imposed one-party rule and consolidated power among his supporters from his home area in central Rwanda. A decade later, Major General Juvenal Habyarimana, a Hutu from northern Rwanda, seized power in a military coup.[11] By the late 1980s, government revenues were declining precipitously as prices for Rwanda's coffee and tea exports were tumbling on the international market. International economic institutions pressured Rwanda to make efficiencies, and the rising unemployment, particularly among young men, pushed Rwanda to the brink of violence and civil war.[12]

Open civil war began in October 1990 when the Tutsi RPF (Rwandan Patriotic Front) launched an invasion of northern Rwanda from their base of exile in southern Uganda. The RPF invasion threatened the Habyarimana government, which then deliberately "awakened the sleeping dogs of ethnic division." In government propaganda, all Tutsi were denounced as alien filth.[13] The RPF's ten thousand troops were soon locked in combat with the Hutu FAR (Forces Armee Rwandaises), who were trained and equipped by the French government, which hoped to keep the "anglo-saxon" forces from winning state power.[14]

In 1992, Rwanda's population was about 9.2 million with 83 percent Hutu and 17 percent Tutsi. However, half the Tutsi population was in exile. The Organization for African Unity (OAU) brokered a cease-fire and a tentative settlement. On 4 August 1993, both sides signed a shaky peace agreement in Arusha, Tanzania. On 5 October 1993, the UN Security Council authorized a peacekeeping force, known as the UN Assistance Mission for Rwanda (UNAMIR) to help implement the Arusha agreement. Neither party was very happy with the peace agreement, but both sides seemed exhausted by the civil war. The Hutu leadership was particularly resistant to the power-sharing agreement arranged in Arusha, and they provoked violent disruptions of the cease-fire. But the qualitative difference in the degree and kind of violence came in 1994.[15]

THE CRIME

On 5 January 1994, President Habyarimana was sworn in as president of a new coalition government. However, not much else could be agreed upon as the ceremonies to install new ministers and deputies were cancelled and the coalition government seemed paralyzed. Instability and violence increased in January and February, such as an attack on an RPF convoy being escorted by the United Nations peacekeeping force in Rwanda (UNAMIR). The roads from Kigali were being mined, and in the capital, demonstrations and attacks on civilians increased. Ominously, the Hutu militia began amassing weapons.[16]

The idea for the genocide seemed to emerge gradually among the extremist Hutu leadership, beginning with the RPF invasion in 1990 and growing into a full-fledged plan by early 1994.[17] In those early months of 1994, extremist Hutu leaders, who included the heads of the defense ministry, the presidential guard, and the chief political party, the *Mouvement Révolutionnaire National pour la Démocratie et de Développement* (MRND[D]), decided to exterminate the entire Tutsi population of Rwanda, as well as any moderate Hutus who dared to oppose them.[18] According to a high-level informant who was being paid by the army chief of staff and the president of the MRND(D) to train special paramilitary units, all Tutsi were to be registered for what the informant assumed was a campaign of final extermination. The informant passed this information on to the United Nations commander in Rwanda, who then sent an urgent fax to UN headquarters in New York warning that genocide was imminent, three months before the genocide actually began.[19] The alert described in some detail Hutu plans to "exterminate" the Tutsi and murder Belgian peacekeepers. This information was also sent to the Belgian, French, and United States embassies in Rwanda.[20]

The extremist Hutus' plan was to organize a society-wide, top-to-bottom genocide of Tutsi. The government administration, the military (FAR), the police, and the party organization right down to the grass-roots level were to implement the genocide.[21] The antagonism between the Tutsi and the Hutu had many and varied roots: social, economic, and political. However, the occasional spikes in ethnic violence did not produce genocide until 1994, when the Hutu extremist leaders decided to commit this horrible crime. This would not be the natural culmination of an ancient African tribal feud, but the cold, calculated plan of ruthless political leaders who saw an opportunity and seized upon it. As Gerard Prunier wrote: "The decision to kill was of course made by politicians for political reasons."[22] These ruthless, criminal conspirators had watched the international community abandon Somalia after the Mogadishu firefight that killed eighteen U.S. soldiers, and fail to stop genocide in Bosnia for three years.[23] They concluded—correctly, as it turned out—that the U.S.-led international community would not have the interest or the stomach to stop genocide in Rwanda.[24]

Through the use of radio and other means of mass communication, the extremist Hutu leadership defined the Tutsi as subhuman "cockroaches" that threatened the existence of Hutus and needed to be wiped out.[25] The triggering event for the genocide, however, was the mysterious shooting down of the airplane carrying Rwandan president Habyarimana and Burundi president Ntaryamira in Kigali on 6 April 1994.[26] Suspicions fell on the twelve-man Hutu group of extremists known as the "social commission," who planned the genocide. The shoot-down, in fact, provided the catalyst for the ensuing genocide.[27] Within an hour of Habyarimana's death, the presidential guard, with prepared lists of priority targets, began the killing in Kigali. These priority targets included Tutsi political leaders, religious leaders, human rights activists, journalists, priests, nuns, and any Hutus moderate enough to resist the slaughter of the Tutsi.[28]

When the genocide began, the RPF broke out of their barracks in Kigali. A larger RPF force soon crossed the border with Uganda and headed south toward Kigali. The RPF had resumed full-scale war to try to stop the genocide. They made rapid progress, quickly defeating Hutu militia and the Rwanda Army. By the end of April, the RPF controlled the northeastern part of the country, but the worst of the genocide spread south and west.[29]

The mass killing spread quickly from the capital to the countryside. There, primarily the two French-trained militias, the Interhamwe and the Impugamugambi, perpetrated the killing.[30] Most Tutsi were killed where they lived or worked or wherever they could be found, most often with machetes, axes, or clubs. In many cases, however, Tutsi were forced to flee into institutions of "sanctuary" such as churches, schools, and hospitals. Here they were often slaughtered en mass.

In one of the worst cases, approximately two thousand Tutsi sought sanctuary at the l'Ecole Technique Officialle (ETO), or what was called the "Don Bosco" school, between 6 April and 11 April 1994. At least four hundred were children. Don Bosco was a technical school in Kigali, and it was protected by ninety Belgian UN peacekeeping troops. However, the Belgian troops were ordered by their superiors at the UN in New York to evacuate only European nationals and to use force only to protect themselves or Europeans nationals. The Belgian peacekeepers were then ordered to withdraw from the school and travel by armed convoy to the airport, where they were then evacuated to safety out of the country. Some of the defenseless Tutsi asked the Belgian troops to shoot them, rather than leave them to be hacked to death by the extremist Hutu militia. When the Belgians began leaving, some Tutsi tried to block their vehicles, but the United Nations Assistance Mission for Rwanda (UNAMIR) troops fired over their heads to scare them away. Within hours of the Belgians' departure, most of the two thousand unarmed Tutsi were slaughtered by Hutu militia using small arms, grenades, and machetes.[31]

In the rural areas, the local Hutu administrators also used the local police to do the killing, but soon the administrators, the police, and the militias were enlisting the aid of ordinary peasants, as killing more than 10 percent of the country's population was hard work and took some time. The Hutu elite were able to convince the ordinary Hutu peasant to participate in the genocide of their Tutsi friends, neighbors, and family members through a carefully planned campaign of hatred, myth, and manipulation. The rape of women before killing them was common, as was sexual mutilation, with breasts and penises being hacked off.[32] Often, the killers stole the possessions of their victims.[33] The genocide, which quickly eclipsed the civil war in casualties, killed twenty thousand in the first week and two hundred thousand in the first month. By the end of the ten-week genocide, some eight hundred thousand Tutsi and moderate Hutus had been slaughtered.[34]

INTERNATIONAL FAILURE

The international community's knowledge of the scope and intensity of the genocide in Rwanda was, in fact, substantial. According to the OAU's International Panel of Eminent Personalities (IPEP):

> [W]hen it was finally over, a major international argument broke out over who knew what about the events unfolding in Rwanda. There can be no doubt on this question: The facts speak for themselves. The world that mattered to Rwanda, its Great Lakes Region neighbors, the UN, all the major western powers—knew exactly what was happening and that it was being masterminded at the highest levels of the Rwandan government.[35]

However, despite having ample warning of the impending genocide and detailed knowledge of the unfolding genocide, and possessing more than sufficient force to stop the perpetrators, the international community took no meaningful action to prevent or suppress the genocide in Rwanda. Again, the words of the IPEP:

> At the UN, the Security Council, led unremittingly by the United States, simply did not care enough about Rwanda to intervene appropriately. What makes the Security Council's betrayal of its responsibility even more intolerable is that the genocide was in no way inevitable. First, it could have been prevented entirely. Then, even once it was allowed to begin, the destruction could have been significantly mitigated. All that was required was a reasonable-sized international military force with a strong mandate.[36]

This last point was corroborated by a study conducted by the Carnegie Commission on Preventing Deadly Conflict, in conjunction with Georgetown University's Institute for the Study of Diplomacy, and the U.S. Army. A panel of ten army generals with significant combat experience studied the feasibility of stopping genocide with the kind of international rapid reaction force that the UNAMIR commander, General

Romeo Dallaire, had asked for: approximately five thousand combat troops. The distinguished military panel concluded the following:

> The hypothetical force described by General Dallaire—at least 5,000 strong, depending on the method of employment, and armed with the equipment and capabilities to employ and sustain a brigade in combat—could have made a significant difference in Rwanda in 1994. . . . The opportunity existed to prevent the killing, to interpose a force between the conventional combatants and reestablish the DMZ, and to put the negotiations back on track.[37]

The panel also concluded that:

> U.S. participation would have been essential. . . . [T]he capabilities for generating political will, forces, and mandates will require study and articulation. . . . Efforts to create a standing peacekeeping force and the delineation of capabilities, responsibilities, and parameters surrounding the use of force in such situations show promise.[38]

The United States government, knowing the full truth about the genocide in Bosnia, "repeatedly and deliberately undermined all attempts to strengthen the UN military presence in Rwanda," and instead relied entirely upon ineffective diplomatic warnings to halt the violence and evaded the central issue of stopping genocide.[39] As David Callahan has explained:

> When reports of genocidal violence first emerged from Rwanda, the U.S. government initiated a diplomatic pressure campaign that combined frequent private appeals with protests by top officials. . . . The killing did not let up. The spectacle of officials in Washington calling long distance to urge restraint on the part of genocidal maniacs in Rwanda was almost comical. Predictably, it was of little use.[40]

U.S. officials did not call the killing "genocide." Instead, they referred to it as "civil war" or "random tribal slaughter." The White House, in fact, forbade its officials to use the word "genocide" for fear that the U.S. would then be obligated to stop it.[41] As Amnesty International, USA, explained:

> In April of 1994, individuals in the legal advisors office of the State Department warned against labeling the massacres as "genocide." The crafters of the subsequent policy toward Rwanda decided instead to use the amorphous term "acts of genocide," citing a difficulty in determining the intent behind the mass killings (despite early evidence to the contrary.) The rationale behind this policy was to first and foremost avoid negative public

reactions triggered by the intervention in Somalia; but the second reason was to avoid the legal obligation to prevent genocide and to punish those responsible, as outlined in the Convention on Genocide.[42]

The UN Security Council had a United Nations peacekeeping force of 2548 troops in Rwanda when the genocide began. On 21 April 1994, two weeks into the genocide, UNAMIR commander General Romeo Dallaire requested reinforcements to put a stop to the genocide. The UN Security Council considered his request, which would have required giving him enforcement powers under Chapter VII of the UN Charter to stop the genocide, but decided against this. Instead, the UN Security Council, at the urging of the United States, voted to *withdraw* 90 percent General Dallaire's peacekeeping forces "for their own safety." The remaining 270 UN troops were to be used only for the evacuation of foreign dependents, and to act as an "intermediary between the parties in an attempt to secure their agreement to a cease-fire."[43] Clearly, the UN Security Council, led by the United States, was determining the nature of the conflict in Rwanda as primarily a civil war, rather than a case of genocide. Also clear is that the U.S.-led Security Council was treating both the perpetrators and the victims of genocide as equally responsible "sides" in a civil war.

If necessary, the remaining UN troops were to use deadly force to defend themselves and the foreign dependents, but not the Rwandans. The IPEP report took particular exception to this behavior:

> This double standard seems to us outrageous. . . . Is there a conclusion we can draw from this incident other than that expatriate lives were considered more valuable than African lives?[44]

For the United States, the memory of the Somalia debacle just five months earlier was still fresh. The working assumption in Washington was that there would be no political support in America for a new, ambiguous, costly intervention in the heart of Africa. Former National Security Council staff member Richard Haass noted:

> The fear of domestic political backlash led to the ignominious pullout from Somalia and the refusal to commit ground forces to Kosovo or forces of any sort to Rwanda.[45]

The IPEP report was even stronger in characterizing America's failure to intervene to stop the genocide in Rwanda:

It was, however, a function of domestic politics and geopolitical indifference. . . . The problem was that nothing was at stake for the U.S. in Rwanda. There were no interests to guard.[46]

Of course, the intentional blurring of the differences between a civil war, as in Somalia, and a maliciously preconceived genocide, as in Rwanda—by avoiding the "g" word—*created* the very ambiguity that served to undercut public support for foreign interventions. And Washington saw no vital interests involved in the Rwanda genocide.[47] Ethnic studies professor Alexandre Kimenyi explained the strategic rationale of U.S. policy: "National interests come first before human rights violations. That's why in Rwanda nobody was in a hurry to intervene."[48]

In May 1994, at the very height of the Rwanda genocide, the White House issued its new policy on U.S. participation in UN peacekeeping operations. *Presidential Decision Directive 25* (PDD 25) laid out in detail the conditions under which the United States would agree to contribute combat troops to a UN peace operation. No American troops would be committed unless there was a vital U.S. national interest at stake, and stopping genocide was not considered a vital U.S. interest. In fact, the word "genocide" did not appear anywhere in the document. This document became the political rationale for the American policy of avoidance and denial regarding genocide in Rwanda.[49] Less than one year after President Clinton castigated the "deniers" of genocide in his speech at the dedication of the Holocaust Memorial Museum, the United States had joined the deniers.[50]

Of course, President Clinton apologized for failing to prevent genocide in Rwanda when he visited Kigali airport in March 1998. He said, in part:

> It may seem strange to you here, especially the many of you who lost members of your family, but all over the world there were people like me sitting in offices, day after day after day, who did not fully appreciate the depth and the speed with which you were being engulfed by this unimaginable terror.[51]

However, the International Panel of Eminent Personalities that investigated the Rwanda genocide was not convinced:

> The U.S. has formally apologized for its failure to prevent genocide. President Clinton insists that his failure was a function of ignorance. The facts show, however, that the American government knew precisely what was happening, not least during the months of genocide . . . Eyewitness accounts were never lacking, whether from Rwandans or expatriates with the International Committee for the Red Cross, Human

Rights Watch, the U.S. Committee for Refugees, or others. Week after week for three months, reports went directly from Rwanda to home governments and international agencies documented the magnitude of the slaughter and made it plain that this was no tribal bloodletting, but the work of hardline political and military leaders. At the same time, the reports spelled how countless people could still be saved, identifying exactly where they were hiding, and what steps were needed to rescue them. Yet the world did less than nothing.[52]

For the ten weeks that the slaughter continued, international leaders delayed, stalled, and vacillated regarding an appropriate response, and they deceived much of the rest of the world about what was actually happening in Rwanda. Only when the genocide was over did they send military forces into Rwanda and the surrounding region, and then only to provide humanitarian assistance, showing "impartiality" and "neutrality" toward both the victims and the perpetrators of genocide. The French launched Operation Turquoise to provide humanitarian assistance to the Hutu *genocidaires* and their dependents in southwest Rwanda, then fleeing the RDF. The U.S., in June, launched Operation Support Hope across the border in the Kivu region of Zaire, objectively assisting the perpetrators of genocide and their dependents, 1.2 million of whom had become refugees from the Tutsi forces suppressing the genocide.[53]

These *genocidaires* in the Kivu refugee camps were committed to retaking power in Rwanda and finishing the genocide they had started. From their refugee camps in Zaire, and with the support of the Mobutu government, they began launching attacks back into Rwanda.[54] The Rwanda government, in league with anti-Mobutu forces in Zaire, and with aid from Uganda, Angola, and Burundi, eventually launched a war to eliminate these camps and to topple Mobutu from power. Mobutu fled Zaire in May 1997 and Laurent Kabila became the head of the new Democratic Republic of Congo. Eventually, however, Kabila turned on his former Rwandan allies, and a continental war broke out involving one-fifth of Africa's governments and armies.[55]

The failure of the international community in Rwanda was unmitigated. Western leaders, beginning with the Clinton administration, misunderstood the strategic nature of the Rwanda crisis. First, they intentionally misidentified the crisis as a "civil war" or an "ancient feud" that was *not vital* to national or international interests.[56] Then the UN Security Council, at the behest of the U.S., eliminated the possibility of using the one tool that could have suppressed the genocide: ground troops. Finally, the Clinton administration, fearing the wrath of domestic public opinion, knowingly misled the public about what was really taking place in Rwanda. The result was the unnecessary deaths of eight hundred thousand innocent Rwandans, the regionalization of ethnic hatred throughout central and eastern Africa, the proliferation of arms throughout central Africa, and the lowering of Rwanda's economic status to the poorest country in the world.[57] Worst of all, perhaps, was that unchecked genocide in Rwanda further damaged the fabric of an already fragile international social order.

CHAPTER 7

Genocide in Kosovo

To look after your own people is the first duty of a statesman. Yet it is a perverted moral code that will allow a million innocent civilians of another country to be made destitute because you are not prepared to risk the life of a single professional soldier of your own. What are soldiers trained for? What kind of a superpower is this? What kind of morality?

—Timothy Garton Ash, 24 June 1999[1]

We now turn to Kosovo. For some, Kosovo does not qualify as a case of genocide. While it is true that the United Nations has not yet formally determined that genocide was perpetrated in Kosovo, the chief prosecutor for the ICTY is, at the time of this writing, still investigating this case, and further indictments, including for genocide, may still be forthcoming.[2] Most importantly, Kosovo cannot be treated as an isolated case, for it is in fact part of a larger pattern of Serbian "ethnic cleansing"—a euphemism for genocide—in which non-Serbs were to be destroyed, defiled, or deported from Greater Serbia, beginning at the periphery in Croatia and Bosnia, and moving toward the center in Kosovo, and eventually in Belgrade itself.

The same perpetrators—Milosevic and company—who were behind the earlier genocide in Bosnia were also at work in Kosovo. Milosevic simply managed to mask his involvement in Bosnia.[3] Milosevic refused to allow a team from the ICTY, led by Chief Prosecutor Louise Arbour, entry into Kosovo to investigate allegations of genocide. The hate rhetoric and the plan were the same as in Bosnia: drive the "Turks" out by death, destruction, and terror. The motives and means of the perpetrators were also the same in Kosovo as in Bosnia: to create a Greater Serbia and in-crease personal political power and wealth through demonization, con-centration, deportation, and annihilation. This chapter, therefore, proceeds on the logical assumption that the murderous ethnic cleansing perpetrated in Kosovo in 1998/99 was an *extension* of Belgrade's systematic genocide perpetrated in Bosnia from 1992 to 1995. Perhaps a domestic analogy is appropriate here. When one is dealing with a serial killer who has already committed a long string of murders, and suddenly another vic-tim is discovered at the feet of the perpetrator, it is prudent to suspect that this most recent murder might be part of a larger pattern.[4]

Finally, on the question of scale, even if there were many fewer mur-dered in the ethnic cleansing of Kosovo than first thought—say ten thou-sand instead of one hundred thousand—it is still genocide if the intent was to destroy, "in whole or in part," the ethnic Albanian community in Kosovo by killing some and driving the rest out. The crime of genocide is not a numbers game. It is a criminal process whether one waits for six mil-lion to be killed or one interrupts it after the first six thousand are killed.[5]

HISTORICAL BACKGROUND

The region of Kosovo has for many centuries been an important part of Serbia's history; Serbian kings built monasteries and churches there, and Kosovo has since been considered the cradle of Serb religion and cul-ture.[6] In the fifteenth century, however, the Ottoman Turks conquered Kosovo and established relatively harsh rule over the Serbs living in the region. In 1912, after five hundred years of Ottoman rule, the Serbs de-feated the Turkish army and liberated Kosovo. At this time, Serbs made up approximately 40 percent of the population of Kosovo.[7]

During World War II, Serbs, Croats, and Muslims in Yugoslavia, when they were not fighting the Allies or the Axis powers, killed each other in large numbers. At the end of World War II, when ultranation-alist Serb Chetnik leaders wanted to "cleanse" Serbia of all non-Serbs, Marshall Tito and his communist Partisans prevented this. Tito, who promulgated a policy of multinationalism and ethnic tolerance in Yu-goslavia, gradually conferred autonomy on Kosovo, as he did with Vojvo-dina to the north, which was dominated by ethnic Hungarians. Continued friction between Serbs and ethnic Albanians during the post–World War II years, as well as declining economic conditions, spurred many Serbs to abandon Kosovo. Between 1974 and 1989, per-haps ten thousand Serbs left Kosovo, in part because of Albanian harass-ment, according to some observers.[8] It was within this seething environment of ethnic tension and periodic violence that Slobodan

Milosevic and his political, military, and intellectual allies hatched their scheme to "ethnically cleanse" Kosovo of its entire Albanian population, killing some and deporting the rest.

The blueprint for the ethnic cleansing of Kosovo and much of the rest of Yugoslavia was drafted by the Serbian Academy of Science and Art and issued on 29 September 1986.[9] This memorandum demanded that Serbia's borders be expanded because the Serbs were allegedly the most mistreated and oppressed nationality in Yugoslavia (despite dominating the Communist Party, the military, the police, the courts, and the financial institutions of Yugoslavia). It argued that all Serbs needed to live in one enlarged Greater Serbia. This document served as the intellectual rationalization and rallying point for a virulent Serb ultranationalist movement, a growing movement that Slobodan Milosevic was soon to hijack.

Kosovo was the original focus of Serbian president Slobodan Milosevic in his rise to power in the late 1980s. A loyal Communist Party bureaucrat, then the head of Yugoslavia's central bank, Milosevic was sent to Kosovo in 1987 to quell growing violence between Serbs and ethnic Albanians. Instead of easing the tensions, he inflamed them by promising the Serbs that he would forcefully support Serbs retaking control of Kosovo.

THE CRIME

In 1989, Milosevic revoked Kosovo's autonomy and began a gradual process of ethnic cleansing. Milosevic began implementing a strategy of gradually increasing persecution of ethnic Albanians in Kosovo, who represented 90 percent of Kosovo's population. Although there had been ethnic tension and occasional violence between Serbs and ethnic Albanians in Kosovo before 1989, none had yet seen anything like the systematic campaign of intimidation and terror that Milosevic's forces waged over the next decade.

From 1989 to 1999, ethnic Albanians were systematically driven from all positions of power and influence in the government, the economy, education, health care, the arts, and all other important institutions in Kosovo society. Ethnic Albanians in Kosovo were systematically stripped of their rights to use their own language, to speak their minds, or to publish their own newspapers. While constituting the overwhelming majority, the ethnic Albanian population in Kosovo gradually became political, economic, social, and cultural outcasts in their own land.[10]

The initial reaction to this campaign of persecution from the leaders of the ethnic-Albanian community in Kosovo was to mount a nonviolent, mass-based campaign of resistance to Serb persecution. Led by Ibrahim Rugova, ethnic Albanians refused to cooperate with Serb institutions and instead set up their own, often clandestine, alternative schools, clinics, libraries, businesses, and government agencies.[11] They also appealed to the West for political support and protection from Serb violence. Soon, this community had created an entire alternative society in Kosovo, which blunted considerably the impact of Serb oppression and frustrated Milosevic and company. However, Milosevic had bigger, more immediate concerns in the early-to-mid-1990s, first among them Bosnia.

The West's failure to halt Serb genocide in Bosnia for three years caused rising fear and anxiety among many ethnic-Albanian leaders. Many ethnic Albanians began to question the efficacy of Rugova's strategy of nonviolent resistance and seeking support from the West. But by far the most shattering developments for the Kosovo Albanians were the fall of Srebrenica with its attendant slaughter under the passive gaze of the West, the failure of UN forces to arrest Bosnian Serb leaders indicted for genocide, and the "nondecision" taken at Dayton regarding the protection of ethnic Albanians in Kosovo. These three disheartening developments—and most especially the failure of Dayton to eliminate the threat from Milosevic—dealt a mortal blow to any lingering hopes among most ethnic-Albanian leaders that Rugova's strategy could protect them from Serb genocide.[12] Warren Bass perhaps summed it up best:

> Dayton's lessons are grimly appropriate when considering the current violence in Kosovo, where Milosevic's demagoguery helped set off Yugoslavia's demise and which is the latest target of his ethnic cleansing. The bloodshed in Kosovo is a symptom of the approach that strengthened Milosevic. . . . As such, today's crisis comes as scant surprise.[13]

This rising fear and bitter disillusionment drove many ethnic Albanians into the arms of the Kosovo Liberation Army (KLA). The KLA had, up until then, been a motley crew of competing clan leaders who nevertheless shared the radical dream of an independent Kosovo. However, most ethnic Albanians in Kosovo were motivated by the more moderate concern of human rights. The KLA launched its first armed attack in May 1993 (after Serb genocide had begun in Bosnia). But most ethnic Albanians rejected the violent strategy of the KLA and maintained their support of Rugova's nonviolent resistance campaign until after Dayton made clear to them the bankruptcy of this approach. The KLA made their first public showing on 28 November 1996, at a funeral of an ethnic-Albanian schoolteacher killed by the Serbs, and as the Serb campaign of ethnic cleansing in Kosovo intensified, ethnic-Albanian sympathy shifted increasingly toward the fledgling and disunited KLA.[14]

In 1998 the Milosevic leadership escalated its persecution of ethnic Albanians and enveloped it in a counterinsurgency campaign aimed at destroying the KLA. This led to an intensification of the struggle between Serb military and police forces, on the one hand, and the growing KLA on the other. Serb forces carried out reprisals against entire families and villages in February 1998. Increasingly, Belgrade tried to justify the growing violence of its original campaign of persecution as necessary to defeat armed "terrorists."[15]

The KLA, buoyed by new support and new recruits, went on the offensive throughout the spring and early summer of 1998, but a Serb counteroffensive forced the lightly armed KLA to abandon open warfare and revert to guerrilla tactics of "hit-and-run."[16] Serb military and police units killed, burned, looted, and deported ethnic Albanians from Kosovo throughout the summer of 1998. Adam Roberts has estimated that during this summer offensive, fifteen hundred ethnic Albanians were killed and three hundred thousand more were displaced and hiding in mountains and forests.[17]

On 23 September 1998, the UN Security Council passed resolution 1199 demanding that Serbia cease all action by security forces against civilians. On 15–16 October, the Serbs agreed in negotiations in Belgrade to reduce to ten thousand their internal security forces and to twelve thousand their military forces. On 24 October 1998, the Security Council demanded in resolution 1203 that Serbia permit unarmed observers from the Organization for Security and Cooperation in Europe (OSCE) to verify the Serb military and police reductions agreed to the previous week in Belgrade.[18] However, according to evidence provided to ICTY chief prosecutor Judge Louise Arbour by the Austrians and the Germans, Milosevic and his generals were already devising a "final solution" to the Kosovo problem: Operation Horseshoe.[19]

In the winter of 1998/99, the Serbs began a systematic, incremental campaign of atrocities against unarmed ethnic Albanian civilians. However, Serb authorities either denied the atrocities or explained them as regrettable but necessary measures to combat "terrorism." Serb leadership was apparently trying to walk a fine line between promulgating their policy of ethnic cleansing in Kosovo and provoking NATO's intervention. Their solution was to ethnically cleanse Kosovo, one village at a time. Or as one Serb diplomat reportedly explained: "A village a day will keep NATO away!"[20]

One such atrocity occurred in Racak in January 1999 and caught the attention of the world as evidence of an apparent Serb massacre of fifty-eight unarmed civilians was made available to the world via reports of the OSCE observers and global television. This massacre finally provoked

NATO to issue an ultimatum to Milosevic demanding that he halt the atrocities, negotiate a peace with the KLA, and withdraw his military and police forces from Kosovo. Racak had finally hardened the West's posture toward Milosevic; compromise with him after the massacre at Racak seemed like a Munich-like appeasement and could not be tolerated.[21] Instead, Milosevic stalled at Rambouillet while he amassed greater forces on the border of Kosovo in preparation for his "final solution" to the Kosovo problem. He assumed that he could ride out any NATO air campaign and that the West was bluffing about using force on the ground. He calculated—correctly, initially—that the West had little stomach for risking military casualties in a ground invasion to stop his ethnic cleansing in Kosovo.[22]

Milosevic's stubborn refusal to negotiate in good faith at Rambouillet or to cease his campaign of ethnic cleansing in Kosovo was a bid to gain time to amass his forces for his Operation Horseshoe. This was his plan for the systematic killing or expulsion of the entire 1.8 million ethnic-Albanian population in Kosovo. This plan began before the NATO bombing campaign started, and intensified after the bombs began falling. On the eve of NATO's bombing campaign, Serbia had sixteen thousand internal security forces, twenty thousand regular army troops, and eight thousand reinforcements on the border with Kosovo. As Mark Danner explained:

> [I]t is now clear, Slobodan Milosevic was preparing his vast operation in Kosovo. In a long career, this would be his masterpiece, cleansing the Serb homeland of its Albanian interlopers in a matter of weeks. This should, again, have come as no surprise; as late as February [1999], George Tenet, the director of Central Intelligence, had actually predicted in public testimony that Milosevic would do precisely this.[23]

This meticulously organized plan was implemented under a single, unified command that oversaw regular army troops, Special Police of the Interior Ministry, and private paramilitary groups such as Arkan's Tigers and the White Eagles. These latter groups were notorious for their central role in Serb genocide in Bosnia a few years earlier. Serb forces began their "final solution" on 19 March 1999 by attacking KLA strongholds on the periphery of Kosovo. On 20 March, the OSCE pulled its unarmed observers out of Kosovo. On 23 March, the Serbs started burning ethnic Albanian villages, and on 24 March, NATO began its bombing campaign against the Serbs. Immediately thereafter, the Serbs greatly intensified their campaign of slaughter in Kosovo.[24]

NATO's credibility was on the line in Kosovo. It appeared to much of the world, the U.S. included, that genocide was again being perpetrated in the Balkans. President Clinton described the stakes involved:

I think there's an important principle here . . . if the world community has the power to stop it, we ought to stop genocide and ethnic cleansing.[25]

British prime minister Tony Blair echoed Clinton's description in a speech in Chicago on 22 April, when he said:

Acts of genocide can never be a purely internal matter. When oppression produces massive flows of refugees which unsettle neighboring countries they can properly be described as "threats to international peace and security."[26]

UN secretary general Kofi Annan also spoke to this concern on 7 April when he said:

Of all gross violations, genocide knows no parallel in human history. . . . Though we have no independent observers on the ground, the signs are that it may be happening, once more, in Kosovo.[27]

Tony Judt, director of the Remarque Institute at New York University, described in a *New York Times* op-ed piece on 5 April what the West needed to do in Kosovo:

The logic of our response must be that the international community or NATO or the United States must be ready to do what is necessary to stop [Milosevic]. Yes, this means ground troops, and yes, that means casualties. If we can't admit this, we lack the military courage of our moral convictions. We must pray for a new political leadership that grasps this and can explain it to the electorate. The alternative is to unlearn every lesson in the past 60 years.[28]

Vaclav Havel, speaking before the Canadian Parliament on 29 April, said:

The alliance of which both Canada and the Czech Republic are now members is waging a struggle against the genocidal regime of Slobodan Milosevic. . . . It is fighting because decent people cannot sit back and watch systematic, state-directed massacres of other people.[29]

However, a political leadership finally willing to speak the "g" word was not yet prepared to use ground troops to stop genocide. Fearing a political backlash from NATO and American casualties, and continuing to misapply the so-called "Vietnam-Beirut-Mogadishu syndrome," U.S. leaders insisted, instead, on a bombing campaign conducted from the safety of fifteen thousand feet over Kosovo and Serbia.[30]

INTERNATIONAL FAILURE

On 24 March 1999, NATO launched a massive bombing campaign against Serb military and police forces in Kosovo, as well as in Serbia proper. NATO's chief objectives were to compel Milosevic to end his brutal campaign of ethnic cleansing and withdraw his armed forces from Kosovo. But rather than end the genocide, Milosevic responded to the NATO bombing campaign by accelerating and intensifying his "final solution." In a little more than ten weeks, according to a U.S. Department of State report, Serb forces expelled more than 90 percent of ethnic Albanians from their homes in Kosovo, creating six hundred thousand internally displaced persons (IDPs) and seven hundred thousand refugees in neighboring Albania, Macedonia, and Montenegro. Serb forces looted and burned homes, schools, hospitals, and mosques in more than five hundred residential areas. They detained military-aged men of an unknown number and fate, and summarily executed intellectuals, professionals, political and community leaders in at least seventy towns and villages, and perpetrated systematic rapes of women in Djakovica and Pec. They systematically confiscated identity papers, passports, and license plates, and destroyed voter and civil registries in towns and villages across Kosovo.[31]

NATO called its bombing campaign Operation Allied Force. It lasted seventy-eight days and involved more than thirty-four thousand sorties, with little or no effect on Milosevic's camouflaged military forces. It also failed to stop the ethnic cleansing and placed a great strain upon NATO unity.[32] General Wesley Clark, supreme allied commander of NATO, and other NATO generals doubted the bombing campaign without a complementary ground component could stop the ethnic cleansing in Kosovo, and they made their doubts known to their civilian superiors early on. However, many political leaders in NATO, misreading the lessons from NATO's bombing campaign in Bosnia in 1995, and desperately seeking a way to avoid troop casualties among NATO troops, assumed the bombing campaign would quickly compel Milosevic to end his "final solution" in Kosovo.[33] As Mark Danner explained:

> Finally, caught in their own ultimatum, they were at last forced to send their warplanes, and this time without Croatian tanks or Bosnian infantry to fight for them on the ground.[34]

Compellence from the air, however, does not work. In order to control the behavior of people on the ground, ground combat forces must be present. Indeed, there never has been a case where bombing alone has forced a government to change its objectives or policy.[35] Strategic bombing failed to break the will of either the German or the British people during World War II, just as it failed to break the will of North Vietnam in the 1960s and early 1970s.[36] Hence, the bombing-only campaign over Kosovo and Serbia had its predictable consequence of uniting the Serb people around their leader, Slobodan Milosevic. Meanwhile, in Kosovo, the ethnic cleansing continued unabated. On 29 May, *New York Times* reporter John Kifner wrote:

> Two months into the campaign now, the terror has been devastatingly effective and virtually unhampered by NATO's bombing campaign, judging by accounts from refugees, relief workers and officials from international agencies, NATO and the United States Government.[37]

As the failure of NATO's bombing campaign to stop the ethnic cleansing in Kosovo became increasingly apparent, there arose a thundering chorus of criticism and outrage. For instance, on 19 April the editors of the *New Republic* described the implications of NATO failing to stop genocide in Kosovo:

> It would be a humiliating defeat for the United States and NATO, a defeat that could ultimately lead to the end of the alliance. It would be a humanitarian and moral catastrophe and a blow to the democratization and stability of Europe as a whole.[38]

On 6 May, Mark Danner, staff writer for the *New Yorker*, wrote:

> Not only is the world's great liberal power, with all its might, unwilling, as we are often told, to be "the policeman of the world" . . . but the idealist values that were proudly assumed to be a vital part of America's vision of itself as a democratic power in the world, and that American leaders so often hailed during the Cold War, appear suddenly desiccated and pale.[39]

On the same day, William Pfaff, Paris-based political columnist for the *International Herald Tribune* wrote:

> If there is not a NATO victory over Serbia there will no longer be a NATO. But no victory now is imaginable without a land campaign.[40]

On 20 May, distinguished Harvard professor of European studies Stanley Hoffmann wrote:

The essence of the issue is simple: at the end of the twentieth century, crimes against humanity are being committed on a scale and with a brutality that one hasn't seen in Europe since Nazi Germany.[41]

On 24 May, President Carter's former national security adviser, Zbigniew Brzezinski, wrote:

President Clinton's conduct of the war over Kosovo has been feckless. His overeager diplomacy has undercut the credibility of his military campaign, while his timid military tactics are depriving his diplomacy of serious clout.... No wonder Serbian strongman Slobodan Milosevic has not yielded. NATO's morally callous failure to take any military risks in order to impede the ethnic cleansing has given Mr. Milosevic's thugs a completely free hand to destroy Kosovar society.[42]

Inevitably, NATO was faced with a critical decision: launch a NATO ground war—with its likelihood of NATO casualties—to stop the genocide, or capitulate to perpetrators of genocide in the belly of Europe. The first seemed to promise a firestorm of domestic political opposition, the second raised the specter of a humiliating defeat for, and the disintegration of, NATO. While leaders in Washington seemed to wring their hands in indecision like modern-day Hamlets, London filled the leadership vacuum by publicly and repeatedly urging preparations for a ground war against the Serbs in Kosovo. At first, the Clinton administration was reluctant—and annoyed at the openness of the call for a ground war—but their growing realization that the alternative—NATO defeat—was even worse, finally moved Washington to reconsider the ground-war option.[43]

Both the British and the Americans began mobilizing the ground forces necessary to execute an overwhelming and decisive victory over Serb forces in Kosovo. Heavy divisions were placed on alert and final preparations were made to call up military reserves in both Britain and the U.S. NATO engineers began widening the road between the Albanian port of Durres and the Kosovo border to accommodate NATO's heaviest tanks, and the size of the NATO ground force in Macedonia was doubled so that it could act as the "spearhead" into Kosovo. Additionally, NATO informed the Russians that unless Milosevic capitulated immediately, the ground invasion of Serbia was coming—and if necessary it would go all the way to Belgrade to apprehend Milosevic—regardless of Russian objections. Russian political and military leaders realized that there was little they could do to challenge superior NATO forces on the ground, given that their "best" troops were bogged down in Chechnya. Furthermore, the Russians decided that an insolent, ultranationalist, recently indicted war criminal like

Milosevic was not worth going to global thermonuclear war to defend. The Russians passed on NATO's message of imminent ground invasion and informed Milosevic that there was nothing more that they could or would do for him. He was now on his own. Faced with compelling evidence of NATO preparations for invasion, globally isolated by the ICTY's indictment of him on charges of war crimes and crimes against humanity, and abandoned by his strongest and closest international allies, Milosevic finally capitulated and the crisis ended.[44]

A STRATEGIC CRITIQUE

Kosovo was an extension of U.S. policy on the Balkans that had suffered for years from confusion, contradiction, and ambiguity.[45] NATO leaders experienced deep shame and bitterness because of their earlier failure to stop the Serb massacre of Bosnian Muslims at Srebrenica. Therefore, NATO leaders were psychologically prepared to prevent a repetition of Serb ethnic cleansing in Kosovo. However, because the leaders of NATO still did not fully appreciate the strategic nature of genocide, they were politically unprepared to adopt the tactics necessary to achieve their goal. Political leaders still did not accept the fact that, objectively, stopping genocide was a vital national interest to every state, especially the most powerful state in the international system. In the words of Tony Judt: "[The lesson] our reluctant leaders either forgot or never knew (was) that the extermination of minorities within national frontiers . . . is illegal, unethical, and threatens the interests of everyone."[46] Consequently, Western leaders, particularly American leaders, were not ready to risk the lives of their ground troops—and the domestic political firestorm they assumed would follow the return of body bags—to stop it.

However, another mistake Western leaders made was, according to Timothy Garton Ash:

> to suggest that the high-altitude bombing campaign, prescribed by the American obsession with achieving "zero casualties," could stop ethnic cleansing on the ground.[47]

This inevitably spelled disaster for their policy until they grudgingly accepted the strategic imperative of a ground invasion more than ten weeks into their bombing campaign.

Some strategists in and out of government argued that preparations for a ground invasion of Kosovo would take up to six months, by which time the ethnic cleansing would have been completed. However, as William Pfaff was quick to point out, this argument was a red herring, meant to hide political opposition to the use of American ground troops. After all, in 1950 General Douglas MacArthur, lacking the modern wonders of rapid transportation, was able to move sufficient U.S. forces across the Pacific to launch the landing at Inchon only eleven and a half weeks after the initial North Korean invasion of South Korea. And just ten years earlier, President Bush's response to the Iraqi invasion of Kuwait was to move ground forces *in days* to Saudi Arabia. What U.S. leaders lacked in the Kosovo crisis was not logistical capability but political will.[48]

A frequent objection to a NATO ground invasion of Kosovo was that the Russians, while just barely tolerating a bombing campaign, would never permit a ground invasion of their Slavic Balkan ally in their historical sphere of influence. However, the leaders of Russian did not much care for Milosevic or his extreme nationalist politics, a brand of hate-politics that threatened their own fledgling Russian democracy. And even if they wanted to preserve Milosevic's regime, the only functioning military option they had left, given the weak and disintegrative state of Russian conventional forces, was nuclear war with the West. The downside of such a radical option, given their limited interests in the former Yugoslavia, was quickly apparent to the Russians.[49]

Another typical objection to a NATO ground war in Kosovo—and to the NATO air war as well—was that the Westphalian norm of nonintervention is sacrosanct and should not be violated. However, as with the crime of aggression, if a state commits genocide against a portion of its own people, it forfeits its legal and moral right to national sovereignty. National sovereignty has never been an absolute right, and states that fail to live up to minimum standards of international obligations (such as eschewing wars of aggression and genocide) endanger their rights and privileges under international law. No state can be permitted to promulgate barbarity with impunity.[50]

Some objected to NATO's use of force in Kosovo without UN Security Council authorization. Although it might have been wiser to put an authorizing resolution to the test in the Security Council before deciding to use NATO air power, it is nevertheless probable that both the Russians and the Chinese would have blocked such a resolution. And although the principle of multilateral legitimacy is highly important, it is trumped by the emergency of needing to rescue the innocent from slaughter. Michael Ignatieff put it this way: "When a house is on fire, you do not seek a search warrant before entering to put out the blaze." Michael Walzer reminded us that the "fire" was "deliberately set, the work of arsonists, aimed to kill, terribly dangerous."[51]

One could also, perhaps, apply the Lockean theory of the "prerogative of the executive" in an international system presented with grave danger but paralyzed by power politics. The most capable member, the functional equivalent of an "executive" in a semi-anarchical system, has the obligation to lead the willing members in an extralegal effort to preserve the fundamental integrity of the system threatened by a grave danger that would destroy the system and the law equally. The invocation of the prerogative power of course runs great risks of arbitrary use, but if the threat to the system—in this case genocide—is truly the *greater* danger to the whole community, then the application of the prerogative power in this instance will eventually be vindicated. However, if cynical leaders, through deception and obfuscation, abuse this prerogative power for their own ends, the larger community will surely hold these leaders accountable once the deception is discovered.[52]

The assumption on the part of Western leaders that their domestic publics would not support a ground invasion to stop genocide in Kosovo was not supported by empirical evidence. Polls in early April showed that 66 percent of British, 58 percent of French, and 54 percent of American respondents supported the use of ground troops to stop the slaughter and mass deportation in Kosovo.[53] Again, though, it depended upon the strategic characterization of the conflict as to whether the public supported the use of force to stop it. For example, when asked on three occasions if it would "be worth the loss of some American soldiers lives to help bring peace to Kosovo," an average of 53 percent of American respondents disagreed. However, when the conflict was described as genocide, the response was quite different. Fully 69 percent agreed with the statement: "The Serbs effort at 'ethnic cleansing' through killing many ethnic Albanians and driving hundreds of thousands of them out of Kosovo is a form of genocide. The U.S. has a moral obligation to join in efforts to stop this genocide." When asked if the U.S. should withdraw if American troops are killed in a ground intervention in Kosovo, only 20–21 percent agreed.[54]

Steven Kull, director of the Program on International Policy Attitudes, found similar patterns in CNN/USA *Today*, CBS, and ABC/*Washington Post* polls. He concluded from this data that:

> Support for involvement in Kosovo is primarily derived from humanitarian concerns and the belief that genocide is occurring. . . . [W]hen the value of ensuring that no American troops are killed is placed against the value of stopping ethnic cleansing in specific scenarios, a majority, in most cases a strong one, accepts some troop fatalities so as to stop ethnic cleansing.[55]

In the conventional wisdom, Kosovo had no U.S. strategic interest. In Kosovo there was no close ally, no geostrategic importance, no oil. However, this conception of "national interest" is far too narrow, simplistic, and short-term to fit the complex, interdependent, rapidly globalizing world in which we now live. A more complex, sophisticated, and holistic—a *grand strategic*—understanding of national interest was required here.

Because unchecked genocide, regardless of where in the world it occurs, violates the most elemental legal and moral rights of human beings to live, it challenges the core norms of the international system dating back to at least the 1648 Treaties of Westphalia, which defined protection for religious minorities.[56] Unchecked genocide also threatens the fundamental integrity of the prevailing liberal international system, which requires at least a minimum of toleration and observance of the rule of law if democracy and prosperity are to survive and grow.[57] Unchecked genocide also threatens the larger region in which it occurs, with sudden and serious political instability and economic disruption, as the effects of the mass crime spill over the borders into neighboring nation-states. Unchecked genocide in Kosovo meant political destabilization, economic disruption, and the growing danger of general war in Europe. The possibility of Albania, Greece, Turkey, Bulgaria, Germany, Russia, the United States, and many other nations being drawn into a widening European conflict was real and could not be long ignored.

Unchecked genocide in Kosovo also threatened both NATO and the UN with greater disunity and dysfunction. The very institutional integrity of these regional and international security organizations was placed in grave jeopardy by unchecked genocide in Kosovo. On the very eve of NATO's fiftieth anniversary, the survival of this security alliance was put in question. The credibility of U.S. leadership in the post–Cold War world was also placed in serious doubt over the American reluctance to risk military casualties to stop genocide in Kosovo. European leaders were so frustrated by America's strategy in Kosovo of airpower only and humiliated by their near-total dependence on U.S. military power, that they have since decided to create their own independent military force. This, in turn, has raised serious questions among some about the future health of NATO.[58]

Taken together, all these elements amounted to genocide posing a grave threat to international peace and security precisely at a critical point of transition from the old Cold War order to some yet undefined international order. The challenge of genocide in Kosovo required enlightened, courageous leadership to recognize the magnitude of the threat posed by genocide. Enlightened leadership should have designated, early on, the task of stopping genocide in Kosovo as a vital national and international interest worthy of significant risk in blood and treasure. Political leaders should have appealed for broad public support for the forceful suppression of genocide in Kosovo and given the American public the chance to respond positively to the challenge instead of being dismissed out of hand as cynical and indifferent.

The price for the U.S. and the international community for failing to demonstrate enlightened leadership in dealing with genocide in Kosovo has been high. Since NATO took control of Kosovo in June 1999, violence and vengeance have run rampant in the region.[59] After allowing so much killing and destruction to be perpetrated by the Serbs, and then allowing the Serb forces to retreat back into Serbia proper with impunity, NATO will have a long and difficult chore keeping the peace in Kosovo.[60] The U.S. itself has ten thousand troops stationed in the Balkans and is spending $4 billion a year on a region it initially saw as too marginal to consider a vital interest.[61] Unfortunately, the legacy for America of waiting too long to confront genocide in the Balkans can be summed up by Timothy Garton Ash's prediction made more than two years ago: "I think the sons of Kansas and the daughters of Ohio will be here for a good long time."[62]

CHAPTER 8

Remedy

Have we learnt anything? . . . Pretty little, so it seems to me. . . . I do not have to tell you that what happened in Rwanda or in Bosnia, happened right next door.

—Yehuda Bauer to the German Bundestag,
Remembrance Day, 27 January 1998[1]

Much that has been recounted in this report is bound to be discouraging for anyone who believed the victors of World War II when they swore "never again" would genocide be tolerated. The atrocities of the Khmer Rouge in Cambodia, the Serbs of the former Yugoslavia, and the Hutu of Rwanda revealed the hollowness of that pledge . . . the readiness of states to declare their concerns about the security of people and respect for human rights within states is not matched by the political will, international capacity, or normative consensus that is required for action.

—John Stremlau, *People in Peril*[2]

It is no tribute to our era that we are becoming experts on the phenomenon of genocide.

—International Panel of Eminent Persons[3]

The cases presented in the three previous chapters clearly demonstrate that the failure of the international community to stop contemporary genocide is due primarily to strategic ignorance about the true nature of genocide. This conceptual mistake led to the misapplication of force in trying to deal with genocide, and it fostered the underestimation of potential domestic support for stopping genocide via decisive force. As we have seen, genocide is a threat to both humanitarian values and traditional national interests, as values and interests are inextricably intertwined when confronting the challenge of contemporary genocide. What is more, genocide threatens the very fabric of our present liberal international order, an order on which all nations depend, but none more so than the leading nation, the United States. Therefore, the international community's unwillingness throughout the 1990s to do what was necessary to stop genocide was a strategic failure of the first magnitude. This pattern of failure has created a tone of dark pessimism among those who study contemporary genocide and crimes against humanity. According to Douglas Simon of Drew University:

> Most of the analyses of the international community's willingness and ability to deal with genocide are characterized by a depressing tone of frustration, cynicism, and pessimism.[4]

However, there are some recent signs of progress on this issue.

SIGNS OF PROGRESS

Over the past couple of years, the consciousness of the scope and depth of international failure regarding genocide has risen. Evidence of this include U.S. secretary of state Madeleine Albright's 1997 acknowledgement of the failure to call the Rwanda slaughter "genocide," President Clinton's 1998 apology for not doing enough to stop genocide in Rwanda, the U.S. establishment of an early warning system to identify signs of genocide quickly, UN secretary-general Kofi Annan's 1999 commitment to stop genocide, and the arrest of higher-ranking Serbs indicted by the ICTY for war crimes, crimes against humanity, and genocide.[5]

Additional signs of advancement on this problem were the adoption of the 1998 Rome statute creating a permanent International Criminal Court, self-critical UN reports on peacekeeping failures at Srebrenica and in Rwanda, the OAU's report on international failure in Rwanda, and reports by prestigious think tanks and NGOs on the dilemmas of humanitarian intervention to halt genocide and other mass murders. These last include Scott Feil's report for the Carnegie Commission on the Prevention of Deadly Conflict, Bruce Jentleson's report for the U.S. Institute for Peace, and the Council on Foreign Relations' memos to the next president.[6]

Finally, several new scholarly books have been published on contemporary genocide and how to stop it, including Neal Riemer's edited volume, *Protection against Genocide,* Isidor Wallimann and Michael Dobkowski's edited volume, rereleased with a new preface, *Genocide and the Modern Age,* and William Schabas's monumental work, *Genocide and International Law.*[7] However, the hope raised by the above evidence of progress has been somewhat offset by the knowledge that this progress has serious limits.

THE LIMITS OF PROGRESS

The progress made on understanding the strategic nature of genocide and what must and can be done to stop it has been incremental and uneven. Some might even call it "glacial." The international community—and its leading power—have yet to produce the firm and consistent political will required to halt genocide. For instance, President Clinton's apology in Kigali, while welcomed, was not followed by any indication of what the United States would do *differently* the next time genocide occurs.[8] The early warning system that the U.S. government created, with the assistance of human rights IGOs and NGOs, though helpful, is still insufficient to stop genocide if there is no political will to act on the early warning. For example, in Kosovo, the international community saw plenty of signs that the Milosevic government was preparing for the massive "ethnic cleansing" of ethnic Albanians, and they had the three-year tragedy of Bosnia as an object lesson. Yet, when it came to producing a credible deterrent, political leaders in the West lacked the wisdom and the fortitude to threaten a ground intervention until it was much too late and Serb forces had already killed thousands of ethnic Albanians and driven more than a million others from Kosovo. In the end, the strategic ignorance of Western leaders cost ethnic Albanians more in death and suffering, and NATO more in resources and integrity, than if Western leaders had correctly recognized the strategic threat and responded to it with a decisive use of force, including ground troops.

While the arrest of higher-ranking Serbs is certainly welcome, the chief architects of the Balkan genocide, Radovan Karadzic, Ratko Mladic, and Slobodan Milosevic, are still at large. The move to create an International Criminal Court is a major step in the right direction, but it has been undercut by the U.S. refusal to sign the Rome treaty.[9]

The UN's self-critical reports regarding the organization's failure to stop genocide in Bosnia and Rwanda are refreshing, but its defeatist attitude in the face of U.S. obstructionism is clearly evident in the UN's embracing of the Brahimi Report at the September 2000 Millennium Conference in New York.[10] After examining the UN's failures at Srebrenica and in Rwanda the Brahimi Report (named after the chairman of the UN panel, Lakhdar Brahimi) calls for major reforms of UN peacekeeping, including improved coordination and support.[11] However, if a reformed peacekeeping strategy is applied to future genocides, what we will inevitably get, given that the strategy of peacekeeping is profoundly inappropriate for stopping genocide, will be better-coordinated, better-supported failures.

BUILDING POLITICAL WILL

As John Stremlau's quote at the head of this chapter points out, three things are necessary for real and sustainable progress in stopping genocide: political will, international capacity, and normative consensus. The think-tank reports seem to offer the most hope for progress in building political will. Because of the content of the reports, the experience of the investigators, and the prestige of these research institutions, the evidence of progress in strategic understanding of genocide contained within them is significant. For instance, U.S. Army Colonel Scott Feil summarized the findings of a panel of ten generals from several NATO and African nations that examined the Rwanda genocide. The panel included the director for operations, U.S. Atlantic Command, the deputy chief of staff for operations, headquarters, U.S. Forces Command, the commanding general of the U.S. First Armored Division in Germany, and the deputy director for strategy, plans, and policy, headquarters, U.S. Department of the Army. The panel concluded that:

> The rapid introduction of robust combat forces, authorized to seize at one time critical points throughout the country, would have changed the political calculations of the participants. The opportunity existed to prevent the killing . . . in the case of Rwanda, U.S. participation would have been essential . . . the capabilities for generating political will, forces, and mandates will require study and articulation.[12]

Bruce Jentleson, director of the Terry Sanford Institute of Public Policy and professor of political science at Duke University, served as special assistant to the director of the State Department's Policy Planning Staff in 1993/94. His report for the U.S. Institute for Peace on coercive prevention is promising for several reasons. Despite the fact that it also fails to focus explicitly on genocide, the report does recognize that the prevention of mass killing requires the early and robust application of military force. In the Summary, Jentleson writes:

> [O]ne of the key lessons of the first decade of the post–Cold War era . . . is that while coercion rarely is sufficient for prevention, it often is necessary. . . . The usual argument from classical geopolitical strategists is that much of the 1990s agenda, however morally commendable, fails the basic

realist calculus of interests (too low), costs (too high), and options (too few). Yet this argument is shown to be flawed on its own terms. It underestimates the interests at stake; it overestimates the costs of acting early compared with acting late; it miscalculates options that narrow rather than stay open over time.[13]

Citing extensively the Feil report, Jentleson argues that in Rwanda "a more credible and robust military strategy could have contained the conflict and prevented the violence from reaching genocidal scale."[14] In Kosovo, Jentleson argues that ground troops should not have been taken off the table at the outset, and that "The shift in late May and early June back to threatening ground troops is widely considered to have been a crucial factor in forcing Milosevic to concede."[15] He also uses extensive polling data to refute the "casualty phobia" thesis regarding public opinion, and to show that Congress is not an insurmountable obstacle for a president determined to intervene to prevent a humanitarian disaster.[16]

The Council on Foreign Relations' policy initiative on humanitarian intervention is in some ways the most promising on the question of stopping genocide. In the forward, Council president Leslie Gelb points out that "No challenge weighs more heavily on American foreign policy at the beginning of the 21st century than that of humanitarian intervention." Gelb informs the reader that the Council commissioned four acknowledged experts with very different backgrounds and perspectives to write policy recommendations for the U.S. president.

Holly Burkhalter, advocacy director for Physicians for Human Rights, which is an NGO specializing in forensic investigations of genocide and other mass murders. She wrote her memorandum from the perspective of the secretary of state. Dov Zakheim is an adjunct senior fellow at the Council on Foreign Relations, consultant to the secretary of defense, and was deputy undersecretary of defense from 1985 to 1987. He wrote from the perspective of the secretary of defense. U.S. Army Colonel Stanley McChrystal, assistant commander for operations in the Eighty-Second Airborne Division, was a military fellow at the Council on Foreign Relations in 1999/2000, a national security fellow at Harvard University's Kennedy School of Government, and commanded both airborne and ranger battalions. He wrote from the perspective of the chairman of the Joint Chiefs of Staff. Finally, Arnold Kanter is a principal and founding member of the Scowcroft Group, a senior fellow at the RAND Corporation, was undersecretary of state from 1991 to 1993, and served on the National Security Council between 1989 and 1991. He wrote from the perspective of the national security adviser.

While there was much disagreement on a number of points regarding humanitarian intervention, there was *unanimity* among the four experts on the need for the U.S. to respond with decisive military force in clear cases of genocide. For example, Holly Burkhalter wrote:

> What must be reversed is the past pattern of American officials repeatedly promising that the United States will never again tolerate genocide (or other forms of mass killings) and repeatedly failing to fulfill this promise. This (incoming) administration can do better by articulating a doctrine that the prevention and suppression of genocide and crimes against humanity are a vital national interest, and offering appropriate resources to realize that commitment—diplomatically where possible, militarily where necessary and feasible.[17]

Dov Zakheim, though highly skeptical of the concept of humanitarian intervention, nevertheless made an exception in cases of genocide. He wrote:

> To counsel a careful calculus of interests when deciding upon intervention is not to foreswear intervention entirely. We must remain ever vigilant to the threat of genocide. As the world's leading democracy, America cannot stand by if one group of people attempts to exterminate another. Passivity in the face of genocide would undermine our very sense of who we are as a nation.[18]

Colonel McChrystal, recognizing the seriousness of sacrifice being asked of American soldiers, wrote the following to the president:

> Before we attempt to define this critical policy, we must recognize the grave implications of our task. We should review the record of past efforts and understand our successes and failures. We should know of the many lives our interventions have saved, and the many they have cost. We should go to Arlington, where you have spoken often of fallen heroes, and there on the hillside ask ourselves what we are willing to have our young die for . . .
> We must recognize several imperatives. It is self-evident that when vital or strategic national interests are at stake, if we have the means, we will intervene. Our record there is clear, but it must also be apparent that in the face of a terrible evil such as genocide, America, preferably in concert with its allies but alone if need be, will intervene to save lives and reduce suffering.[19]

Finally, Arnold Kanter sums up the collective position of these National Security Council "principals" favoring the prevention and suppression of genocide:

Not only is it very much in the U.S. national interest to foster an international environment that is compatible with our values—including democratic norms, human rights, and free markets—but from a purely pragmatic perspective, our moral authority is an indispensable element of American leadership and influence. Moreover, we as Americans sooner or later must face ourselves, live with the consequences of our action or inaction, and decide what it says about who we are and what we stand for. All of your senior advisers share this perspective, at least to the extent that they believe the United States should be prepared to consider the use of military force in clear cases of genocide.[20]

Adding to the promise of a better understanding of, and more effective action to stop genocide, are the recently published books dealing comparatively with this crime. In the new preface to their 1987 text, Wallimann and Dobkowski remind the reader that "the notion of genocide has been a difficult one to grasp, to define, and a phenomenon not sufficiently studied."[21] They conclude their preface with the following:

In addition to the urgent necessity of creating political mechanisms and the political will for timely international interventions, the fundamental and no less urgent task before us is to confront and overcome the spirit of avoidance, indifference, and pusillanimity that has inhibited our ability to act quickly and intelligently when faced with this profound human tragedy.[22]

In Neal Riemer's edited volume, the dean of genocide scholars, Helen Fein, writes that crimes such as genocide and mass murder are scarcely recognized by the international community in this post–Cold War period. She contends that:

Such crimes are distanced by framing them with a neutral label that avoids perception of the criminal causes of such events: refugee or humanitarian crises, complex humanitarian emergencies, or ethnic conflict, implying there are two equally culpable parties. This serves to obscure both cause and perpetrator; thus, there is no crime, such as genocide, requiring international attention.[23]

Schabas's exhaustive treatment of genocide in international law fills in the legal history of the struggle to stop genocide, and examines in great detail the many controversies that have arisen from the judicial interpretation of the Genocide Convention. In particular, he explores the controversial question of the *right* versus the *duty* of states under international law to prevent, suppress, and punish genocide.[24]

ENHANCING INTERNATIONAL CAPACITY

A successful global governance antigenocide strategy would address *all three* stages of the process: prevention, suppression, and punishment. It would construct an early warning system—such as the Forum on Early Warning (FEWER)[25]—that would be centrally coordinated in a legally competent Genocide Convention monitoring body, a sort of standing Commission of Experts that would supervise the application of the Genocide Convention and save valuable time in alerting the UN secretary-general to imminent or occurring genocide.[26] Such a strategy would also create a standing UN rapid reaction force, perhaps trained and equipped by NATO or a private firm such as Military Professional Resources, Inc. This UN force would be ready on a moment's notice to intervene with decisive force anywhere around the world to stop or prevent genocide.[27] This strategy would also support the establishment of the new International Criminal Court by arresting suspected perpetrators and holding them for trial.[28] Additionally, NGOs such as Prevent Genocide International[29] would aid in the mobilization of global public support for a transnational antigenocide network.[30]

CONSOLIDATING NORMATIVE CONSENSUS

The community of experts concerned with the task of creating the political will to stop genocide must reinforce and extend this recent progress in understanding the nature of genocide and the political and military strategy necessary to prevent and suppress it. Scholars and policy analysts must broaden and deepen this understanding among policymakers and convince them that stopping genocide is a *vital national interest,* worth taking the political risks inherent in using (or credibly threatening) decisive force to achieve. We academic and policy experts must persuade U.S. decisionmakers to transform this new knowledge into changed policy: that is, to incorporate a *strategic* understanding of genocide into national security strategy, use of force doctrine, and public affairs policy. Accomplishing these goals is the only way to build the "political will" necessary to break the international logjam that currently exists regarding this greatest problem of the post–Cold War era.

However, before such a strategy can be implemented successfully, we experts must consolidate our own understanding of genocide. For far too long, specialists in international law, human rights, humanitarian assistance, international security, peace and conflict resolution, ethnic conflict studies, and regional studies (for example, the Balkans, the Great Lakes region of Central Africa) have blithely assumed that we did not need the genocide scholars to tell us what genocide is. Most of the time, we have been wrong! In virtually every case where a think tank, national government, or IGO put together a panel of "experts" to investigate the international community's failure to stop contemporary genocide, the genocide scholars have been strangely absent! (My own field, international relations, is at least as guilty of this oversight as most others. While the study of war—especially nuclear war—has proliferated in the IR literature throughout the Cold War era, neither of the leading foreign policy and IR journals, *Foreign Affairs* or *International Affairs* [London], published a single article on genocide in the half century between 1945 and 1995! And the professional journal of the International Studies Association, *International Studies Quarterly*, published only one article on genocide in the past quarter-century, that of Harff and Gurr in 1988.)[31]

We "experts" must first overcome our own intellectual ignorance (and arrogance) regarding genocide if we hope to be effective in convincing busy policymakers to think differently about genocide and the national interest. Indeed, it is high time to bring in the genocide scholars. They are the best prepared to address the definitional, historical, motivational, quantitative, process, and remedial controversies regarding genocide. And what the genocide scholars do not know about humanitarian intervention, regional politics, refugee problems, public opinion, the proper use of force, and global governance, we can provide. By bringing together the best minds and experience regarding the nature of genocide, the use of military force, and public opinion, we may finally be able to offer policymakers a way to stop this scourge of humanity.

Toward a Better Twenty-First Century

... because each one's need to maintain his own respect for himself was more important to him than his popularity with others—because his desire to win or maintain a reputation for integrity and courage was stronger than his desire to maintain his office—because his conscience, his personal standard of ethics, his integrity or morality, call it what you will—was stronger than the pressure of public disapproval—because his faith that his course was the best one, and would ultimately be vindicated, outweighed fear of public reprisal.

—John F. Kennedy, *Profiles in Courage*

Contemporary cases of genocide are not isolated crimes. The thinking that underpinned the actions of the perpetrators of genocide in the former Yugoslavia, in Rwanda, and in Kosovo is part of a growing global trend of violent hate ideology. From Memphis to Marseilles to Moscow, the forces of hatred, intolerance, and mass murder, if left unchallenged, will only gain strength. The simple old myth that these forces perished in the ashes of the Third Reich will no longer suffice. And every time confused and indecisive leadership capitulates to these forces, more innocents perish, and many more times their number are placed in mortal danger.

It does not have to be this way. Nothing about this pathetic process of international failure is inevitable. The global proliferation of genocide, war, starvation, disease, and death is not predetermined. We do have a choice. Not only do we possess the informational knowledge and the physical power to put an immediate stop to this downward spiral into barbarism, but we all possess within us the moral fiber to use that knowledge and power to do what we know to be right. What remains, though, is for each of us to make this choice and to steel ourselves for the trial of seeing it through, because a global campaign to suppress genocide will not be casualty-free. If our political leaders lack the will to do what is right, then we must be prepared to apply the kind of political pressure that will stiffen their spines. If they actively obstruct a campaign to suppress genocide, then we must use the democratic process to move them out of the way.

Some will object that the strategy proposed above is naively utopian. However, far greater progress has been made where cynical realists doubted the possibilities. Few know the power of democratic moral politics better than playwright and statesman Vaclav Havel. Speaking directly to the skepticism of policymakers and academics long hardened by their adopted paradigm of realism, he said:

> We are living in extraordinary times. The human face of the world is changing so rapidly that none of the familiar political indicators are adequate. We playwrights, who have to cram a lifetime or an entire historical era into a two-hour play, can scarcely understand this rapidity ourselves. And if it gives us trouble, think of the trouble it must give to political scientists, who spend their whole lives studying the realm of the probable and have even less experience with the realm of the improbable than playwrights do.[1]

Still others will criticize the above proposals for not going far enough. Crimes less severe than genocide are left out, and given the "statist" bias in the Westphalian international system; genocide perpetrated by a permanent member of the UN Security Council can still go unsuppressed and unpunished. While this is true, improving the capacity of the international community to respond to mass murder to the point where the crimes such as occurred in Bosnia, Rwanda, and Kosovo can be stopped would be no small gain.[2] The strategy proposed above splits the difference between those who insist on perfection and those who despair of making any progress.

Improving our capacity to respond effectively to genocide is the only choice we can make if we want to pass on to succeeding generations a "Global Village" rather than Dante's "Inferno." Our children and their children deserve no less from us.

The Nuremberg Principles (1946)

(Principles of International Law Recognized in the Charter of the Nuremberg Tribunal and Judgment of the Tribunal) 1950 U.N. GAOR, 5th Sess., Supp. No. 12 (A/1316)

PRINCIPLE I

Any person who commits an act which constitutes a crime under international law is responsible therefor and liable to punishment.

PRINCIPLE II

The fact that internal law does not impose a penalty for an act which constitutes a crime under international law does not relieve the person who committed the act from responsibility under international law.

PRINCIPLE III

The fact that a person who committed an act which constitutes a crime under international law acted as Head of State or responsible Government official does not relieve him from responsibility under international law.

PRINCIPLE IV

The fact that a person acted pursuant to order of his Government or of a superior does not relieve him from responsibility under international law, provided a moral choice was in fact possible to him.

PRINCIPLE V

Any person charged with a crime under international law has the right to a fair trial on the facts and law.

PRINCIPLE VI

The crimes hereinafter set out are punishable as crimes under international law:

a. Crimes against peace:
   i. Planning, preparation, initiation or waging a war of aggression or a war in violation of international treaties, agreements or assurances;
   ii. Participation in a common plan or conspiracy for the accomplishment of any of the acts mentioned under (I).

b. War crimes: Violations of the laws or customs of war which include, but are not limited to, murder, ill-treatment of prisoners of war or of persons on the seas, killing of hostages, plunder of public or private property, wanton destruction of cities, towns, or villages, or devastation not justified by military necessity.

c. Crimes against humanity: Murder, extermination, enslavement, deportation and other inhuman acts done against any civilian population, or persecutions on political, racial or religious grounds, when such acts are done or such persecutions are carried on in execution of or in connection with any crime against peace or any war crime.

PRINCIPLE VII

Complicity in the commission of a crime against peace, a war crime, or a crime against humanity as set forth in Principle VI is a crime under international law.

UN General Assembly Resolution on the Crime of Genocide

A/RES/96 (I), 11 December 1946

Genocide is a denial of the right of existence of entire human groups, as homicide is the denial of the right to live of individual human beings; such denial of the right of existence shocks the conscience of mankind, results in great losses to humanity in the form of cultural and other contributions represented by these human groups, and is contrary to moral law and to the spirit and aims of the United Nations.

Many instances of such crimes of genocide have occurred when racial, religious, political and other groups have been destroyed, entirely or in part.

The punishment of the crime of genocide is a matter of international concern.

The General Assembly, therefore,

Affirms that genocide is a crime under international law which the civilized world condemns, and for the commission of which principals and accomplices—whether private individuals, public officials or statesmen, and whether the crime is committed on religious, racial, political or any other grounds—are punishable;

Invites the Member States to enact the necessary legislation for the prevention and punishment of this crime;

Recommends that international cooperation be organized between States with a view to facilitating the speedy prevention and punishment of the crime of genocide, and, to this end,

Requests the Economic and Social Council to undertake the necessary studies, with a view to drawing up a draft convention on the crime of genocide to be submitted to the next regular session of the General Assembly.

UN Convention on the Prevention and Punishment of the Crime of Genocide

A/RES/260 A (III), 9 December 1948

The Contracting Parties,

Having considered the declaration made by the General Assembly of the United Nations in its resolution 96 (1) dated 11 December 1946 that genocide is a crime under international law, contrary to the spirit and aims of the United Nations and condemned by the civilized world,

Recognizing that at all periods of history genocide has inflicted great losses on humanity, and

Being convinced that, in order to liberate mankind from such an odious scourge, international cooperation is required,

Hereby agree as hereinafter provided:

ARTICLE I

The contracting parties confirm that genocide, whether committed in time of peace or in time of war, is a crime under international law which they undertake to prevent and to punish.

ARTICLE II

In the present Convention, genocide means any of the following acts committed with intent to destroy, in whole or in part, a national, ethnical, racial or religious group, as such:

a. Killing members of the group;
b. Causing serious bodily or mental harm to members of the group;
c. Deliberately inflicting on the group conditions of life calculated to bring about its physical destruction in whole or in part;
d. Imposing measures intended to prevent births within the group;
e. Forcibly transferring children of the group to another group.

ARTICLE III

The following acts shall be punishable:
a. Genocide;
b. Conspiracy to commit genocide;
c. Direct and public incitement to commit genocide;
d. Attempt to commit genocide;
e. Complicity in genocide.

ARTICLE IV

Persons committing genocide or any of the other acts enumerated in article III shall be punished, whether they are constitutionally responsible rulers, public officials or private individuals.

ARTICLE V

The Contracting Parties undertake to enact, in accordance with their respective Constitutions, the necessary legislation to give effect to the provisions of the present Convention, and, in particular, to provide effective penalties for persons guilty of genocide or any of the other acts enumerated in article III.

ARTICLE VI

Persons charged with genocide or any of the other acts enumerated in article III shall be tried by a competent tribunal of the State in the territory of which the act was committed, or by such international penal tribunal as may have jurisdiction with respect to those Contracting Parties which shall have accepted its jurisdiction.

ARTICLE VII

Genocide and other acts enumerated in article III shall not be considered as political crimes for the purpose of extradition.

The Contracting Parties pledge themselves in such cases to grant extradition in accordance with their laws and treaties in force.

ARTICLE VIII

Any Contracting Party may call upon the competent organs of the United Nations to take such action under the Charter of the United Nations as they consider appropriate for the prevention and suppression of acts of genocide or any other acts enumerated in article III.

ARTICLE IX

Disputes between the Contracting Parties relating to the interpretation, application or fulfillment of the present Convention, including those relating to the responsibility of a State for genocide or any of the other acts enumerated in article III, shall be submitted to the International Court of Justice at the request of any of the parties in the dispute.

ARTICLE X

The present Convention, of which the Chinese, English, French, Russian and Spanish texts are equally authentic, shall bear the date of 9 December 1948.

ARTICLE XI

The present Convention shall be open until 31 December 1949 for signatures on behalf of any Member of the United Nations and any non-member State to which an invitation to sign has been addressed by the General Assembly.

The present Convention shall be ratified, and the instruments of ratification shall be deposited with the Secretary-General of the United Nations.

After 1 January 1950, the present Convention may be acceded to on behalf of any Member of the United Nations and of any non-member State which has received an invitation as aforesaid.

Instruments of accession shall be deposited with the Secretary-General of the United Nations.

ARTICLE XII

Any Contracting Party may at this time, by notification addressed to the Secretary-General of the United Nations, extend the application of the present Convention to all or any of the territories for the conduct of whose foreign relations that Contracting Party is responsible.

ARTICLE XIII

On the day when the first twenty instruments of ratification or accession have been deposited, the Secretary-General shall draw up a procès-verbal and transmit a copy thereof to each Member of the United Nations and to each of the non-member States contemplated in article XI.

The present Convention shall come into force on the ninetieth day following the day of deposit of the twentieth instrument of ratification or accession.

Any ratification or accession effected, subsequent to the latter date shall become effective on the ninetieth day following the deposit of the instrument of ratification or accession.

ARTICLE XIV

The present Convention shall remain in effect for a period of ten years as from the date of its coming into force.

It shall thereafter remain in force for successive periods of five years for such Contracting Parties as have not denounced it at least six months before the expiration of the current period.

Denunciation shall be effected by a written notification addressed to the Secretary-General of the United Nations.

ARTICLE XV

If, as a result of denunciations, the number of Parties to the present Convention should become less than sixteen, the Convention shall cease to be in force as from the date on which the last of these denunciations shall become effective.

ARTICLE XVI

A request for the revision of the present Convention may be made at any time by any Contracting Party by means of a notification in writing addressed to the Secretary-General.

The General Assembly shall decide upon the steps, if any, to be taken in respect of such request.

ARTICLE XVII

The Secretary-General of the United Nations shall notify all Members of the United Nations and the non-member States contemplated in article XI of the following:

  a. Signatures, ratifications and accessions received in accordance with article XI;
  b. Notifications received in accordance with article XII;
  c. The date upon which the present Convention comes into force in accordance with article XIII;
  d. Denunciations received in accordance with article XIV;
  e. The abrogation of the Convention in accordance with article XV;
  f. Notifications received in accordance with article XVI.

ARTICLE XVIII

The original of the present Convention shall be deposited in the archives of the United Nations.

A certified copy of the Convention shall be transmitted to each Member of the United Nations and to each of the non-member States contemplated in article XI.

ARTICLE XIX

The present Convention shall be registered by the Secretary-General of the United Nations on the date of its coming into force.

Notes

1. Geoffrey Best wrote that he learned as a young scholar at Edinburgh the value of "points of entry" to new areas of knowledge from one of his senior colleagues, John Mitchell. See Best, "Justice, International Relations and Human Rights," *International Affairs* 71 (1995): 775.

2. For my earliest attempt at analyzing the problem of post–Cold War genocide, see my unpublished paper: "The International Use of Force to Suppress Genocide: Necessary and Realistic," at the International Symposium on Contemporary Forms of Genocide, University of Nebraska-Lincoln, 15–16 April 1996.

3. For further elaboration on this point, see Elliott L. Meyrowitz and Kenneth J. Campbell, "Vietnam Veterans and War Crimes Hearings," in *Give Peace a Chance: Exploring the Vietnam Antiwar Movement,* edited by Melvin Small and William D. Hoover (Syracuse: Syracuse University Press, 1992), 129–140. Also see Kenneth J. Campbell, "The International War Crimes Conference, Oslo, June 1971: Excerpts from the Diary of One of the Witnesses," in *Nobody Gets Off the Bus: The Viet Nam Generation Big Book,* edited by Kali Tal and Dan Duffy (Woodbridge, CT: Viet Nam Generation, 1994), 148–151; and my interview included in Robert A. Gross, "Lieutenant Calley's Army: Following Orders in Vietnam," *Esquire* 76 (October 1971): 154–158, 196–197, 199.

4. See Kenneth J. Campbell, "Once Burned, Twice Cautious: Explaining the Weinberger-Powell Doctrine," *Armed Forces & Society* 24 (summer 1998): 357–374.

1. Raphael Lemkin, "Genocide: A Modern Crime," *Free World* 4 (April 1945): 39–43; republished at www.preventgenocide.com (accessed 23 October 2000).

2. See, for example, Max Singer and Aaron Wildavsky, *The Real World Order: Zones of Peace/Zones of Turmoil* (Chatham, NJ: Chatham House, 1993); James

N. Rosenau, *Turbulence in World Politics: A Theory of Change and Continuity* (Princeton: Princeton University Press, 1990); Samuel P. Huntington, "The Clash of Civilization?" *Foreign Affairs* 72 (summer 1993): 22–49; and Robert D. Kaplan, "The Coming Anarchy," *Atlantic Monthly* (February 1994): 44–76. Other contributions to this pessimistic "doom and gloom" literature were Zbigniew Brzezinski, *Out of Control: Global Turmoil on the Eve of the Twenty-First Century* (New York: Charles Scribner's Sons, 1993); Daniel Patrick Moynihan, *Pandaemonium: Ethnicity in International Politics* (Oxford: Oxford University Press, 1993); and William Pfaff, *The Wrath of Nations: Civilization and the Furies of Nationalism* (New York: Touchstone, 1993).

3. See John G. Ikenberry, "The Myth of Post–Cold War Chaos," *Foreign Affairs* 75 (May/June 1996): 76–91; and Joseph S. Nye Jr., "Redefining the National Interest," *Foreign Affairs* 78 (July/August 1999): 22–35.

4. See Bruce Cronin, "Changing Norms of Sovereignty and Multilateral Intervention," in *Collective Conflict Management and Changing World Politics,* edited by Joseph Lepgold and Thomas G. Weiss (Albany: State University of New York Press, 1998), 159–180; also Jennifer M. Hazen, "The Rhetoric of Genocide: Signs of Shifting Norms of Intervention," paper presented at the annual meeting of the International Studies Association, Los Angeles, 16 March 2000.

5. See John L. Davies and Ted Robert Gurr, *Preventive Measures: Building Risk Assessment and Crisis Early Warning Systems* (Lanham, MD: Rowman & Littlefield, 1998); Chantel de Jonge Oudraat, "Intervention in Internal Conflicts: Legal and Political Conundrums," *Working Paper* 15, Carnegie Endowment for International Peace, August 2000; *Report of the Panel on United Nations Peace Operations (Brahimi Report),* www.un.org (accessed 1 September 2000); "Problems and Prospects for Humanitarian Intervention," the Stanley Foundation's Thirty-fifth United Nations of the Next Decade Conference, Vail, Colorado, 11–16 June 2000.

6. Timothy Garton Ash, "Kosovo: Was It Worth It?" *New York Review of Books* 47 (21 September 2000): 60.

7. See Martha Minow, "Why Try?" in *Kosovo: Contending Voices on Balkan Interventions,* edited by William Joseph Buckley (Grand Rapids, MI: Eerdmans, 2000), 465–466; also Richard J. Goldstone, *For Humanity: Reflections of a War Crimes Investigator* (New Haven: Yale University Press, 2000).

8. For example, see Scott R. Feil, "Preventing Genocide: How the Early Use of Force Might Have Succeeded in Rwanda," *A Report to the Carnegie Commission on Preventing Deadly Conflict* (New York: Carnegie Corporation, April 1998); Jeffrey Laurenti, "International Intervention—Humanitarian or Otherwise?" paper presented at the International Symposium on Humanitarian Intervention and the United Nations, Japan Association of United Nations Studies, Aoyama Gakuin Daigaku, Tokyo, 27 May 2000; and the International Panel of Eminent Personalities, "Rwanda: The Preventable Genocide," Report to the Organization for African Unity, 29 May 2000, www.oau-oua.org (accessed 23 August 2000).

9. Michael Howard, "The Strategic Approach to International Relations," in Michael Howard, *The Causes of War* (Cambridge: Harvard University Press, 1983), 36; also see Bernard Brodie, *War and Politics* (New York: Macmillan, 1973), especially chapter one, "*De quoi s'agit-il?*" (What is it all about?), 1–28.

10. See Inis L. Claude Jr., "The Common Defense and Great Power Responsibilities," *Political Science Quarterly* 101 (1986): 719–732.

11. Roger Hilsman, *To Move a Nation: The Politics of Foreign Policy in the Administration of John F. Kennedy* (New York: Dell, 1967), 12.

12. On the central role of morality in international politics, see E.H. Carr, *The Twenty Years' Crisis, 1919–1939* (New York: Harper & Row, 1964); also, Stanley Hoffmann, *Duties Beyond Borders: On the Limits and Possibilities of Ethical International Politics* (Syracuse, NY: Syracuse University Press, 1981). On tangible and intangible elements of power, including morality, see Hans J. Morgenthau, *Politics among Nations: The Struggle for Power and Peace,* 4th ed. (New York: Alfred A. Knopf, 1967). For a neoliberal institutionalist analysis of international relations, see Robert O. Keohane and Joseph S. Nye Jr., *Power and Interdependence,* 2nd ed. (Glenview, IL: Scott Foresman/Little, Brown, 1989). A fine social constructivist treatment of nationalism and extremist violence is Ernst B. Haas, *Nationalism, Liberalism, and Progress, vol. 1, The Rise and Decline of Nationalism* (Ithaca, NY: Cornell University Press, 1997).

13. B.H. Liddell Hart defined "grand strategy" as the coordination of all power resources—military, economic, political, and moral—of a nation or group of nations for the attainment of peace, security, and prosperity. In other words, it goes far beyond the traditional use of "strategy" as meaning *military* strategy in wartime. See his classic work, *Strategy,* 2nd rev. ed. (New York: Praeger, 1968), 335–336.

14. See, for example, Charles B. Strozier and Michael Flynn, eds., *Genocide, War, and Human Survival* (Lanham, MD: Rowman & Littlefield, 1996); Aryeh Neier, *War Crimes: Brutality, Genocide, Terror, and the Struggle for Justice* (New York: Times Books, 1998); and Neal Riemer, ed., *Protection against Genocide: Mission Impossible?* (Westport, CT: Praeger, 2000).

CHAPTER 1

1. Edward Hallett Carr, *The Twenty Years' Crisis, 1919–1939* (New York: Harper & Row, 1964), 41.

2. James N. Rosenau, *Along the Domestic-Foreign Frontier: Exploring Governance in a Turbulent World* (Cambridge: Cambridge University Press, 1997), 172–173.

3. David Held and Anthony McGrew, with David Goldblatt and Jonathan Perraton, "Managing the Challenge of Globalization and Institutionalizing Cooperation through Global Governance," in *The Global Agenda: Issues and Perspectives,* 6th ed., edited by Charles W. Kegley Jr., and Eugene R. Wittkopf (New York: McGraw-Hill, 2001), 141.

4. See, for example, Maryann K. Cusimano, ed., *Beyond Sovereignty: Issues for a Global Agenda* (Boston/New York: Bedford/St. Martin's Press, 2000); Rosenau, *Along the Domestic-Foreign Frontier;* Richard Falk, *On Humane Governance: Toward a New Global Politics* (University Park: Pennsylvania State University Press, 1995); Robert O. Keohane and Joseph S. Nye Jr., "Globalization: What's New? What's Not? (And So What?)," *Foreign Policy* 118 (spring 2000): 104–119; Princeton N. Lyman, "Globalization and the Demands of Governance," *Georgetown Journal of International Affairs* 1 (winter/spring 2000): 89–97; and Raimo Vayrynen, ed., *Globalization and Global Governance* (Lanham, MD: Rowman & Littlefield, 1999)

5. Keohane and Nye, "Globalization," 104.

6. Ibid., 128–129.

7. Rosenau, *Along the Domestic-Foreign Frontier,* 172; Karen A. Mingst, "Global Governance: The American Perspective," in Vayrynen, *Globalization,* 92.

8. Vayrynen, "Preface," in *Globalization,* xi.

9. Mingst, "Global Governance," 92, 94.

10. I use here a hybrid of several definitions put forward in the leading literature, but acknowledge that the definition of global governance is continually contested in this period. See Mingst, "Global Governance," 94.

11. Ibid., 92–93.

12. Keohane and Nye, "Globalization," 113, 118.

13. See Inis L. Claude Jr., *Swords into Plowshares: The Problems and Progress of International Organization,* 4th ed. (New York: Random House, 1971), 57.

14. See Robert Gilpin, *War and Change in World Politics* (Cambridge: Cambridge University Press, 1981), especially chapter 5, "Hegemonic War and International Change."

15. John G. Ikenberry, "The Myth of Post–Cold War Chaos," *Foreign Affairs* 75 (May/June 1996): 90–91.

16. Christian P. Scherrer, "Preventing Genocide: The Role of the International Community," *Prevent Genocide International,* www.preventgenocide.org (accessed 1 April 2000).

17. For the historical roots of genocide, see Frank Chalk and Kurt Jonassohn, *The History and Sociology of Genocide* (New Haven: Yale University Press, 1990).

18. Inis L. Claude Jr., "The Common Defense and Great Power Responsibilities," *Political Science Quarterly* 101 (1986): 724, 726–727. Also see Hedley Bull, *The Anarchical Society* (New York: Columbia University Press, 1995), 194–222.

19. W. Bowman Cutter, Joan Spero, and Laura D'Andrea Tyson, "New World, New Deal," *Foreign Affairs* 79 (March/April 2000): 80.

20. Lyman, "Globalization," 90, 96.

21. Michael E. Brown and Richard N. Rosecrance, "Comparing Costs of Prevention and Costs of Conflict: Toward a New Methodology," in *The Costs of Conflict: Prevention and Cure in the Global Arena,* edited by Michael E.

Brown and Richard N. Rosecrance (Lanham, MD: Rowman & Little-field/Carnegie Commission on Preventing Deadly Conflict, 1999), 17.

CHAPTER 2

1. Clausewitz, *On War* (Princeton: Princeton University Press, 1976), 88–89.
2. Quoted in Bernard Brodie, *War and Politics* (New York: Macmillan, 1973), 1.
3. Herbert Hirsch, *Genocide and the Politics of Memory: Studying Death to Preserve Life* (Chapel Hill: University of North Carolina Press, 1995), 184.
4. Roger W. Smith, "Human Destructiveness and Politics: The Twentieth Century as an Age of Genocide," in *Genocide and the Modern Age: Etiology and Case Studies of Mass Death,* edited by Isidor Wallimann and Michael N. Dobkowski (Syracuse, NY: Syracuse University Press, 2000), 21–39.
5. John G. Ikenberry, "The Myth of Post–Cold War Chaos," *Foreign Affairs* 75 (May/June 1996), 76–91.
6. Raphael Lemkin, a noted Polish scholar and attorney, first used the term "genocide" in his *Axis Rule in Occupied Europe* (Washington: Carnegie Endowment for International Peace, 1944). The term is made up of the ancient Greek word *genos,* which means "race" or "tribe," and the Latin *cide,* which means "killing."
7. See Frank Chalk and Kurt Jonassohn, *The History and Sociology of Genocide* (New Haven: Yale University Press, 1990), 32.
8. Michael Howard, George J. Andreopoulos, and Mark R. Shulman, eds., *The Laws of War: Constraints on Warfare in the Western World* (New Haven: Yale University Press, 1994), especially chapters 2, 3, and 4.
9. Howard Ball, *Prosecuting War Crimes and Genocide: The Twentieth Century Experience* (Lawrence: University Press of Kansas, 1999), 12, 26–30. Also see George S. Yacoubian Jr., "Reconciling the Causation of Genocide: A Theoretical Perspective on the Armenian Tragedy," unpublished paper presented at the International Symposium on Contemporary Forms of Genocide, University of Nebraska-Lincoln, 15–16 April 1996.
10. Lemkin, *Axis Rule;* also Raul Hilberg, *The Destruction of the European Jews* (Chicago: Quadrangle Books, 1961).
11. Lemkin, *Axis Rule,* 81.
12. Hilberg, *Destruction,* 31.
13. For an examination of the destruction of Europe's Gypsies during the Holocaust, see: Sybil Milton, "Holocaust: The Gypsies" in *Century of Genocide: Eyewitness Accounts and Critical Views,* edited by Samuel Totten, William S. Parsons, and Israel W. Charney (New York: Garland Publishing, 1997), 171–188.
14. See for instance, Martin Gilbert, *Auschwitz and the Allies* (New York: Henry Holt, 1981); and David S. Wyman, *The Abandonment of the Jews: America and the Holocaust, 1941–1945* (New York: New Press, 1998).

15. See Dwight D. Eisenhower, *Crusade in Europe* (Garden City, NY: Doubleday, 1948), 408–409; also Tom Infield, "Witness," *Philadelphia Inquirer Magazine* (9 April 1995): 12–15, 24–26, 28, 31.

16. Harry S. Truman, "Message to the Congress Transmitting First Annual Report on U.S. Participation in the United Nations, February 5, 1947," in *Public Papers of the Presidents: Harry S. Truman, 1947* (Washington, D.C.: U.S. Government Printing Office, 1963), 121–122.

17. Louis Henkin, *The Age of Rights* (New York: Columbia University Press, 1990), 1. For a detailed account of the International Military Tribunal at Nuremberg, see Eugene Davidson, *The Trial of the Germans* (New York: Macmillan, 1966); and Michael R. Marrus, *The Nuremberg War Crimes Trial, 1945–46: A Documentary History* (Boston: Bedford Books, 1997). For the political and historical origins of the Nuremberg Trials, see Bradley F. Smith, *The Road to Nuremberg* (New York: Basic Books, 1981). For analysis of the significance of the IMT, see Max Radin, "Justice at Nuremberg," *Foreign Affairs* 24 (April 1946): 369–384; Henry L. Stimson, "The Nuremberg Trial: Landmark in Law," *Foreign Affairs* 25 (January 1947): 179–189; and Telford Taylor, *The Anatomy of the Nuremberg Trials* (New York: Alfred A. Knopf, 1992). Critics who argue that Nuremberg amounted to "victors' justice" must take into account the fact that the defendants were permitted a legal defense, established rules of evidence were applied, only twelve of the twenty-two received the death sentence, while seven received prison terms of varying length and three were acquitted outright. Perhaps more importantly, the only other alternatives to trial were the summary execution of between five thousand (Churchill's preference) and fifty thousand (Stalin's preference) of the leading Nazis. The Nuremberg Trial, by comparison, looks like a good deal.

18. Marrus, *Nuremberg War Crimes Trial,* 80.

19. Stimson, "Nuremberg Trial," 179, 189.

20. United Nations, *The United Nations and Human Rights, 1945–1995* (New York: UN Department of Public Information, 1995), 18, 19.

21. Henkin, *Age of Rights,* 16, 75.

22. Ibid., 67.

23. William Schabas, "Special Report: The Genocide Convention at Fifty," United States Institute of Peace, 7 January 1999, Washington, D.C., www.usip.org/oc/sr/sr990107.html (accessed 25 June 2000).

24. Smith, *Road to Nuremberg,* 253.

25. Allan Dowty and Gil Lowscher, "Refugee Flows as Grounds for International Action," *International Security* 21 (summer 1996): 61–62.

26. For a sound scholarly treatment of the 1990/91 Gulf War, see Lawrence Freedman and Efraim Karsh, *The Gulf Conflict, 1990–1991: Diplomacy and War in the New World Order* (Princeton: Princeton University Press, 1993).

27. See, for example, Frank Chalk, "Redefining Genocide," and Israel W. Charney, "Toward a Generic Definition of Genocide," in *Genocide: Concep-*

tual and Historical Dimensions, edited by George J. Andreopoulos (Philadelphia: University of Pennsylvania Press, 1994), 47–63 and 64–94.

28. W. Michael Reisman and Chris T. Antoniou, eds., *The Laws of War: A Comprehensive Collection of Primary Documents on International Laws Governing Armed Conflict* (New York: Vintage Books, 1994), 84–85.

29. See Alain Destexhe, "The Third Genocide," *Foreign Policy* 97 (winter 1994–95): 4.

30. Schabas, "Special Report."

31. William A. Schabas, *Genocide in International Law* (Cambridge: Cambridge University Press, 2000), 233–234.

32. Author's conversation with Helen Fein, New York City, 3 December 1998.

33. My search was conducted on 21 September 1998, and the ICRC's list was dated 1 May 1998.

34. See Markus Schmidt, "Treaty-Based Human Rights Complaints Procedures in the UN: Remedy or Mirage for Victims of Human Rights Violations?" *Human Rights* 2 (spring 1998): 13–18. It may be instructive (if not disturbing) to the reader to learn that the crime of genocide is never mentioned in this article. One might reasonably conclude from this that the UNHCHR considers monitoring compliance with the Genocide Convention to be someone else's problem.

35. In a conversation with this author in Oslo on 18 June 2000, Phil Williams, a leading scholarly expert on transnational organized crime, conceded that genocide was, regrettably, outside the normal domain of scholars of international criminal activity. For a brief overview of international criminal law, see Gerhard Von Glahn, *Law among Nations: An Introduction to Public International Law,* 7th ed. (Boston: Allyn & Bacon, 1996), 256–293.

36. E-mail response to author's query, 4 November 1998.

37. See M. Cherif Bassiouni, "The United Nations Commission of Experts Established Pursuant to Security Council Resolution 780 (1992)," *American Journal of International Law* 88 (1994): 784–805.

38. Roger Winter, "Never Again—Again," U.S. Committee for Refugees, (www.refugees.org), February 1999.

39. Quoted in Martin Gilbert, *Auschwitz and the Allies* (New York: Henry Holt, 1981), 341.

40. See Lori Fisler Damrosch, "Genocide and Ethnic Conflict," in *International Law and Ethnic Conflict,* edited by David Wippman (Ithaca: American Society of International Law/Cornell University Press, 1998), 258.

41. Quoted in William R. Slomanson, *Fundamental Perspectives on International Law* (St. Paul, MN: West Publishing, 1990), 247.

42. For a good examination of globalization and the challenge of transsovereign problems, see Maryann K. Cusimano, ed., *Beyond Sovereignty: Issues for a Global Agenda* (Boston: Bedford Books; St. Martin's Press, 2000).

43. Rosenau, *Along the Domestic-Foreign Frontier,* 180.

44. Tony Judt, "On Kosovo: The Reason Why," *New York Review of Books* 45 (20 May 1999): 16.
45. See Michael J. Glennon, "The New Interventionism: The Search for a Just International Law," *Foreign Affairs* 78 (May/June 1999): 2.
46. Raphael Lemkin, "Genocide as a Crime under International Law," *American Journal of International Law* 4 (1947): 150.
47. Richard B. Lillich, *Humanitarian Intervention and the United Nations* (Charlottesville: University Press of Virginia, 1973), vii.
48. Hilaire McCoubrey and Nigel D. White, *International Organizations and Civil Wars* (Aldershot: Dartmouth, 1995), 14.
49. From the "Vienna Convention on the Law of Treaties" (1969), quoted in William R. Slomanson, *Fundamental Perspectives on International Law* (St. Paul, MN: West Publishing, 1990), 267.
50. Simon, "Grading Harms," 32–37.
51. McCoubrey and White, *International Organizations and Civil Wars,* 14.
52. Quoted at www.un.org/icc/index.html (accessed 6 July 2000.)
53. Damrosch, "Genocide and Ethnic Conflict," 271.
54. Rein Mullerson and David J. Scheffer, "Legal Regulation of the Use of Force," in *Beyond Confrontation: International Law for the Post–Cold War Era,* edited by Lori Fisler Damrosch, Gennady M. Danilenko, and Rein Mullerson (Boulder, CO: Westview Press, 1995), 123.
55. David J. Scheffer, "International Judicial Intervention," *Foreign Policy* 102 (spring 1996): 37; also Kevin R. Chaney, "Pitfalls and Imperatives: Applying the Lessons of Nuremberg to the Yugoslav War Crimes Trials," *Dickinson Journal of International Law* 14 (fall 1995): 65.
56. Michael Walzer, *Just and Unjust Wars: A Moral Argument with Historical Illustrations* (New York: Basic Books, 1977), 106–107.
57. Michael Walzer, *Thick and Thin: Moral Argument at Home and Abroad* (Notre Dame, IN: University of Notre Dame, 1994), 1–6.
58. Michael Walzer, "The Politics of Rescue," *Social Research* 62 (spring 1995): 59–60.
59. J. Bryan Hehir, "Expanding Military Intervention: Promise or Peril?" *Social Research* 62 (spring 1995): 46.
60. Stanley Hoffmann, "The Politics and Ethics of Military Intervention," *Survival* 37 (winter 1995–96): 38, 49.
61. Scheffer, "International Judicial Intervention," 35.
62. Gerald W. Scully, "Genocide Is Bad for the Economy," *New York Times,* 14 December 1997, sec. 4, p. 7.
63. See for instance, Lynne Duke, "Genocide's Legacy: Tourist Killings Highlight Continuing Role Hutus Play in Central Africa's Conflicts," *Washington Post,* 10 March 1999, A17.
64. Andrew S. Natsios, *U.S. Foreign Policy and the Four Horsemen of the Apocalypse: Humanitarian Relief in Complex Emergencies* (Westport, CT: Praeger/Center for Strategic and International Affairs, 1997), 29.

65. Myron Weiner, "Security, Stability, and International Migration," *International Security* 17 (winter 1992–93): 91–126.

66. Such unilateral interventions for ostensibly humanitarian purposes occurred when India invaded East Pakistan (Bangladesh) in 1971, when Vietnam invaded Cambodia in 1978, and when Tanzania invaded Uganda in 1979. See Alan Dowty and Gil Loescher, "Refugee Flows As Grounds for International Action," *International Security* 21 (summer 1996): 61–62.

67. For example, see Charles Trueheart, "Journalists Take Aim at Policymakers: In Europe and U.S., Media Mirror Mood," *Washington Post*, 21 July 1995, A27.

68. Natsios, *Four Horsemen*, 23, 31.

69. David Mitrany, *A Working Peace System* (Chicago: Quadrangle Books, 1966).

70. Carr, *Twenty Years' Crisis*; Charles P. Kindleberger, *The World in Depression, 1929–1939* (Berkeley: University of California Press, 1973); Robert O. Keohane and Joseph S. Nye Jr., *Power and Interdependence*, 2nd ed. (Glenview, IL: Scot Foresman/Little, Brown, 1989).

71. W. Bowman Cutter, Joan Spero, and Laura D'Andrea Tyson, "New World, New Deal," *Foreign Affairs* 79 (March/April 2000): 98.

72. Keohane and Nye, "Globalization," 118.

73. John F. Murphy, "International Crimes," in *United Nations Legal Order*, vol. 2, edited by Oscar Schacter and Christopher C. Joyner (Cambridge: Cambridge University Press, 997–1000).

74. See Thomas W. Simon, "Grading Harms: Giving Genocide Its Due," paper presented at the International Symposium on Contemporary Forms of Genocide, University of Nebraska-Lincoln, 15–16 April 1996.

75. See, for instance, Thomas G. Weiss, *Military-Civilian Interactions*; Natsios, *U.S. Foreign Policy*; Chris Seiple, *The U.S. Military/NGO Relationship in Humanitarian Interventions* (Carlisle Barracks, PA: Peacekeeping Institute, 1996); Thomas G. Weiss and Cindy Collins, *Humanitarian Challenges and Intervention: World Politics and the Dilemmas of Help* (Boulder, CO: Westview Press, 1996); and Stanley Hoffmann (with contributions by Robert C. Johansen, James P. Sterba, and Raimo Vayrynen), *The Ethics and Politics of Humanitarian Intervention* (Notre Dame, IN: Notre Dame Press, 1996).

76. Helen Fein, "The Three P's of Genocide Prevention: With Application to a Genocide Foretold—Rwanda," in *Protection against Genocide: Mission Impossible?*, edited by Neal Riemer (Westport, CT: Praeger, 2000), 42.

77. Charles W. Kegley Jr., and Eugene R. Wittkopf, *World Politics: Trend and Transformation*, 7th ed. (New York: St. Martin's Press/Worth, 1999), 367–368; Ted Robert Gurr and Barbara Harff, *Ethnic Conflict in World Politics* (Boulder, CO: Westview Press, 1994), appendix, 160–166.

78. IPEP, *Rwanda: The Preventable Genocide*, report to the OAU, 29 May 2000, sec. 1, para. 4, www.oau-oua.org (accessed 23 August 2000).

79. Tonya Langford, "Things Fall Apart: State Failure and the Politics of Intervention," *International Studies Review* 1 (spring 1999): 61. Also see I. William Zartman, ed., *Collapsed States: The Disintegration and Restoration of Legitimate Authority* (Boulder, CO: Lynne Rienner, 1995).

80. See, for instance, Terrence Lyons and Ahmed I. Samatar, *Somalia: State Collapse, Multilateral Intervention, and Strategies for Political Reconstruction* (Washington, D.C.: Brookings Institution, 1995).

81. Smith, "Human Destructiveness," 23.

82. Reisman and Antoniou, *The Laws of War*, 335–336.

83. Several good treatments of war crimes and the laws of war (otherwise known as international humanitarian law) have been published in recent years. See, for instance, Geoffrey Best, *War and Law Since 1945* (Oxford: Clarendon Press, 1994); and Michael Howard, George J. Andreopoulos, and Mark R. Shulman, eds., *The Laws of War: Constraints on Warfare in the Western World* (New Haven: Yale University Press, 1994). An older, but still quite useful, treatment is Richard A. Falk, Gabriel Kolko, and Robert J. Lifton, eds., *Crimes of War: A Legal, Political-Documentary, and Psychological Inquiry into the Responsibility of Leaders, Citizens, and Soldiers for Criminal Acts in War* (New York: Vintage Books, 1971).

84. Gilbert, *Auschwitz and the Allies*, 131–136.

85. Hirsch, *Genocide and the Politics of Memory*, 185; Douglas W. Simon, "The Evolution of the International System and Its Impact on Protection against Genocide," in *Protection Against Genocide: Mission Impossible?* edited by Neal Riemer (Westport, CT: Praeger, 2000), 17–30.

CHAPTER 3

1. Quoted in Telford Taylor, *Nuremberg and Vietnam: An American Tragedy* (Chicago: Quadrangle Books, 1970), 9.

2. Brian Urquhart, "In the Name of Humanity," *New York Review of Books* 47 (27 April 2000): 19.

3. Kenneth J. Campbell, "Once Burned, Twice Cautious: Explaining the Weinberger-Powell Doctrine," *Armed Forces & Society* 24 (spring 1998): 357–374. Also see David Petraeus, "Military Influence and the Post-Vietnam Use of Force," *Armed Forces & Society* 15 (summer 1989): 489–505; Christopher M. Gacek, *The Logic of Force* (New York: Columbia University Press, 1994); Frank G. Hoffman, "Decisive Force: The New American Way of War?" *Strategic Review* (winter 1995): 23–34; and Charles A. Stevenson, "The Evolving Clinton Doctrine on the Use of Force," *Armed Forces & Society* 22 (summer 1996): 511–535.

4. Richard N. Haass, *Intervention: The Use of American Military Force in the Post–Cold War World* (Washington, D.C.: Carnegie Endowment for International Peace, 1994), 1–2.

5. Philip Everts, "When the Going Gets Rough: Does the Public Support the Use of Military Force?" *World Affairs* 162 (winter 2000): 91.

6. For a good contemporary treatment of this issue, see Robert Buzzanco, *Vietnam and the Transformation of American Life* (Malden, MA: Blackwell, 1999).

7. See, for instance, William J. Taylor Jr., and David H. Petraeus, "The Legacy of Vietnam for the U.S. Military," in *Democracy, Strategy, and Vietnam: Implications for American Policymaking*, edited by George K. Osborn, Asa A. Clark IV, Daniel J. Kaufman, and Douglas E. Lute (Lexington, MA: Lexington Books, 1987), 249–268.

8. Telford Taylor, *Nuremberg and Vietnam: An American Tragedy* (Chicago: Quadrangle Books, 1970).

9. Ibid., 189, 207.

10. Bernard Brodie, *War and Politics* (New York: Macmillan, 1973).

11. Ibid., 1.

12. Ibid., vii.

13. Ibid., chapters 4 and 5.

14. Ibid., 192–195.

15. Ibid., 8.

16. John E. Mueller, *War, Presidents and Public Opinion* (New York: John Wiley & Sons, 1973).

17. Ibid., vii, 266.

18. Michael Walzer, *Just and Unjust Wars: A Moral Argument with Historical Illustrations*, 2nd ed. (New York: Basic Books, 1992).

19. Ibid., 97–101, 186–196, 299.

20. Leslie H. Gelb and Richard K. Betts, *The Irony of Vietnam: The System Worked* (Washington, D.C.: Brookings Institution, 1979.)

21. Ibid., 332.

22. Colonel Harry G. Summers Jr., *On Strategy: A Critical Analysis of the Vietnam War* (Novato, CA: Presidio Press, 1982; New York: Dell, 1984).

23. See, for instance, Colonel Robert D. Heinl, "Collapse of the Armed Forces," *Armed Forces & Society* (7 June 1971); reprinted in *Vietnam and America*, edited by Marvin E. Gettleman et al. (New York: Grove Press, 1995), 326–327; Edward L. King, *Death of an Army* (New York: Saturday Review Press, 1972); William Hauser, *America's Army in Crisis* (Baltimore: Johns Hopkins University Press, 1973); David Cortright, *Soldiers in Revolt* (Garden City, NJ: Anchor Press, 1975); Richard A. Gabriel and Paul L. Savage, *Crisis in Command* (New York: Hill & Wang, 1978).

24. Ibid., 56.

25. Ibid.

26. Ibid., 18–29, 33–44, 62–65, 264–270.

27. Ibid., 33.

28. John P. Lovell, "Vietnam and the U.S. Army: Learning to Cope with Failure," in Osborn et al., *Democracy, Strategy and Vietnam*, 136; Colonel Harry G. Summers Jr. (Ret.), *On Strategy II: A Critical Analysis of the Gulf War* (New York: Dell, 1992), 133.

29. Ibid., 134.

30. Ibid., 135.

31. Andrew J. Bacevich, "The Limits of Orthodoxy: The Use of Force after the Cold War," in *The United States and the Use of Force in the Post–Cold War Era*, the Aspen Strategy Group (Queenstown, MD: Aspen Institute, 1995), 182.

32. See Alexander M. Haig, *Caveat: Realism, Reagan, and Foreign Policy* (New York: Macmillan, 1984), 127–128; Drew Middleton, "U.S. Generals Are Leery of Latin Intervention," *New York Times*, 21 June 1983, A9; Richard Halloran, *To Arm a Nation* (New York: Macmillan, 1986), chapter 1.

33. Secretary of State George Shultz, "Terrorism and the Modern World," address before the Park Avenue Synagogue, New York City, 25 October 1984, *Department of State Bulletin* 84 (December 1984): 14–17.

34. See James A. Nathan and James K. Oliver, *Foreign Policy Making and the American Political System*, 3rd ed. (Baltimore: Johns Hopkins University Press, 1994), 20.

35. George P. Shultz, *Turmoil and Triumph: My Years As Secretary of State* (New York: Charles Scribner's Sons, 1993), 650.

36. The full text of the speech can be found in "The Uses of Military Power," *Defense* (January 1985): 2–11.

37. Excerpted from Haass, *Intervention*, appendix C, 173–180.

38. Colin Powell, with Joseph E. Persico, *My American Journey* (New York: Random House, 1995), 303.

39. Hoffman, "Decisive Force," 23–34. In fact, General Powell informed the author in a personal note (6 April 1998) that he never liked his name affixed to the Weinberger Doctrine but could do little about it.

40. Petraeus, "Military Influence"; Haass, *Intervention*, 25–31.

41. Summers, *On Strategy II*, 157.

42. Central Command figures quoted in Lawrence Freedman and Efraim Karsh, *The Gulf Conflict, 1990–1991: Diplomacy and War in the New World Order* (Princeton: Princeton University Press, 1993), 389.

43. Ibid., 387–389.

44. Bacevich, "Limits of Orthodoxy," 183, 185; Nathan and Oliver, *Foreign Policy Making*, 21; Bob Woodward, *The Commanders* (New York: Simon & Schuster, 1991); Summers, *On Strategy II*, 1–3.

45. Les Aspin, "The Use and Usefulness of Military Forces in the Post–Cold War, Post-Soviet World," in Haass, *Intervention*, appendix D, 183–185.

46. Powell, *My American Journey*, 580; Haass, *Intervention*, 61, 134–135; Weiss, *Military-Civilian Interactions*, 69–96.

47. "The Clinton Administration's Policy on Reforming Multilateral Peace Operations," in Haass, *Intervention*, appendix H, 212–215.

48. John Stone, "Air-Power, Land-Power and the Challenge of Ethnic Conflict," *Civil Wars* 2 (autumn 1999), 30–32; John M. Rothgeb Jr., *Defining Power: Influence and Force in the Contemporary International System* (New York: St. Martin's Press, 1993), 152.

49. See, for example, William Safire, "General Shilly-Shali," *New York Times*, 21 April 1994, A19; Trudy Rubin, "Gen. Powell's Perplexing Policy,"

Philadelphia Inquirer, 22 September 1995, A23; Georgie Anne Geyer, "Blame Pentagon for Being Bogged Down in Bosnia," *News Journal* (Wilmington, DE), 26 February 1996, A11.

CHAPTER 3

1. Quoted in Mike Allen, "On Campus: Student Insularity Mutes Their Outrage," *New York Times,* 11 April 1999, p. 13.
2. Catherine McArdle Kelleher, "Security in the New Order: Presidents, Polls and the Use of Force," in *Beyond the Beltway: Engaging the Public in U.S. Foreign Policy,* edited by Daniel Yankelovich and I.M. Destler (New York: Norton, 1994), 226–227.
3. Ibid., 243; Thomas G. Weiss, *Military-Civilian Interactions: Intervening in Humanitarian Crises* (Lanham, MD: Rowman & Littlefield, 1999), 3.
4. Philip Everts, "When the Going Gets Rough: Does the Public Support the Use of Military Force?" *World Affairs* 162 (winter 2000): 93. Also see Joseph S. Nye Jr., "Redefining the National Interest," *Foreign Affairs* 78 (July/August 1999): 27.
5. Saul Mendlovitz and John Fousek, "A UN Constabulary to Enforce the Law on Genocide and Crimes against Humanity," in *Protection against Genocide: Mission Impossible?,* edited by Neal Riemer (Westport, CT: Praeger, 2000), 118–119.
6. This quoted phrase was used repeatedly by a number of U.S. officials with whom I spoke privately as they passed through the University of Delaware between 1993 and 1996. It seemed to me almost a mantra.
7. Kelleher, "Security in the New Order," 242.
8. The TMC, NBC, and *New York Times* polling data can be found in Andrew Kohut and Robert C. Toth, "Arms and the People," *Foreign Affairs* 73 (November/December 1994): 53–55.
9. Weiss, *Military-Civilian Interactions,* 149.
10. Steven Kull, *Americans on Kosovo: A Study of U.S. Public Attitudes* (summary findings), program on international policy attitudes, School of Public Affairs, University of Maryland, 27 May 1999.
11. Benjamin L. Page and Jason Barabas, "Foreign Policy Gaps between Citizens and Leaders," *International Studies Quarterly* 44 (September 2000): 355–356.
12. Steven Kull, "What the Public Knows That Washington Doesn't," *Foreign Policy* 101 (winter 1995–96): 113–114.
13. Steven Kull and I.M. Destler, *Misreading the Public: The Myth of a New Isolationism* (Washington, D.C.: Brookings Institution, 1999), 95–96.
14. Ibid., 198–199.
15. Steven Kull and Clay Ramsay, "Challenging U.S. Policymakers' Image of an Isolationist Public," *International Studies Perspectives* 1 (April 2000): 109.
16. Kull, *Americans on Kosovo,* 2, 4, 9, 10.

17. Ibid., 113.
18. Ibid., 114.
19. Everts, "When the Going Gets Rough," 102–103, 105.
20. Roy Gutman, *Witness to Genocide,* (New York: Macmillan, 1993), xiii–xiv; Holly J. Burkhalter, "The Question of Genocide: The Clinton Administration and Rwanda," *World Policy Journal* 11 (winter 1994–95): 44–48, 54; Weiss, *Military-Civilian Interactions,* 148.
21. *White House Virtual Library,*. www.whitehouse.gov (search conducted 3 February 1998).

CHAPTER 5

1. "U.S. Holocaust Museum Dedicated," *U.S. Department of State DISPATCH* 4 (10 May 1993): 323.
2. Ambassador-at-Large for War Crimes Issues David J. Scheffer, "The United States: Measures to Prevent Genocide and Other Atrocities,." address at the conference on "Genocide and Crimes against Humanity: Early Warning and Prevention," U.S. Holocaust Memorial Museum, Washington, D.C., 10 December 1998 (www.state.gov).
3. U.S. National Security Adviser Anthony Lake, "Defining Mission, Setting Deadlines: Meeting New Security Challenges in the Post–Cold War World," address at George Washington University, 6 March 1996 (Gopher/White House, 95030702.TXT).
4. James Gow, *Triumph of the Lack of Will: International Diplomacy and the Yugoslav War* (New York: Columbia University Press, 1997), 6.
5. David Rieff, *Slaughterhouse: Bosnia and the Failure of the West* (New York: Simon & Schuster, 1995), 27.
6. Roy Gutman, *Witness to Genocide* (New York: Macmillan, 1993), xviii–xix; International Commission on the Balkans, *Unfinished Peace: Report of the International Commission on the Balkans* (Washington, D.C.: Carnegie Endowment for International Peace/Aspen Institute Berlin, 1996), 32.
7. International Commission, *Unfinished Peace,* 15–17; Richard Holbrooke, *To End a War* (New York: Random House, 1998), 23.
8. International Commission, *Unfinished Peace,* 15, 20, 24; Misha Glenny, *The Fall of Yugoslavia: The Third Balkan War* (New York: Penguin Books, 1992), 15, 33, 60; Peter Maass, *Love Thy Neighbor: A Story of War* (New York: Alfred A. Knopf, 1996), 28; Laura Silber and Allan Little, *Yugoslavia: Death of a Nation* (New York: Penguin Books, 1997), 25–57; Warren Zimmermann, "The Last Ambassador: A Memoir of the Collapse of Yugoslavia," *Foreign Affairs* 74 (March/April 1995): 5.
9. Philip J. Cohen, "The Complicity of Serbian Intellectuals in Genocide in the 1990s," in *This Time We Knew: Western Responses to Genocide in Bosnia,* edited by Thomas Cushman and Stjepan G. Mestrovic (New York: New York University Press, 1996), 39.

10. Ibid., 45; International Commission, *Unfinished Peace*, 25–26; Glenny, *The Fall of Yugoslavia*, 20–21, 78; Gutman, *Witness to Genocide*, xviii, xxi–xxii; Holbrooke, *To End a War*, 24.

11. Cohen, "The Complicity of Serbian Intellectuals," 40.

12. Gutman, *Witness to Genocide*, 109–119; Norman Cigar, *Genocide in Bosnia* (College Station, TX: Texas A&M University Press, 1995), 58.

13. Gutman, *Witness to Genocide*, 38, 109–119; Cigar, *Genocide in Bosnia*, 51, 56.

14. Gutman, *Witness to Genocide*, 77–78; Cigar, *Genocide in Bosnia*, 60; Francis A. Boyle, *The Bosnian People Charge Genocide: Proceedings at the International Court of Justice Concerning Bosnia v. Serbia on the Prevention of the Crime of Genocide* (Amherst, MA: Aletheia Press, 1996), 14–15; UN Commission on Human Rights, *Resolution 1995/89 "Situation of Human Rights in the Republic of Bosnia and Herzegovina, the Republic of Croatia and the Federal Republic of Yugoslavia (Serbia and Montenegro)*, 8 March 1995.

15. UN Commission, Resolution 1995/89.

16. Gutman, *Witness to Genocide*, 20–21, 36–37.

17. Ibid., 34–35, 50–52; Boyle, *Bosnian People Charge Genocide*, 32–34; Maass, *Love Thy Neighbor*, 36–49.

18. Maass, *Love Thy Neighbor*, 45.

19. Boyle, *Bosnian People Charge Genocide*, 30–31; Gutman, *Witness to Genocide*, 68–76.

20. See Roger Cohen, "C.I.A. Report Finds Serbs Guilty in Majority of Bosnian War Crimes," *New York Times*, 9 March 1995, A1, A8.

21. David Rieff, speaking perhaps for many correspondents, confessed that "it is hard to be dispassionate about ethnic cleansing and mass murder!" See Rieff, *Slaughterhouse*, 9.

22. For detailed accounts of the Srebrenica massacre, see Human Rights Watch/Helsinki, *Bosnia-Hercegovina: The Fall of Srebrenica and the Failure of U.N. Peacekeeping*, a Human Rights Watch-Helsinki Report, vol. 7, no. 13 (October 1995); Jan Willem Honig and Norbert Both, *Srebrenica: Record of a War Crime* (New York: Penguin Books, 1997); and David Rohde, *End Game: The Betrayal and Fall of Srebrenica, Europe's Worst Massacre since World War II* (New York: Farrar, Straus & Giroux, 1997).

23. Helen Fein, executive director, Institute for the Study of Genocide, "Reassessing Contemporary Genocide: Such Mass Murders Can Be Stopped," paper presented at the International Symposium on Contemporary Forms of Genocide, University of Nebraska-Lincoln, 15–16 April 1996, 7.

24. Mark Danner, "America and the Bosnia Genocide," *New York Review of Books* 44 (4 December 1997): 64–65.

25. His collection of stories on Bosnia can be found in Gutman, *Witness to Genocide*.

26. UN Security Council, *Final Report of the Commission of Experts Established Pursuant to Security Council Resolution 780 (1992)*; UN Commission, *Resolution 1995/89*; Boyle, *Bosnian People Charge Genocide*, 99; ICTY indictments in

appendix 3 in Cushman and Mestrovic, eds., *This Time We Knew,* 363–401; Human Rights Watch/Helsinki, *Fall of Srebrenica,* 3; Amnesty International, *Report 1996.*

27. United Nations, *The Blue Helmets: A Review of United Nations Peace-keeping,* 3rd ed. (New York: UN Department of Public Information, 1996), 505–506; M. Cherif Bassiouni, "The United Nations Commission of Experts Established Pursuant to Security Council Resolution 780 (1992)," *American Journal of International Law,* vol. 88, no. 4 (1994): 784–805.

28. UN Security Council, *Final Report of the Commission of Experts Established Pursuant to Security Council Resolution 780 (1992),* para. 142, 147–150.

29. Bassiouni, "United Nations Commission of Experts," 784–805.

30. Copies of these indictments can be found in Cushman and Mestrovic, eds., *This Time We Knew,* appendix 3, 363–401.

31. See Boyle, *Bosnian People Charge Genocide,* 177.

32. Section one, paragraph 28 of the text of the Vienna Declaration, in *United Nations and Human Rights,* 453.

33. Richard J. Goldstone, "War Crimes: When Amnesia Causes Cancer," *Washington Post,* 2 February 1997, C4; Thomas G. Weiss, *Military-Civilian Interactions: Intervening in Humanitarian Crises* (Lanham, MD: Rowman & Littlefield, 1999), 115: Amnesty International, "CBS Crew Tapes SFOR Soldiers Sipping Coffee As Indicted War Crimes Suspect Sits Nearby," amnesty-usa.bestware.net (accessed 15 October 1997).

34. Weiss, *Military-Civilian Interaction,* 130.

35. Fein, "Reassessing Contemporary Genocide," 7–8.

36. See, for instance, Mark Danner, "Slouching Toward Dayton," *New York Review of Books* 45 (23 April 1998): 62.

37. Holbrooke, *To End a War,* 217.

38. Gow, *Triumph of the Lack of Will,* 9–10.

39. Weiss, *Military-Civilian Interactions,* xiv; also Philip H. Gordon, "Their Own Army? Making European Defense Work," *Foreign Affairs* 79 (July/August 2000): 12–17.

40. David Callahan, *Unwinnable Wars: American Power and Ethnic Conflict* (New York: Twentieth Century Fund Book/Hill & Wang, 1997), 98.

41. Gow, *Triumph of the Lack of Will,* 307.

42. Aryeh Neier, *War Crimes: Brutality, Genocide, Terror, and Struggles for Justice* (New York: Times Books, 1998), 112.

43. Mark Danner, "Kosovo: The Meaning of Victory," *New York Review of Books* 46 (15 July 1999): 53; Winston S. Churchill, *The Second World War, Volume I: The Gathering Storm* (Boston: Houghton Mifflin, 1983), 283.

44. Rieff, *Slaughterhouse,* 119; Donald Rothchild and David A. Lake, "Containing Fear: The Management of Transnational Ethnic Conflict," in *The International Spread of Ethnic Conflict: Fear, Diffusion, and Escalation,* edited by David A. Lake and Donald Rothchild (Princeton: Princeton University Press, 1998), 205.

45. Madeleine K. Albright, "Use of Force in a Post–Cold War World," address at the National War College, National Defense University, Fort McNair, Washington, D.C., 23 September 1993, *U.S. Department of State Dispatch*, vol. 4, no. 39 (27 September 1993): 666.

46. Anthony Lake, "Principles Governing U.S. Use of Force," remarks at George Washington University, 6 March 1996 (GOPHER/WHITE-HOUSE*95030702.TXT).

47. White House, *A National Security Strategy for a New Century*, May 1997 (www.whitehouse.gov).

48. Quoted in Joshua Muravchik, *The Imperative of American Leadership: A Challenge to Neo-Isolationism* (Washington, D.C.: American Enterprise Institute Press, 1996), 103. Also see Susan L. Woodward, *Balkan Tragedy: Chaos and Dissolution after the Cold War* (Washington, D.C.: Brookings Institution, 1995), 2; Callahan, *Unwinnable Wars*, 97.

49. See, for instance, Richard K. Betts, "The Delusion of Impartial Intervention," *Foreign Affairs* 73 (November/December 1994): 20–33.

50. Weiss, *Military-Civilian Interactions*, 107–108, 113.

51. Ibid., 125; and Roger Cohen, "Honor, Too, Is Put to Flight in Bosnia," *New York Times*, 16 July 1995, sec. 4, pp. 1, 4.

52. For an official account of UN peacekeeping operations in Bosnia during this period, see United Nations, *The Blue Helmets*, 485–566.

53. Warren Bass, "The Triage of Dayton," *Foreign Affairs* 77 (September/October 1998): 99–100.

54. Danner, "Slouching Toward Dayton," 64–65.

55. International Commission, *Unfinished Peace*, 55.

56. Ibid., 61; also Woodward, *Balkan Tragedy*, 2–3; Gow, *Triumph of the Lack of Will*, 217; Richard Holbrooke, *To End a War* (New York: Random House, 1998), 84.

57. See Colin L. Powell, "Why Generals Get Nervous," *New York Times*, 8 October 1992, A35; and Barton Gellman, "U.S. Military Fears Balkan Intervention," *Washington Post*, 12 August 1992, A24.

58. Mark Thompson, "Generals for Hire," *Time* (15 January 1996): 34–36.

59. Timothy Garton Ash, "Cry the Dismembered Country," *New York Review of Books* 46 (14 January 1999): 32.

60. Holbrooke, *To End a War*, 73.

61. Michael O'Hanlon, *Saving Lives with Force: Military Criteria for Humanitarian Intervention* (Washington, D.C.: Brookings Institution, 1997), 81.

62. Timothy Garton Ash, "Kosovo: Was It Worth It?" *New York Review of Books* 47 (21 September 2000): 58.

63. Raymond Bonner, "Tactics Were Barrier to Top Serb's Indictment," *New York Times*, 29 March 1999, A9.

64. UN General Assembly, "The Fall of Srebrenica," a *Report to the Secretary-General Pursuant to General Assembly Resolution 53/35*. A/54/549, 15 November 1999, 108–109.

65. Michael Ignatieff, *Virtual War: Kosovo and Beyond* (New York: Metropolitan Books, 2000), 178.

66. See Alain Destexhe, "The Third Genocide," *Foreign Policy* 97 (winter 1994–95): 3–17; Destexhe, *Rwanda and Genocide in the Twentieth Century* (New York: New York University Press, 1995). At an international conference in Quebec City in August 2000, a representative of MSF restated this position in a discussion following panel presentations on mass crimes and genocide. (Source: author's conference notes.)

67. For an interesting examination of this question by a Balkan scholar, see Steven L. Burg, "Afterward: Genocide in Bosnia-Herzegovina?" in *Century of Genocide: Eyewitness Accounts and Critical Views,* edited by Samuel Totten, William S. Parsons, and Israel W. Charney (New York: Garland Publishing, 1997), 424–433. Another prominent Balkan scholar explained to this author at a conference of international security scholars in 1996 that, while she was unfamiliar with the scholarly literature on genocide (*sic*), she was convinced that *all three sides* were guilty of committing genocide in Bosnia!

68. Callahan, *Unwinnable Wars,* 101. Also see "At Least Slow the Slaughter," (editorial) *New York Times,* 4 October 1992, E16; William Safire, "General Shilly-Shali," *New York Times,* 21 April 1994, A19; Trudy Rubin, "Gen. Powell's Perplexing Policy," *Philadelphia Inquirer,* 22 September 1995, A23; and Georgie Anne Geyer, "Blame Pentagon for Being Bogged Down in Bosnia," *News Journal* (Wilmington, DE), 26 February 1996, A11.

69. General Powell expressed his disdain for having his name on a doctrine that has been policy under *all* the Joint Chiefs since the early 1980s. Source: personal note to this author, 6 April 1996.

70. Colin Powell, with Joseph E. Persico, *My American Journey* (New York: Random House, 1995), 576–577.

71. ICB, *Report,* 21.

CHAPTER 6

1. Gerard Prunier, *The Rwanda Crisis: History of a Genocide* (New York: Columbia University Press, 1997), 237–238.

2. International Panel of Eminent Personalities, "Rwanda: The Preventable Genocide," *Report to the Organization of African Unity,* 29 May 2000 (www.oau-oua.org) (accessed 23 August 2000), 10.1. The members of the panel were Ketumile Masire, former president of Botswana (chair), Lisbet Palme, chairperson of the Swedish Committee for UNICEF, Stephen Lewis, former Canadian ambassador to the UN, Ellen Johnson-Sirleaf of Liberia, former director of the regional bureau for Africa of the UN Development Program, Hocine Djoudi, former Algerian ambassador to France, P.N. Bhagwati, former chief justice of the supreme court of India.

3. Quoted in IPEP, *Rwanda,* 10.6.

4. IPEP, *Rwanda,* E. S. 8

5. Prunier, *Rwanda Crisis,* 14–15, 19–21, 39; Matthew J. Vaccaro, "The Politics of Genocide: Peacekeeping and Disaster Relief in Rwanda," in *UN Peacekeeping, American Policy, and Uncivil Wars of the 1990s,* edited by William J. Durch (New York: St. Martin's Press/Henry L. Stimson Center, 1996), 369; Edmond J. Keller, "Transnational Ethnic Conflict in Africa," in *The International Spread of Ethnic Conflict: Fear, Diffusion, and Escalation,* edited by David A. Lake and Donald Rothchild (Princeton: Princeton University Press, 1998), 282.

6. Prunier, *Rwanda Crisis,* 14–15, 39.

7. Ibid., 5–28.

8. Ibid., 26–33; Vaccaro, "Politics of Genocide," 369.

9. Keller, "Transnational Ethnic Conflict," 281–282.

10. Ibid., 282; Vaccaro, "Politics of Genocide," 369–370.

11. Vaccaro, "Politics of Genocide," 369.

12. IPEP, *Rwanda,* E.S. 15.

13. Ibid., E.S. 17.

14. Ibid., E.S. 18; Prunier, *Rwanda Crisis,* 93–191; also Alain Destexhe, *Rwanda and Genocide in the Twentieth Century* (New York: New York University Press, 1995); Fergal Keane, *Season of Blood: A Rwandan Journey* (New York: Penguin Books, 1996); United Nations, *The United Nations and Rwanda, 1993–1996,* United Nations Blue Books Series, vol. 10 (New York: UN Department of Public Information, 1996); and Philip Gourevitch, *We Wish to Inform You That Tomorrow We Will Be Killed with Our Families: Stories from Rwanda* (New York: Farrar, Straus & Giroux, 1998).

15. United Nations, *The Blue Helmets: A Review of United Nations Peace-keeping,* 3rd ed. (New York: Department of Public Information, 1996), 341–344; Prunier, *Rwanda Crisis,* 191.

16. Andrea Kathryn Talentino, "Rwanda," in *The Costs of Conflict: Prevention and Cure in the Global Arena,* edited by Michael E. Brown and Richard N. Rosecrance (Lanham, MD: Rowman & Littlefield/Carnegie Commission on Preventing Deadly Conflict, 1999), 59–60.

17. IPEP, *Report,* E.S. 23.

18. Prunier, *Rwanda Crisis,* 240–241.

19. Gourevitch, *We Wish to Inform You,* 103–104.

20. Philip Gourevitch, "The Genocide Fax," *New Yorker* (11 May 1998): 42–46.

21. Prunier, *Rwanda Crisis,* 213–280.

22. Ibid., 4.

23. A detailed account of the U.S. military debacle in Mogadishu can be found in Mark Bowden, *Black Hawk Down: A Story of Modern War* (New York: Penguin Books, 2000).

24. Gourevitch, *We Wish to Inform You,* 102–103.

25. Ibid.; and Frank Chalk, "Hate Radio in Rwanda," paper presented at the International Symposium on Contemporary Forms of Genocide, University of Nebraska-Lincoln, 15–16 April 1996.

26. Prunier, *Rwanda Crisis,* 211–212.
27. Talentino, "Rwanda," 53, 60.
28. Prunier, *Rwanda Crisis,* 223–243.
29. Keller, "Transnational Ethnic Conflict," 283; Talentino, "Rwanda," 61.
30. Prunier, *Rwanda Crisis,* 165, 240–245.
31. IPEP, *Rwanda,* 10.13, 15.47; Alison Des Forges, *"Leave None to Tell the Story":
    Genocide in Rwanda* (New York: Human Rights Watch, 1999), 610–618.
32. Prunier, *Rwanda Crisis,* 256.
33. Ibid., 40, 246–248.
34. Talentino, "Rwanda," 53, 61; Keller, "Transnational Ethnic Conflict," 283.
35. IPEP, *Rwanda,* E.S. 24.
36. Ibid., E.S. 33.
37. Scott Feil, *Preventing Genocide: How the Early Use of Force Might Have Succeeded in
    Rwanda* (New York: Carnegie Corporation, 1998), 26–27. The members
    of the panel were: Brigadier General Henry K. Anyidoho, Commander,
    2nd Infantry Brigade, Ghana; Major General Greg Gile, U.S. Atlantic
    Command, USA; Major General Romeo Dallaire, Chief of Staff, Na-
    tional Defense Headquarters, Canada; Major General James Hill,
    Deputy Chief of Staff for Operations, United States Forces Command;
    General Vigleik Eide, OSCE, Austria; Major General (Ret.) John Arch
    MacInnis (Chair), Chief, Mine Clearance and Policy Unit, UN;
    Brigadier General Bo Wranker, Commander, UNPREDEP, Macedonia;
    Major General William Nash, U.S. Army, Commander, 1st Armored Di-
    vision, Germany; Brigadier General Bruce Scott, Deputy Director, Strat-
    egy, Plans, and Policy, U.S. Army; Major General Franklin van Kappen,
    Military Advisor, Department of Peacekeeping Operations, UN;
    Casimir Yost, Director, Institute for the Study of Diplomacy, George-
    town University; Jane Holl, Ph.D., Executive Director, Carnegie Com-
    mission, USA; Colonel Scott Feil, U.S. Army, Senior Service College
    Fellow, ISD, Georgetown University.
38. Ibid.
39. IPEP, *Rwanda,* E.S. 42.
40. David Callahan, *Unwinnable Wars: American Power and Ethnic Conflict* (New
    York: Twentieth Century Fund/Hill & Wang, 1997), 144.
41. Ibid., 144–145; Holly J. Burkhalter, "The Question of Genocide: The
    Clinton Administration and Rwanda," *World Policy Journal* 11 (winter
    1994–95): 44–48; David Aronson, "Congo Games," *New Republic* (5 and
    12 January 1998): 13; Thomas G. Weiss, *Military-Civilian Interactions: Inter-
    vening in Humanitarian Crises* (Lanham, MD: Rowman & Littlefield, 1999),
    148.
42. Amnesty International, USA, "The World Fails to Respond," *Forsaken
    Cries,* 3–4.
43. United Nations, *The Blue Helmets,* 347; Callahan, *Unwinnable Wars,* 114;
    Weiss, *Military-Civilian Interactions,* 163, 165.
44. IPEP, *Rwanda,* 10.15.

45. Richard N. Haass, "The Squandered Presidency," *Foreign Affairs* 79 (May/June 2000): 139.
46. IPEP, *Rwanda*, 12.32–33.
47. Weiss, *Military-Civilian Interactions*, xi, 149.
48. Brad Knickerbocker, "Grappling with the Century's Most Heinous Crimes," *Christian Science Monitor* (12 April 1999): 12.
49. Burkhalter, "The Question of Genocide," 48; Weiss, *Military-Civilian Interactions*, 149; the White House, *Presidential Decision Directive 25: The Clinton Administration's Policy on Reforming Multilateral Peace Operations* (May 1994).
50. See President Clinton, "U.S. Holocaust Museum Dedicated," (address at the dedication ceremony, Washington, D.C., 22 April 1993), *US Department of State Dispatch* 4 (10 May 1993): 322–324.
51. Bill Clinton, "Remarks by the President to Genocide Survivors, Assistance Workers, and U.S. and Rwandan Government Officials, Kigali, Rwanda," the White House, Office of the Press Secretary, 25 March 1998.
52. IPEP, *Rwanda*, E.S. 34; 10.7.
53. IPEP, *Report*, E.S. 53–54; Weiss, *Military-Civilian Interactions*, 150–156.
54. Kate Halvorsen, "Protection and Humanitarian Assistance in the Refugee Camps in Zaire: The Problem of Security," in *The Path of a Genocide: The Rwandan Crisis from Uganda to Zaire*, edited by Howard Adelman and Astri Suhrke (New Brunswick, NJ: Transaction, 1999), 309–310.
55. IPEP, *Report*, E.S. 57–58.
56. Ibid., 10.6.
57. Ibid., 20.54–20.58, 20.71; Felix Egboo, "Rwanda," in *Africa Review: The Economic and Business Report* (London: Walden Publishing, 1997), 171.

CHAPTER 7

1. Timothy Garton Ash, "Kosovo and Beyond," *New York Review of Books* 46 (24 June 1999): 7.
2. Michael Ignatieff, *Virtual War: Kosovo and Beyond* (New York: Metropolitan Books, 2000), 124.
3. Warren Zimmerman, "Milosevic's Final Solution," *New York Review of Books* 46 (10 June 1999): 42; Dusko Doder and Louise Branson, *Milosevic: Portrait of a Tyrant* (New York: Free Press, 1999), 152.
4. The author first made this argument in an op-ed piece in the wake of the Racak massacre, two months before NATO began its air war against Serbia. See Kenneth J. Campbell, "Massacre in Kosovo Is Genocide—and World Must Act Accordingly," *Philadelphia Inquirer*, 19 January 1999, A 11.
5. Steven Erlanger and Christopher S. Wren, "Early Count Hints at Fewer Kosovo Deaths," *New York Times*, 11 November 1999, A6; Aryeh Neier, *War Crimes: Brutality, Genocide, Terror, and the Struggle for Justice* (New York: Times Books, 1998), 121.

6. Timothy Garton Ash, "Cry, the Dismembered Country," *New York Review of Books* 46 (14 January 1999): 31.

7. Aleksa Djilas, "Imagining Kosovo," *Foreign Affairs* 77 (September/October 1998): 124–130.

8. Ibid., 125, 130; Chris Hedges, "Kosovo's Brutal Game of See-Saw," *New York Times,* 28 March 1999, 6.

9. Philip J. Cohen, "The Complicity of Serbian Intellectuals in Genocide in the 1990s," in *This Time We Knew: Western Responses to Genocide in Bosnia,* edited by Thomas Cushman and Stjepan G. Mestrovic (New York: New York University Press, 1996), 39–40.

10. Djilas, "Imagining Kosovo," 127.

11. Chris Hedges, "Kosovo's Next Masters?" *Foreign Affairs* 78 (May/June 1999): 24–31.

12. Ibid.; Ignatieff, *Virtual War,* 126; Ash, "Cry," 30.

13. Warren Bass, "The Triage of Dayton," *Foreign Affairs* 77 (September/October 1998): 96.

14. Hedges, "Kosovo's Next Masters?" 36; Ash, "Cry," 29; Tim Judah, "Impasse in Kosovo," *New York Review of Books* 45 (8 October 1998): 4.

15. Ash, "Cry," 30.

16. Judah, "Impasse," 4–5.

17. Adam Roberts, "NATO's 'Humanitarian War' over Kosovo," *Survival* 41 (autumn 1999): 113.

18. Ibid., 105, 111.

19. Ignatieff, *Virtual War,* 121–122.

20. Ibid., 41, 60.

21. Ibid., 60–61; Roberts, "NATO's 'Humanitarian War,'" 104.

22. Ignatieff, *Virtual War,* 203–204; Mark Danner, "Endgame in Kosovo," *New York Review of Books* 46 (6 May 1999): 11.

23. Danner, "Endgame," 11; Roberts, "NATO's 'Humanitarian War,'" 111, 114; Zimmerman, "Milosevic's Final Solution," 42; John Kifner, "How Serb Forces Purged One Million Albanians," *New York Times,* 29 May 1999, A1.

24. Kifner, "How Serb Forces," A1, A4; Danner, "Endgame in Kosovo," 11.

25. Quoted in Ivo H. Daalder and Michael E. O'Hanlon, "Unlearning the Lessons of Kosovo," *Foreign Policy* 116 (fall 1999): 128; also see Francis X. Clines, "NATO Hunting for Serb Forces; U.S. Reports Signs of 'Genocide,'" *New York Times,* 30 March 1999, 1.

26. Quoted in Roberts, "NATO's 'Humanitarian War,'" 119.

27. Quoted in Brad Knickerbocker, "Grappling with the Century's Most Heinous Crimes," *Christian Science Monitor* 12 April 1999, 12.

28. Tony Judt, "Tyrannized by Weaklings," *New York Times,* 5 April 1999, (www.nytimes.com).

29. Vaclav Havel, "Kosovo and the End of the Nation-State," *New York Review of Books* 46 (10 June 1999): 6.

30. Ignatieff, *Virtual War*, 187; Roberts, "NATO's 'Humanitarian War,'" 10, 112, 120; William Pfaff, "Land War in Kosovo?" *New York Review of Books* 46 (6 May 1999): 20.

31. U.S. Department of State, "Erasing History: Ethnic Cleansing in Kosovo," May 1999 (www.state.gov). Also, see Ignatieff, *Virtual War*, 55; Roberts, "NATO's 'Humanitarian War,'" 113; Judah, "Impasse," 4; Carlotta Gall, "Fleeing Kosovars Tell of Death and Pillage," *New York Times*, 28 March 1999, 16; International Crisis Group, "Atrocities in Kosovo Must Be Stopped," *ISG Briefing*, 28 March 1999 (www.intl-crisis-group.org); Clines, "NATO Hunting for Serb Forces," 1, 8; John Kifner, "Countless Refugee Accounts Give Details of Mass Killings," *New York Times*, 6 April 1999, 1; Holly Burkhalter, advocacy director, Physicians for Human Rights, "Editorial on Kosovo Genocide," *National Public Radio*, 9 April 1999 (JUSTWATCH-L@LISTSERV.ACSU.BUFFALO.EDU); Steven Erlanger, "With Demographics Changed, Serbs Urge Some Albanians to Remain, Diplomat Says," *New York Times*, 25 April 1999, 16. Craig R. Whitney, "Confident in Their Bombs, Allies Still Plan for Winter," *New York Times*, 5 May 1999, A9.

32. Peter W. Rodman, "The Fallout from Kosovo," *Foreign Affairs* 78 (July/August 1999): 47.

33. Timothy Garton Ash, "Kosovo: Was It Worth It?" *New York Review of Books* 47 (21 September 2000): 58.

34. Danner, "Endgame," 11; also see Ignatieff, *Virtual War*, 62–63; Roberts, "NATO's 'Humanitarian War,'" 109–111.

35. See Colonel Harry G. Summers Jr. (Retired), *On Strategy II: A Critical Analysis of the Gulf War* (New York: Dell, 1992), 134; J. Bryan Hehir, "Kosovo: A War of Values and the Values of War," in *Kosovo: Contending Voices on Balkan Interventions*, edited by William Joseph Buckley (Grand Rapids, MI: Eerdmanns Publishing, 2000), 404.

36. See John M. Rothgeb Jr., *Defining Power: Influence and Force in the Contemporary International System* (New York: St. Martin's Press, 1993), 152.

37. Kifner, "How Serb Forces," A4.

38. "Going to Ground," *New Republic* (19 April 1999) (www.thenewrepublic.com).

39. Danner, "Endgame," 11.

40. Pfaff, "Land War in Kosovo?" 20.

41. Stanley Hoffmann, "On Kosovo: What Is to Be Done?" *New York Review of Books* 46 (20 May 1999): 17.

42. *Wall Street Journal*, 24 May 1999, reprinted in Buckley, ed. *Kosovo: Contending Voices*, 324.

43. Ignatieff, *Virtual War*, 62–63.

44. See Steven Erlanger, "NATO Was Closer to Ground War in Kosovo Than Is Widely Realized," *New York Times*, 7 November 1999, 6; also see Doder and Branson, *Milosevic*, 271; Roberts, "NATO's 'Humanitarian War'" 118; Ignatieff, *Virtual War*, 62–64, 109–110.

45. Ignatieff, *Virtual War*, 65.

46. Tony Judt, "On Kosovo: The Reason Why," *New York Review of Books* 45 (20 May 1999): 16.

47. Ash, "Kosovo: Was It Worth It?" 58.

48. Pfaff, "Land War," 20.

49. Ignatieff, *Virtual War*, 202.

50. Ash, "Cry," 33; Judt, "On Kosovo," 16; Michael Walzer, "Kosovo," *Dissent* (Summer 1999): 5–7; Michael Walzer, "The Politics of Rescue," *Social Research* 62 (spring 1995): 53–66; William A. Schabas, *Genocide in International Law* (Cambridge: Cambridge University Press, 2000), 2, 24–26, 444–445.

51. Ignatieff, *Virtual War*, 182; Walzer, "Kosovo," 7.

52. See John Locke, "The Second Treatise of Civil Government," chap. 14, in *Two Treatises on Government* (New York: Hafner, 1947), para. 158–159, pp. 203–207.

53. Pfaff, "Land War," 20.

54. Steven Kull, *Americans on Kosovo: A Study of U.S. Public Attitudes* (summary findings), program on international policy attitudes, School of Public Affairs, University of Maryland, 27 May 1999, 2, 4, 9–10.

55. Ibid., 10.

56. Schabas, *Genocide in International Law*, 15.

57. See Michael Walzer, *On Toleration* (New Haven, CT: Yale University Press, 1997).

58. See, for instance, Philip H. Gordon, "Their Own Army?" *Foreign Affairs* 79 (July/August 2000): 12–17.

59. Timothy Garton Ash, "Anarchy and Madness," *New York Review of Books* 47 (10 February 2000): 48–53.

60. David Rohde, "Kosovo Seething," *Foreign Affairs* 79 (May/June 2000): 65–79.

61. ABC *Nightly News*, 6 October 2000.

62. Ash, "Cry," 33.

CHAPTER 8

1. Yehuda Bauer, speech to the German Bundestag on Remembrance Day, 27 January 1998 (English text), Information Services, Yad Vashem, Jerusalem.

2. John Stremlau, "People in Peril: Human Rights, Humanitarian Action, and Preventing Deadly Conflict," *A Report to the Carnegie Commission on Preventing Deadly Conflict,* (New York: Carnegie Corporation, May 1998), 41.

3. International Panel of Eminent Persons, "Rwanda: The Preventable Genocide," *Report to the OAU, 29 May 2000,* sec. 1, para. 5, www.oau-oua.org (accessed 23 August 2000).

4. Douglas W. Simon, "The Evolution of the International System and Its Impact on Protection against Genocide," in *Protection against Genocide: Mission Impossible?* edited by Neal Riemer (Westport, CT: Praeger, 2000), 17.

5. Secretary of State Madeleine K. Albright, "Remarks at the Organization of African Unity, Economic Commission for Africa," Addis Ababa, Ethiopia, 9 December 1997, www.state.gov (accessed 3 March 1998); "Remarks by the President to Genocide Survivors, Assistance Workers, and U.S. and Rwanda Government Officials," the White House, Office of the Press Secretary (Kampala, Uganda) 25 March 1998; David J. Scheffer, Ambassador-at-Large for War Crimes Issues, U.S. Department of State, "The United States: Measures to Prevent Genocide and Other Atrocities," address to the Conference on "Genocide and Crimes against Humanity: Early Warning and Prevention," U.S. Holocaust Memorial Museum, Washington, D.C., 10 December 1998, www.state.gov (accessed 14 December 1998); "Kofi Annan Emphasizes Commitment to Enabling UN Never Again to Fail in Protecting Civilian Population from Genocide or Mass Slaughter," UN press release, SG/SM/7263/AFR/196, 16 December 1999; Associated Press, "Bosnia War Crimes Suspect Kills Self," 13 October 2000, www.aol.com/news (accessed 13 October 2000); and David Rohde, "Jury in New York Orders Bosnian Serb to Pay Billions," *New York Times,* 26 September 2000, www.nytimes.com (accessed 6 October 2000).

6. The Rome Statute on the International Criminal Court and the UN reports on Srebrenica and Rwanda can be found at www.un.org; OAU, "International Panel of Eminent Personalities to Investigate the 1994 Genocide in Rwanda and the Surrounding Events," www.oau-oua.org (accessed 23 August 2000); Scott Feil, *Preventing Genocide: How the Early Use of Force Might Have Succeeded in Rwanda* (New York: Carnegie Corporation, 1998); Bruce W. Jentleson, *Coercive Prevention: Normative, Political, and Policy Dilemmas* (Washington, D.C.: United States Institute of Peace, October 2000); and Alton Frye, project director, *Humanitarian Intervention: Crafting a Workable Doctrine* (New York: Council on Foreign Relations, 2000).

7. Neal Riemer, ed., *Protection against Genocide: Mission Impossible?* (Westport, CT: Praeger, 2000); Isidor Wallimann and Michael N. Dobkowski, eds., *Genocide and the Modern Age: Etiology and Case Studies of Mass Death* (Syracuse, NY: Syracuse University Press, 2000); William A. Schabas, *Genocide in International Law: The Crime of Crimes* (Cambridge: Cambridge University Press, 2000).

8. When I asked the director of a prestigious Washington think tank how the U.S. would respond the next time genocide occurred in the heart of Africa, he provided an answer indicative of the foreign-policy community's cynicism regarding the political will to stop genocide: "The president will simply apologize, again."

9. See Ruth Wedgwood, "Fiddling in Rome," *Foreign Affairs* 77 (November/December 1998): 20–24.

10. Barbara Crossette, "Leaders Envision Broad New Role for UN Council," *New York Times,* 8 September 2000, A1, A10.

11. *Report of the Panel on United Nations Peace Operations (Brahimi Report),* 17 August 2000, www.un.org/peace/reports (accessed 1 September 2000). Though the failures of the UN to stop genocide in Bosnia and Rwanda were the catalyst for this study, the report rarely mentions the "g" word.

12. Feil, *Preventing Genocide,* 26–27.

13. Jentleson, *Coercive Prevention,* 5.

14. Ibid., 16.

15. Ibid., 35.

16. Ibid., 24–30.

17. Frye, *Humanitarian Intervention,* 37.

18. Ibid., 50.

19. Ibid., 54, 55.

20. Ibid., 7.

21. Wallimann and Dobkowski, *Genocide and the Modern Age,* ix.

22. Ibid., xiii.

23. Helen Fein, "The Three P's of Genocide Prevention: With Application to a Genocide Foretold—Rwanda," in Riemer, ed., *Protection against Genocide,* 42.

24. Schabas, *Genocide in International Law,* especially chapter 10, "Prevention of Genocide."

25. FEWER is a global organization of NGOs, academics, UN agencies, and governments, founded in 1996 in the wake of the Rwanda genocide, to exchange knowledge and experience, and to generate the political will to stop genocide, www.fewer.org (accessed 9 January 2000).

26. See Schabas, *Genocide in International Law,* 472.

27. See, for example, Brian Urquhart, "For a UN Volunteer Force," *New York Review of Books* 40 (10 June 1993): 3–4; Carl Kaysen and George Rathjens, *Peace Operations by the United Nations: The Case for a Volunteer UN Military Force* (Cambridge, MA: Committee on International Security Studies/American Academy of Arts and Sciences, 1996); and Saul Mendlovitz and John Fousek, "A UN Constabulary to Enforce the Law on Genocide and Crimes against Humanity," in Riemer, ed., *Protection against Genocide,* 105–122.

28. Norman Dorsen and Morton H. Halperin, "Justice after Genocide," Policy in Perspective, the Century Fund, www.tcf.org (accessed 29 March 2000); David Wippman, "Can an International Criminal Court Prevent and Punish Genocide?" in *Protection against Genocide: Mission Impossible?* edited by Neal Riemer (Westport, CT: Praeger, 2000), 85–104.

29. Prevent Genocide International was founded in 1998 to use the internet to link individuals and organizations in a transnational network dedicated to eliminating genocide, www.preventgenocide.org (accessed 1 May 2000).

30. Craig Warkentin and Karen Mingst, "International Institutions, the State, and Global Civil Society in the Age of the World Wide Web," *Global Governance* 6 (April–June 2000): 237–257.

31. See Barbara Harff and Ted Robert Gurr, "Toward Empirical Theory of Genocides and Politicides: Identification and Measurement of Cases Since 1945," *International Studies Quarterly* 32 (1988): 359–371.

CONCLUSION

1. Speech to a Joint Session of the U.S. Congress, 21 February 1990, in Vaclav Havel, *The Art of the Impossible: Politics as Morality in Practice* (New York: Alfred A. Knopf, 1997), 11.

2. See Edward Mortimer, "Under What Circumstances Should the UN Intervene Militarily in a 'Domestic' Crisis?" in *Peacemaking and Peacekeeping for the New Century,* edited by Olara A. Otunnu and Michael W. Doyle (Lanham, MD: Rowman & Littlefield, 1998), 137.

Bibliography

ABC Nightly News. Friday, 6 October 2000.

Addis Ababa, Ethiopia (9 December 1997): www.state.gov (accessed 3 March 1998).

Adelman, Howard, and Astri Suhrke, eds. *The Path of a Genocide: The Rwanda Crisis from Uganda to Zaire.* New Brunswick, NJ: Transaction Publishers, 1999.

Akhavan, Payam. "The Yugoslav Tribunal at a Crossroads: The Dayton Peace Agreement and Beyond." *Human Rights Quarterly* 18 (1996): 259–285.

Albright, Madeleine K. "Use of Force in a Post–Cold War World." Address at the National War College, National Defense University, Fort McNair, Washington, D.C., 23 September 1993. *U.S. Department of State Dispatch* 4 (27 September 1993): 665–668.

———. "Remarks at the Organization of African Unity, Economic Commission for Africa."

Allen, Mike. "On Campus: Student Insularity Mutes Their Outrage." *New York Times,* 11 April 1999, 13.

Ambrose, Stephen E., and Douglas G. Brinkley. *Rise to Globalism: American Foreign Policy since 1938.* 8th rev. ed. New York: Penguin Books, 1997.

Amnesty International, *Amnesty International Report, 1996.* www.amnesty.org.

———. "CBS Crew Tapes SFOR Soldiers Sipping Coffee As Indicted War Crimes Suspect Sits Nearby." www.amnesty-usa.bestware.net (15 October 1997).

———. "Agreement on Kosovo Must Include Immediate Action and a Long-Term Commitment to Human Rights." *News Release,* 13 October 1998. www.amnesty.org.

———. *Forsaken Cries: The Story of Rwanda/Educating for Action.* Information materials and primary documents on key themes from the video.

Aronson, David. "Congo Games." *New Republic* (5 and 12 January 1998): 13–15.

Ash, Timothy Garton. "Cry, the Dismembered Country." *New York Review of Books* 46 (14 January 1999): 29–33.

———. "Kosovo and Beyond." *New York Review of Books* 46 (24 June 1999): 4–7.

———. "Anarchy and Madness." *New York Review of Books* 47 (10 February 2000): 48–53.

———. "Kosovo: Was It Worth It?" *New York Review of Books* 47 (21 September 2000): 50–60.

Aspin, Les. "The Use and Usefulness of Military Force in the Post–Cold War, Post-Soviet World." In *Intervention*, by Richard N. Haass. Washington, D.C.: Carnegie Endowment for International Peace, 1994. Appendix D.

Associated Press. "Balkan Countries Ready to Do Business with Yugoslavia." www.nando.net (accessed 24 November 1995).

————. "Bosnia War Crimes Suspect Kills Self." (13 October 2000): www. aol.com (accessed 13 October 2000).

Bacevich, Andrew J. "The Limits of Orthodoxy: The Use of Force after the Cold War." In *The United States and the Use of Force in the Post–Cold War Era*, edited by the Aspen Strategy Group, 171–190. Queenstown, MD: Aspen Institute, 1995.

Bachrach, Peter, and Morton S. Baratz. "Two Faces of Power." In *Classic Readings in American Politics*, edited by Pietro S. Nivola and David H. Rosenbloom, 142–151. New York: St. Martin's Press, 1986.

Ball, Howard. *Prosecuting War Crimes and Genocide: The Twentieth Century Experience.* Lawrence: University Press of Kansas, 1999.

Bass, Warren. "The Triage of Dayton." *Foreign Affairs* 77 (September/October 1998): 95–108.

Bassiouni, M. Cherif, ed. *International Criminal Law.* Vol. 1, *Crimes.* Dobbs Ferry, NY: Transnational Publishers, 1986.

————. "International Criminal Law and Human Rights." In *International Criminal Law.* Vol. 1, *Crimes*, edited by M. Cherif Bassiouni, 15–32. Dobbs Ferry, NY: Transnational, 1986.

————. "Introduction to the Genocide Convention." In *International Criminal Law.* Vol. 1, *Crimes*, edited by M. Cherif Bassiouni, 281–286. Dobbs Ferry, NY: Transnational, 1986.

————. "The United Nations Commission of Experts Established Pursuant to Security Council Resolution 780 (1992)." *American Journal of International Law* 88 (1994): 784–805.

Bauer, Yehuda. *The Holocaust in Historical Perspective.* Seattle: University of Washington Press, 1978.

————. "Speech to the German Bundestag on Remembrance Day, 27 January 1998." Information Services, Yad Vashem, Jerusalem.

Bennett, A. Leroy. *International Organization: Principles and Issues.* 5th ed. Englewood Cliffs, NJ: Prentice Hall, 1991.

Beres, Louis Rene. "Genocide and Genocide-Like Crimes." In *International Criminal Law.* Vol. 1, *Crimes*, edited by M. Cherif Bassiouni, 271–279. Dobbs Ferry, NY: Transnational, 1986.

Bert, Wayne. *The Reluctant Superpower: United States' Policy in Bosnia, 1991–1995.* New York: St. Martin's Press, 1997.

Best, Geoffrey. *War and Law since 1945.* Oxford: Clarendon Press, 1994.

————. "Justice, International Relations and Human Rights." *International Affairs* 71 (1995): 775–799.

Betts, Richard K. "The Delusion of Impartial Intervention." *Foreign Affairs* 73 (November/December 1994): 20–33.

Blakesley, Christopher L. "Atrocity and Its Prosecution: The Ad Hoc Tribunals for the Former Yugoslavia and Rwanda." In *The Law of War Crimes*, edited by

Timothy L.H. McCormack and Gerry J. Simpson, 189–228. The Hague: Kluwer Law International, 1997.

Bonner, Raymond. "Tactics Were Barrier to Top Serb's Indictment." *New York Times*, 29 March 1999, A9.

Bowden, Mark. *Black Hawk Down: A Story of Modern War*. New York: Penguin Books, 2000.

Boyle, Francis A. *The Bosnian People Charge Genocide: Proceedings at the International Court of Justice Concerning Bosnia v. Serbia on the Prevention of the Crime of Genocide*. Amherst, MA: Alethia Press, 1996.

Breitman, Richard. *Official Secrets: What the Nazis Planned, What the British and Americans Knew*. New York: Hill & Wang, 1999.

Broder, John M. "NATO Attacks Serb Ground Units in Kosovo." *New York Times*, 28 March 1999, 1, 16.

Brodie, Bernard. *War and Politics*. New York: Macmillan, 1973.

Brown, Chris. "Human Rights." In *The Globalization of World Politics: An Introduction to International Relations*, edited by John Baylis and Steve Smith, 469–482. Oxford: Oxford University Press, 1997.

Brown, Michael E., and Richard N. Rosecrance. "Comparing Costs of Prevention and Costs of Conflict: Toward a New Methodology." In *The Costs of Conflict: Prevention and Cure in the Global Arena*, edited by Michael E. Brown and Richard N. Rosecrance, 1–22. Lanham, MD: Rowman & Littlefield, 1999.

Brzezinski, Zbigniew. *Out of Control: Global Turmoil on the Eve of the Twenty-First Century*. New York: Robert Steward Books/Charles Scribner's Sons, 1993.

———. Compromise over Kosovo Means Defeat." *Wall Street Journal*, 24 May 1999. Reprinted in *Kosovo: Contending Voices on Balkan Intervention*, edited by William Joseph Buckley, 324–325. Grand Rapids, MI: Eerdmans, 2000.

Bull, Hedley. *The Anarchical Society: A Study of Order in World Politics*. 2nd ed. New York: Columbia University Press, 1995.

Burg, Steven L. "Afterward: Genocide in Bosnia-Herzegovina?" In *Century of Genocide: Eyewitness Accounts and Critical Views*, 424–433. New York: Garland Publishing, 1997).

Burkhalter, Holly J. "The Question of Genocide: The Clinton Administration and Rwanda." *World Policy Journal* 11 (winter 1994–95): 44–54.

———. Editorial on Kosovo Genocide. *National Public Radio*, 9 April 1999. Justwatch-L@listserv.acsu.guffalo.edu

Buzzanco, Robert. *Vietnam and the Transformation of American Life*. Oxford: Blackwell, 1999.

Callahan, David. *Unwinnable Wars: American Power and Ethnic Conflict*. New York: Twentieth Century Fund Book/Hill & Wang, 1997.

Campbell, Kenneth J. "The International War Crimes Conference, Oslo, June 1971: Excerpts from the Diary of One of the Witnesses." In *Nobody Gets Off the Bus: The Viet Nam Generation Big Book*, edited by Kali Tal and Dan Duffy, 148–151. Woodbridge, CT: Viet Nam Generation, 1994.

———. "The International Use of Force to Suppress Genocide: Necessary and Realistic." Paper presented at the International Symposium on Contemporary Forms of Genocide, University of Nebraska-Lincoln, 15–16 April 1996.

————. "The Role of Force in Humanitarian Intervention." *Airman-Scholar* 3 (spring 1997):20–27.

————. "Genocide and the New World Order." *Injustice Studies* 1 (November 1997): www.wolf.its.ilstu.edu/injustice

————. "Once Burned, Twice Cautious: Explaining the Weinberger-Powell Doctrine." *Armed Forces and Society* 24 (spring 1998): 357–374.

————. "Clausewitz and Genocide: Bosnia, Rwanda, and Strategic Failure." *Civil Wars* 1 (summer 1998): 26–37.

————. "Massacre in Kosovo Is Genocide—and World Must Act Accordingly." *Philadelphia Inquirer*, 19 January 1999, A11.

Carr, E.H. *The Twenty Years' Crisis, 1919–1939.* New York: Harper & Row, 1964.

Carter, Hodding. "Punishing Serbia." *Foreign Policy* 96 (fall 1994): 49–56.

Chalk, Frank, and Kurt Jonassohn. *The History and Sociology of Genocide.* New Haven: Yale University Press/Montreal Institute for Genocide Studies, 1990.

Chalk, Frank. "Redefining Genocide." In *Genocide: Conceptual and Historical Dimensions,* edited by George J. Andreopoulos, 47–63. Philadelphia: University of Pennsylvania Press, 1994.

————. "Rwanda in the History of Genocide." Paper presented at the International Symposium on Contemporary Forms of Genocide, University of Nebraska-Lincoln, 15–16 April 1996.

————. "Hate Radio in Rwanda." Paper presented at the International Symposium on Contemporary Forms of Genocide, University of Nebraska-Lincoln, 15–16 April 1996.

Chaney, Kevin R. "Pitfalls and Imperatives: Applying the Lessons of Nuremberg to the Yugoslav War Crimes Trials." *Dickinson Journal of International Law* 14 (fall 1995): 57–94.

Charney, Israel W. "Toward a Generic Definition of Genocide." In *Genocide: Conceptual and Historical Dimensions,* edited by George J. Andreopoulos, 64–94 Philadelphia: University of Pennsylvania Press, 1994.

Chicago Manual of Style. 14th ed. Chicago: University of Chicago Press, 1993.

Churchill, Winston S. *The Gathering Storm. Vol. 1 of The Second World War.* Boston: Houghton Mifflin, 1985.

Cigar, Norman. *Genocide in Bosnia: The Policy of "Ethnic Cleansing."* College Station, TX: Texas A&M University Press, 1995.

Clark, Roger S. "Nuremberg and Tokyo in Contemporary Perspective." In *The Law of War Crimes,* edited by Timothy L.H. McCormack and Gerry J. Simpson, 171–187. The Hague: Kluwer Law International, 1997.

Claude, Inis L. Jr. *Swords into Plowshares: The Problems and Progress of International Organizations.* 4th ed. New York: Random House, 1971.

————. "The Common Defense and Great-Power Responsibilities." *Political Science Quarterly* 101 (1986): 719–732.

Clausewitz, Carl von. *On War.* Princeton: Princeton University Press, 1976.

Clines, Francis X. "NATO Hunting for Serb Forces; U.S. Reports Signs of 'Genocide.'" *New York Times,* 30 March 1999, 1, 8.

Clinton, Bill. "U.S. Holocaust Museum Dedicated." Address at the Dedication Ceremony, Washington, D.C., 22 April 1993. *U.S. Department of State Dispatch* 4 (10 May 1993): 322–324.

———. *Remarks by the President to White House Conference on Africa,* 27 June 1994, www.whitehouse.gov.

———. "Remarks by the President to Genocide Survivors, Assistance Workers, and U.S. and Rwandan Government Officials, Kigali, Rwanda." The White House, 25 March 1998.

———. Letter to the author, 4 May 1999.

Cohen, Philip J. "The Complicity of Serbian Intellectuals in Genocide in the 1990s." In *This Time We Knew: Western Responses to Genocide in Bosnia,* edited by Thomas Cushman and Stjepan G. Mestrovic, 39–64. New York: New York University Press, 1996.

Cohen, Roberta, and Francis M. Deng. "Exodus within Borders." *Foreign Affairs* 77 (July/August): 12–16.

Cohen, Roger. "C.I.A. Report Finds Serbs Guilty in Majority of Bosnian War Crimes." *New York Times,* 9 March 1995, A1, A8.

———. "Honor, Too, Put to Flight in Bosnia." *New York Times,* 16 July 1995, sec. 4, pp. 1, 4.

Collingwood, R.G. *The New Leviathan, Or Man, Society, Civilization and Barbarism.* rev. ed. Oxford: Clarendon Press, 1992.

Cortright, David. *Soldiers in Revolt.* Garden City, NJ: Anchor Press, 1975.

Craig, Gordon A., and Alexander L. George. *Force and Statecraft: Diplomatic Problems of Our Time.* 3rd ed. New York: Oxford University Press, 1995.

Cronin, Bruce. "Changing Norms of Sovereignty and Multilateral Intervention." In *Collective Conflict Management and Changing World Politics,* edited by Joseph Lepgold and Thomas G. Weiss, 159–180. Albany, NY: University of New York Press, 1998.

Crossette, Barbara. "Leaders Envision Broad New Role for UN Council." *New York Times,* 8 September 2000, A1, A10.

Cushman, Thomas, and Stjepan G. Mestrovic, eds. *This Time We Knew: Western Responses to Genocide in Bosnia.* New York: New York University Press, 1996.

Cusimano, Maryann K., ed. *Beyond Sovereignty: Issues for a Global Agenda.* Boston/New York: Bedford/St. Martin's Press, 2000.

Cutter, W. Bowman, Joan Spero, and Laura D'Andrea Tyson. "New World, New Deal." *Foreign Affairs* 79 (March/April 2000): 80–98.

Czuczka, Tony. "A Day of Remembrance." *Philadelphia Inquirer,* 28 January 1998, A2.

Daalder, Ivo H., and Michael E. O'Hanlon. "Unlearning the Lessons of Kosovo." *Foreign Policy* 116 (fall 1999): 128–140.

Damrosch, Lori Fisler. "Introduction." In *Enforcing Restraint: Collective Intervention in Internal Conflicts,* edited by Lori Fisler Damrosch, 1–26. New York: Council on Foreign Relations, 1993.

———. "Concluding Reflections." In *Enforcing Restraint: Collective Intervention in Internal Conflicts,* edited by Lori Fisler Damrosch, 348–367. New York: Council on Foreign Affairs, 1993.

————, and Rein Mullerson. "The Role of International Law in the Contemporary World." In *Beyond Confrontation: International Law for the Post–Cold War Era*, edited by Lori Fisler Damrosch, Gennady M. Danilenko, and Rien Mullerson, 1–21. Boulder, CO: Westview Press, 1995.

————. "Genocide and Ethnic Conflict." In *International Law and Ethnic Conflict*, edited by David Wippman, 256–279. Ithaca, NY: American Society of International Law/Columbia University Press, 1998.

Danner, Mark. "The U.S. and the Yugoslav Catastrophe." *New York Review of Books* 44 (20 November 1997): 56–64.

————. "America and the Bosnia Genocide." *New York Review of Books* 44 (4 December 1997): 55–65.

————. "Clinton, the UN, and the Bosnian Disaster." *New York Review of Books* 44 (18 December 1997): 65–81.

————. "Bosnia: The Turning Point." *New York Review of Books* 45 (5 February 1998): 34–41.

————. "Bosnia: Breaking the Machine." *New York Review of Books* 45 (19 February 1998): 41–45.

————. "Bosnia: The Great Betrayal." *New York Review of Books* 45 (26 March 1998): 40–52.

————. "Slouching Toward Dayton." *New York Review of Books* 45 (23 April 1998): 59–65.

————. "The Killing Fields of Bosnia." *New York Review of Books* 45 (24 September 1998): 63–77.

————. "Operation Storm." *New York Review of Books* 45 (22 October 1998): 73–79.

————. "Endgame in Kosovo." *New York Review of Books* 46 (6 May 1999): 8–11.

————. "Kosovo: The Meaning of Victory." *New York Review of Books* 46 (15 July 1999): 53–54.

Davidson, Eugene. *The Trial of the Germans*. New York: Macmillan, 1966.

Davies, John L., and Ted Robert Gurr. *Preventive Measures: Building Risk Assessment and Crisis Early Warning Systems*. Lanham, MD: Rowman & Littlefield, 1998.

Des Forges, Alison. *"Leave None to Tell the Story: Genocide in Rwanda*. New York: Human Rights Watch, 1999.

Destexhe, Alain. *Rwanda and Genocide in the Twentieth Century*. New York: New York University Press, 1995.

————. "The Third Genocide." *Foreign Policy* 97 (winter 1994–95): 3–17.

Djilas, Aleksa. "Imagining Kosovo." *Foreign Affairs* 77 (September/October 1998): 124–131.

Doctors Without Borders USA. "Medical Personnel Targeted in Kosovo." News Release (9 October 1998): www.dwb.org.

Doder, Dusko, and Louise Branson. *Milosevic: Portrait of a Tyrant*. New York: Free Press, 1999.

Donnelly, Jack. *International Human Rights*. 2nd ed. Boulder, CO: Westview Press, 1998.

Dorsen, Norman, and Morton H. Halperin. "Justice after Genocide." Policy in Perspective, The Century Fund: www.tcf.org (accessed 29 March 2000).

Dowty, Alan, and Gil Loescher. "Refugee Flows as Grounds for International Action." *International Security* 21 (summer 1996): 61–62.

Duke, Lynne. "Genocide's Legacy: Tourist Killings Highlight Continuing Role Hutus Play in Central Africa's Conflicts." *Washington Post*, 10 March 1999, A17.

Egboo, Felix. "Rwanda." *Africa Review: The Economic and Business Report.* London: Walden Publishing, 1997.

Eisenhower, Dwight D. *Crusade in Europe.* Garden City, NY: Doubleday, 1948.

Erdheim, Stuart G. "Could the Allies Have Bombed Auschwitz-Birkenau?" *Holocaust and Genocide Studies* 11 (1997): 129–170.

Erlanger, Steven. "With Demographics Changed, Serbs Urge Some Albanians to Remain, Diplomat Says." *New York Times*, 25 April 1999, 16.

———. "NATO Was Closer to Ground War in Kosovo Than Is Widely Realized." *New York Times*, 7 November 1999, 6.

———, and Christopher S. Wren. "Early Count Hints at Fewer Kosovo Deaths." *New York Times*, 11 November 1999, A6.

Everts, Philip. "When the Going Gets Rough: Does the Public Support the Use of Military Force?" *World Affairs* 162 (winter 2000): 91–107.

Falk, Richard A., Gabriel Kolko, and Robert Jay Lifton, eds. *Crimes of War: A Legal, Political-Documentary, and Psychological Inquiry into the Responsibility of Leaders, Citizens, and Soldiers for Criminal Acts in War.* New York: Vintage Books, 1971.

Falk, Richard A. "The Complexities of Humanitarian Intervention: A New World Order Challenge." *Michigan Journal of International Law* 17 (winter 1996): 491–513.

———. "Meeting the Challenge of Genocide in Bosnia: Reconciling Moral Imperatives with Political Constraints." In *Genocide, War, and Human Survival,* edited by Charles B. Strozier and Michael Flynn, 125–135. Lanham, MD: Rowman & Littlefield, 1996.

Farer, Tom. "A Paradigm of Legitimate Intervention." In *Enforcing Restraint: Collective Intervention in Internal Conflicts,* edited by Lori Fisler Damrosch, 316–347. New York: Council on Foreign Relations, 1993.

Fearon, James D. "Commitment Problems and the Spread of Ethnic Conflict." In *The International Spread of Ethnic Conflict: Fear, Diffusion, and Escalation,* edited by David A. Lake and Donald Rothchild, 107–126. Princeton: Princeton University Press, 1998.

Feil, Scott. *Preventing Genocide: How the Early Use of Force Might Have Succeeded in Rwanda.* A Report to the Carnegie Commission on Preventing Deadly Conflict. New York: Carnegie Corporation, April 1998.

Fein, Helen. "Reassessing Contemporary Genocide: Such Mass Murders Can Be Stopped." Paper presented at the International Symposium on Contemporary Forms of Genocide. University of Nebraska-Lincoln, April 1996.

———. "The Three P's of Genocide Prevention: With Application to a Genocide Foretold—Rwanda." In *Protection against Genocide: Mission Impossible?,* edited by Neal Riemer, 41–66. Westport, CT: Praeger, 2000.

Fisher, Ian. "Rwanda's Huge Stake in Congo's War." *New York Times,* 27 December 1998, 12.

Freedman, Lawrence, ed. *Military Intervention in European Conflicts*. Oxford: Blackwell, 1994.

———, and Efraim Karsh. *The Gulf Conflict, 1990–1991: Diplomacy and War in the New World*. Princeton: Princeton University Press, 1993.

Friedman, Thomas L. "Bosnia Reconsidered." *New York Times*, 8 April 1993, A6.

Frontline: "The Triumph of Evil." PBS, 26 January 1999.

Frye, Alton. *Humanitarian Intervention: Crafting a Workable Doctrine*. New York: Council on Foreign Relations, 2000.

Fukuyama, Francis. *The End of History and the Last Man*. New York: Avon Books, 1992.

Gabriel, Richard A., and Paul L. Savage. *Crisis in Command*. New York: Hill & Wang, 1978.

Gacek, Christopher M. *The Logic of Force*. New York: Columbia University Press, 1994.

Gall, Carlotta. "Fleeing Kosovars Tell of Death and Pillage." *New York Times*, 28 March 1999, 16.

Ganguly, Rajat, and Ray Taras. *Understanding Ethnic Conflict: The International Dilemma*. New York: Longman, 1998.

Gelb, Leslie H., and Richard K. Betts. *The Irony of Vietnam*. Washington, D.C.: Brookings Institution, 1979.

Gellman, Barton. "U.S. Military Fears Balkan Intervention." *Washington Post*, 12 August 1992, A24.

George, Alexander L. *Bridging the Gap: Theory and Practice in Foreign Policy*. Washington, D.C.: United States Institute of Peace Press, 1993.

Geyer, Georgie Anne. "Blame Pentagon for Being Bogged Down in Bosnia." *News Journal* (Wilmington, DE), 26 February 1996, A16.

Gilbert, Martin. *Auschwitz and the Allies*. New York: Henry Holt, 1981.

Gilpin, Robert. *War and Change in World Politics*. Cambridge: Cambridge University Press, 1981.

Glahn, Gerhard Von. *Law among Nations: An Introduction to International Public Law*. 7th ed. Boston: Allyn & Bacon, 1996.

Glennon, Michael J. "The New Interventionism: The Search for a Just International Law." *Foreign Affairs* 78 (May/June 1999): 2–7.

Glenny, Misha. *The Fall of Yugoslavia: The Third Balkan War*. New York: Penguin Books, 1992.

Goble, Paul. "Yugoslavia: Analysis from Washington—Fighting over 'Genocide.'" *Central Europe Online*. www.centraleurope.com (accessed 9 April 1999).

Goldstone, Richard J. "War Crimes: When Amnesia Causes Cancer." *Washington Post*, 2 February 1997, C4.

———. "No Justice in Bosnia." *New York Times*, 3 March 1997, A25.

———. *For Humanity: Reflections of a War Crimes Investigator*. New Haven: Yale University Press, 2000.

Gordon, Philip H. "Their Own Army? Making European Defense Work." *Foreign Affairs* 79 (July/August 2000): 12–17.

Gourevitch, Philip. *We Wish to Inform You That Tomorrow We Will Be Killed with Our Families: Stories from Rwanda*. New York: Farrar, Straus & Giroux, 1998.

———. "The Genocide Fax." *New Yorker*, 11 May 1998, 42–46. Gow, James. *Triumph of the Lack of Will: International Diplomacy and the Yugoslav War.* New York: Columbia University Press, 1997.

Gross, Robert A. "Lieutenant Calley's Army: Following Orders in Vietnam." *Esquire* 76 (October 1971): 154–158, 196–197, 199.

Gurr, Ted Robert, and Barbara Harff. *Ethnic Conflict in World Politics.* Boulder, CO: Westview Press, 1994.

———. "Ethnic Conflict on the Wane." *Foreign Affairs* 79 (May/June 2000): 52–64.

Gutman, Roy. *Witness to Genocide.* New York: Macmillan, 1993.

Haas, Ernst B. *Nationalism, Liberalism, and Progress. Vol. 2, The Rise and Decline of Nationalism.* Ithaca: Cornell University Press, 1997.

———. "Failed Interventions Discredit the Intervener." *Currents: Institute of International Studies* (online edition, spring 1997).

Haass, Richard N. *Intervention: The Use of American Military Force in the Post–Cold War World.* Washington, D.C.: Carnegie Endowment for International Peace, 1994.

———. *The Reluctant Sheriff: The United States after the Cold War.* New York: Council on Foreign Relations, 1997.

———. "The Squandered Presidency." *Foreign Affairs* 79 (May/June 2000): 136–140.

Haig, Alexander M. *Caveat: Realism, Reagan, and Foreign Policy.* New York: Macmillan, 1984.

Halloran, Richard. *To Arm a Nation.* New York: Macmillan, 1986.

Halperin, Sandra. "The Spread of Ethnic Conflict in Europe: Some Comparative Historical Reflections." In *The International Spread of Ethnic Conflict: Fear, Diffusion, and Escalation,* edited by David A. Lake and Donald Rothchild, 151–184. Princeton: Princeton University Press, 1998.

Halvorsen, Kate. "Protection and Humanitarian Assistance in the Refugee Camps in Zaire: The Problem of Security." In *The Path of a Genocide: The Rwandan Crisis from Uganda to Zaire,* edited by Howard Adelman and Astri Suhrke, 307–320. New Brunswick, NJ: Transaction, 1999.

Harden, Baine. "What It Would Take to Cleanse Serbia." *New York Times,* 9 May 1999, sec. 4, pp. 1, 6.

Harff, Barbara, and Ted Robert Gurr. "Toward Empirical Theory of Genocides and Politicides: Identification and Measurement of Cases since 1945." *International Studies Quarterly* 32 (1988): 359–371.

———. "Early Warning of Humanitarian Crises: Sequential Models and the Role of Acceleration." In *Preventive Measures: Building Risk Assessment and Crisis Early Warning Systems,* edited by John L. Davies and Ted Robert Gurr, 70–78. Lanham, MD: Rowman & Littlefield, 1998.

Hart, B.H. Liddell. *Strategy.* 2nd rev. ed. New York: Praeger, 1968.

Hassner, Pierre. *Violence and Peace: From the Atomic Bomb to Ethnic Cleansing.* Budapest: Central European University Press, 1997.

Hauser, William. *America's Army in Crisis.* Baltimore, MD: Johns Hopkins University Press, 1973.

Havel, Vaclav. *The Art of the Impossible: Politics as Morality in Practice; Speeches and Writings, 1990–1996.* New York: Alfred A. Knopf, 1997.

———. "Kosovo and the End of the Nation-State." *New York Review of Books* 46 (10 June 1999): 4–6.

Hazen, Jennifer M. "The Rhetoric of Genocide: Signs of Shifting Norms of Intervention." Paper presented to the Annual Meeting of the International Studies Association, Los Angeles, 16 March 2000.

Hedges, Chris. "Kosovo's Brutal Game of See-Saw." *New York Times*, 28 March 1999, 6.

———. "Kosovo's Next Masters?" *Foreign Affairs* 78 (May/June 1999): 24–42.

Hehir, Bryan J. "Expanding Military Intervention: Promise or Peril?" *Social Research* 62 (spring 1995): 41–51.

———. "Military Intervention and National Sovereignty: Recasting the Relationship." In *Hard Choices: Moral Dilemmas in Humanitarian Intervention,* edited by Jonathan Moore, 29–54. Lanham, MD: Rowman & Littlefield, 1998.

———. "Kosovo: A War of Values and the Values of War." In *Kosovo: Contending Voices on Balkan Interventions,* edited by William Joseph Buckley, 399–405. Grand Rapids, MI: Eerdmans, 2000.

Heinl, Robert D. "Collapse of the Armed Forces." In *Vietnam and America,* edited by Marvin E. Gettleman et al., 326–327. New York: Grove Press, 1995.

Held, David, and Anthony McGrew, with David Goldblatt and Jonathan Perratos. "Managing the Challenge of Globalization and Institutionalizing Cooperation through Global Governance." In *The Global Agenda: Issues and Perspectives.* 6th ed., edited by Charles W. Kegley Jr. and Eugene R. Wittkopf, 134–146. New York: McGraw-Hill, 2001.

Henkin, Louis. *The Age of Rights.* New York: Columbia University Press, 1990.

Hilberg, Raul. *The Destruction of the European Jews.* Chicago: Quadrangle Books, 1961.

Hilsman, Roger. *To Move a Nation.* New York: Dell, 1967.

Hirsch, Herbert. *Genocide and the Politics of Memory: Studying Death to Preserve Life.* Chapel Hill, NC: University of North Carolina Press, 1995.

Hoffman, Eva. "The Uses of Hell." *New York Review of Books* 47 (9 March 2000): 19–23.

Hoffman, Fred G. "Decisive Force: A New American Way of War." *Strategic Review* (winter 1995): 23–34.

Hoffmann, Stanley. *Duties beyond Borders: On the Limits and Possibilities of Ethical International Politics.* Syracuse, NY: Syracuse University Press, 1981.

———. "The Politics and Ethics of Humanitarian Intervention." *Survival* 37 (winter 1995– 96): 29–51.

———, ed. *The Ethics and Politics of Humanitarian Intervention.* Notre Dame, IN: Notre Dame University Press, 1996.

———. "On Kosovo: What Is to Be Done?" *New York Review of Books* 46 (20 May 1999): 17–18.

———. "In Defense of Mother Theresa: Morality in Foreign Policy." *Foreign Affairs* 75 (March/April 1996): 172–175.

Holbrooke, Richard C. "Advancing U.S. Interests in Europe." *U.S. Department of State Dispatch* 6 (20 March 1995): 209–216.

————. *To End a War*. New York: Random House, 1998.

Holsti, K.J. *War, the State, and the State of War*. Cambridge: Cambridge University Press, 1996.

Honig, Jan Willem, and Norbert Both. *Srebrenica: Record of a War Crime*. New York: Penguin Books, 1997.

Howard, Michael, George J. Andreopoulos, and Mark R. Shulman, eds. *The Laws of War: Constraints on Warfare in the Western World*. New Haven: Yale University Press, 1994.

————. *The Causes of Wars, and Other Essays*. Cambridge, MA: Harvard University Press, 1983.

Human Rights Watch/Helsinki. *Bosnia-Hercegovina: The Fall of Srebrenica and the Failure of UN Peacekeeping*. A Human Rights Watch-Helsinki Report 7 (October 1995).

Huntington, Samuel P. "The Clash of Civilizations?" *Foreign Affairs* 72 (summer 1993): 22–49.

————. *The Clash of Civilizations: Remaking of World Order*. New York: Touchstone Books, 1996.

Ignatieff, Michael. *The Warrior's Honor: Ethnic War and the Modern Conscience*. New York: Metropolitan Books/Henry Holt, 1997.

————. "Human Rights: The Midlife Crisis." *New York Review of Books* 46 (20 May 1999): 58–62.

————. "The New American Way of War." *New York Review of Books* 47 (20 July 2000): 42–46.

————. *Virtual War: Kosovo and Beyond*. New York: Metropolitan Books, 2000.

Ikenberry, G. John. "The Myth of Post–Cold War Chaos." *Foreign Affairs* 75 (May/June 1996): 76–91.

Infield, Tom. "Witness." *Philadelphia Inquirer Magazine*, 9 April 1995, 12–15, 24–26, 28, 31.

International Commission on the Balkans. *Unfinished Peace: Report of the International Commission on the Balkans*. Washington, D.C.: Carnegie Endowment for International Peace/Aspen Institute Berlin, 1996.

International Crisis Group. "Atrocities in Kosovo Must Be Stopped." *ISG Briefing* (28 March 1999): www.intl-crisis-group.org.

International Panel of Eminent Personalities. *Rwanda: The Preventable Genocide*. Report to the Organization of African Unity (29 May 2000): www.oau-oua.org (accessed 23 August 2000).

Jentleson, Bruce W. "Preventive Diplomacy and Ethnic Conflict: Possible, Difficult, Necessary." In *The International Spread of Ethnic Conflict: Fear, Diffusion, and Escalation*, edited by David A. Lake and Donald Rothchild, 293–316. Princeton: Princeton University Press, 1998.

————. "Coercive Prevention: Normative, Political, and Policy Dilemmas." *Peaceworks* 35 (October 2000). Washington, D.C.: United States Institute of Peace.

Jonassohn, Kurt, and Frank Chalk. "A Typology of Genocide and Some Implications for the Human Rights Agenda." In *Genocide and the Modern Age: Etiology and Case Studies of Mass Death*, edited by Isidor Wallimann and Michael N. Dobkowski, 3–20. Syracuse, NY: Syracuse University Press, 2000.

Joyner, Christopher C. "Strengthening Enforcement of Humanitarian Law: Reflections on the International Criminal Tribunal for the Former Yugoslavia." *Duke Journal of Comparative and International Law* 6 (1995): 94–101.

———, ed. *The United Nations and International Law.* Cambridge: Cambridge University Press/American Society of International Law, 1997.

Judah, Tim. "Will There Be a War in Kosovo?" *New York Review of Books* 45 (14 May 1998): 35–38.

———. "Impasse in Kosovo." *New York Review of Books* 45 (8 October 1998): 4–6.

Judt, Tony. "Tyrannized by Weaklings." *New York Times,* 5 April 1999, www.nytimes.com.

———. "On Kosovo: The Reason Why." *New York Review of Books* 46 (20 May 1999): 16.

Kaplan, Robert D. "The Coming Anarchy." *Atlantic Monthly* (February 1994): 44–76.

Kartashkin, Vladimir A., and Stephen P. Marks. "International Human Rights." In *Beyond Confrontation: International Law for the Post–Cold War Era.* A joint research project of the ASIL (Washington, D.C.) and the Institute of State and Law (Moscow), edited by Lori Fisler Damrosch, Gennady M. Danilenko, and Rein Mullerson, 275–307. Boulder, CO: Westview Press, 1995.

Kay, Sean. "After Kosovo: NATO's Credibility Dilemma." *Security Dialogue* 31 (March 2000): 71–84.

Kaysen, Carl, and George Rathjens. *Peace Operations by the United Nations: The Case for a Volunteer UN Military Force.* Cambridge, MA: Committee on International Security Studies, American Academy of Arts and Sciences, 1996.

Keane, Fergal. *Season of Blood: A Rwandan Journey.* London: Penguin Books, 1995.

Keegan, John. *A History of Warfare.* New York: Vintage Books, 1993.

Kegley, Charles W. Jr., and Eugene R. Wittkopf. *World Politics: Trend and Transformation.* 7th ed. New York: St. Martin's Press/Worth, 1999.

Kelleher, Catherine McArdle. "Security in the New Order: Presidents, Polls, and the Use of Force." In *Beyond the Beltway: Engaging the Public in U.S. Foreign Policy,* edited by Daniel Yankelovich and I.M. Destler, 225–252. New York: Norton, 1994.

Keller, Edmond J. "Transnational Ethnic Conflict in Africa." In *The International Spread of Ethnic Conflict: Fear, Diffusion, and Escalation,* edited by David A. Lake and Donald Rothchild, 275–292. Princeton: Princeton University Press, 1998.

Kennan, George F. "Morality and Foreign Policy." *Foreign Affairs* 64 (winter 1985): 205–218.

Keohane, Robert O., and Joseph S. Nye Jr. *Power and Interdependence.* 2nd ed. Glenview, IL: Scott Foresman/Little Brown, 1989.

———. "Globalization: What's New? What's Not? (And So What?)" *Foreign Policy* 118 (spring 2000): 104–119.

Khan, Sadruddin Aga. "A Fig Leaf on Serbian Genocide." *New York Times,* 12 April 1993, A17.

Kifner, John. "Countless Refugee Accounts Give Details of Mass Killings." *New York Times,* 6 April 1999, 1, 10.

———. "How Serb Forces Purged One Million Albanians." *New York Times,* 29 May 1999, A1, A4.

Kindleberger, Charles P. *The World in Depression, 1929–1939*. Berkeley: University of California Press, 1973.

King, Edward L. *Death of an Army*. New York: Saturday Review Press, 1972.

Knickerbocker, Brad. "Grappling with the Century's Most Heinous Crimes." *Christian Science Monitor*, 12 April 1999, 1, 12.

Kohut, Andrew, and Robert C. Toth. "Arms and the People." *Foreign Affairs* 73 (November/December 1993): 47–61.

Krasner, Stephen D., and Daniel T. Froats. "Minority Rights and the Westphalian Model." In *The International Spread of Ethnic Conflict: Fear, Diffusion, and Escalation*, edited by David A. Lake and Donald Rothchild, 227–250. Princeton: Princeton University Press, 1998.

Kressel, Neil J. *Mass Hate: The Global Rise of Genocide and Terror*. New York: Plenum Press, 1996.

Krumm, Donald. "Early Warning: An Action Agenda." In *Preventive Measures: Building Risk Assessment and Crisis Early Warning Systems*, edited by John L. Davies and Ted Robert Gurr, 248–254. Lanham, MD: Rowman & Littlefield, 1998.

Kull, Steven. "What the Public Knows That Washington Doesn't." *Foreign Policy* 101 (winter 1995–96): 102–115.

———. *Americans on Kosovo: A Study of U.S. Public Attitudes* (summary findings). Program on International Policy Attitudes, School of Public Affairs, University of Maryland (27 May 1999).

Kull, Steven, and I.M. Destler. *Misreading the Public: The Myth of a New Isolationism*. Washington, D.C.: Brookings Institution, 1999.

Kull, Steven, and Clay Ramsay. "Challenging U.S. Policymakers' Image of an Internationalist Public." *International Studies Perspectives* 1 (April 2000): 105–117.

Kuper, Leo. *The Prevention of Genocide*. New Haven: Yale University Press, 1985.

Kuran, Timur. "Ethnic Dissimulation and Its International Diffusion." In *The International Spread of Ethnic Conflict: Fear, Diffusion, and Escalation*, edited by David A. Lake and Donald Rothchild, 35–60. Princeton: Princeton University Press, 1998.

Lake, Anthony. "Principles Governing U.S. Use of Force." Remarks at George Washington University, 6 March 1996. www.whitehouse.com

Lake, David A., and Donald Rothchild. "Spreading Fear: The Genesis of Transnational Ethnic Conflict." In *The International Spread of Ethnic Conflict: Fear, Diffusion, and Escalation*, edited by David A. Lake and Donald Rothchild, 3–32. Princeton: Princeton University Press, 1998.

Langford, Tonya. "Things Fall Apart: State Failure and the Politics of Intervention." *International Studies Review* 1 (spring 1999): 59–79.

Laurenti, Jeffrey. "International Intervention—Humanitarian or Otherwise?" Paper presented at the International Symposium on Humanitarian Intervention and the United Nations, Japan Association for United Nations Studies, Aoyama Gakuin Daigaku, Tokyo, 27 May 2000.

Lemkin, Raphael. *Axis Rule in Occupied Europe*. Washington, D.C.: Carnegie Endowment for International Peace, 1944.

———. "Genocide: A Modern Crime." *Free World* 4 (April 1945): 39–43. Republished at www.preventgenocide.org (accessed 23 October 2000).

Lepgold, Joseph, and Thomas G. Weiss, eds. *Collective Conflict Management and Changing World Problems*. Albany, NY: State University of New York Press, 1998.

Levy, Richard. "The Bombing of Auschwitz Revisited: A Critical Analysis." In *FDR and the Holocaust*, edited by Verne W. Newton, 219–272. New York: St. Martin's Press, 1996.

Lillich, Richard B. *Humanitarian Intervention and the United Nations*. Charlottesville, VA: University Press of Virginia, 1973.

Lin, Jennifer. "Russia, China Call for End to NATO Attacks." *Philadelphia Inquirer*, 12 May 1999, A1, A11.

Lippman, Thomas W., and Ann Devoy. "Matching Policy to Rhetoric." *Washington Post National Weekly Edition*, 18–24 September 1995, 6–7.

Lippmann, Walter. *U.S. Foreign Policy: Shield of the Republic*. Boston: Little, Brown, 1943.

Littell, Franklin H. "Holocaust Education After '40 Years in the Wilderness.'" In *The Holocaust Forty Years After*, edited by Marcia Littell, Richard Libowitz, and Evelyn Bodek Rosen, 1–6. Lewiston, NY: Edwin Mellen Press, 1989.

Locke, John. *Two Treatises on Government*. New York: Hafner, 1947.

Loescher, Gil. *Refugee Movements and International Security*. Adelphi Paper 268. London: Brassey's for the IISS, 1992.

———. *Beyond Charity: International Cooperation and the Global Refugee Crisis*. New York: Oxford University Press/Twentieth Century Fund, 1993.

Lovell, John P. "Vietnam and the U.S. Army: Learning to Cope with Failure." In *Democracy, Strategy, and Vietnam: Implications for American Policymaking*, edited by George K. Osborn, Asa A. Clark IV, Daniel J. Kaufman, and Douglas E. Lute, 121–154. Lexington, MA: Lexington Books, 1987.

Luttwak, Edward N. "Where Are the Great Powers? At Home with the Kids." *Foreign Affairs* 73 (July/August 1994): 23–28.

Lyman, Princeton N. "Globalization and the Demands of Governance." *Georgetown Journal of International Affairs* 1 (winter/spring 2000): 89–97.

Lyons, Terrence, and Ahmed I. Samatar. *Somalia: State Collapse, Multilateral Intervention, and Strategies for Political Reconstruction*. Washington, D.C.: Brookings Institution, 1995.

Maass, Peter. *Love Thy Neighbor: A Story of War*. New York: Alfred A. Knopf, 1996.

Mandel, Robert. "Perceived Security Threat and the Global Refugee Crisis." *Armed Forces and Society* 24 (fall 1997): 77–103.

Marrus, Michael R. *The Nuremberg War Crimes Trial, 1945–46: A Documentary History*. Boston: Bedford Books, 1997.

Marschik, Axel. "The Politics of Prosecution: European Approaches to War Crimes." In *The Law of War Crimes*, edited by Timothy L.H. McCormack and Gerry J. Simpson, 65–101. The Hague: Kluwer Law International, 1997.

Maull, Hanns W. " Germany in the Yugoslav Crisis." *Survival* 37 (winter 1995/96): 99–130.

Maykuth, Andrew. "Burundi Heads for Genocidal War." *Philadelphia Inquirer*, 26 May 1996, A4.

McCoubrey, Hilaire, and Nigel D. White. *International Organizations and Civil Wars*. Aldershot: Dartmouth, 1995.

Mendlovitz, Saul, and John Fousek. "The Prevention and Punishment of the Crime of Genocide." In *Genocide, War and Human Survival,* edited by Charles B. Strozier and Michael Flynn, 137–151. Lanham, MD: Rowman & Littlefield, 1996.

———. "A UN Constabulary to Enforce the Law on Genocide and Crimes Against Humanity." In *Protection against Genocide: Mission Imposssible?,* edited by Neal Riemer, 104–122. Westport, CT: Praeger, 2000.

Meron, Theodor. "Answering for War Crimes." *Foreign Affairs* 76 (January/February 1997): 2–8.

Meyrowitz, Elliott L., and Kenneth J. Campbell. "Vietnam Veterans and War Crimes Hearings." In *Give Peace a Chance: Exploring the Vietnam Antiwar Movement,* edited by Melvin Small and William D. Hoover, 129–140. Syracuse, NY: Syracuse University Press, 1992.

Middleton, Drew. "U.S. Generals Are Leery of Latin Intervention." *New York Times,* 21 June 1983, A9.

Miller, Lynn H. *Global Order: Values and Power in International Politics.* 4th ed. Boulder, CO: Westview Press, 1998.

Milton, Sybil. "Holocaust: The Gypsies." In *Century of Genocide: Eyewitness Accounts and Critical Views,* edited by Samuel Totten, William S. Parsons, and Israel W. Charney, 171–188. New York: Garland Publishing, 1997.

Mingst, Karen. *Essentials of International Relations.* New York: W.W. Norton, 1999.

———. "Global Governance: The American Perspective." In *Globalization and Global Governance,* edited by Raimo Vayrynen, 87–102. Lanham, MD: Rowman & Littlefield, 1999.

Minow, Martha. "Why Try?" In *Kosovo: Contending Voices on Balkan Intervention,* edited by William Joseph Buckley, 465–466. Grand Rapids, MI: Eerdmans, 2000.

Mitrany, David. *A Working Peace System.* Chicago: Quadrangle Books, 1966.

Morgenthau, Hans J. *Politics among Nations: The Struggle for Power and Peace.* 4th ed. New York: Alfred A. Knopf, 1967.

Mortimer, Edward. "Under What Circumstances Should the UN Intervene Militarily in a 'Domestic' Crisis?" In *Peacemaking and Peacekeeping for the New Century,* edited by Olara A. Otunnu and Michael W. Doyle, 111–144. Lanham, MD: Rowman & Littlefield, 1998.

Moss, George Donelson. *Vietnam: An American Ordeal.* Englewood Cliffs, NJ: Prentice Hall, 1990.

Moynihan, Daniel Patrick. *Pandaemonium: Ethnicity in International Politics.* Oxford: Oxford University Press, 1993.

Mueller, John E. *War, Presidents and Public Opinion.* New York: John Wiley & Sons, 1973.

Mullerson, Rein, and David J. Scheffer. "Legal Regulations of the Use of Force." In *Beyond Confrontation: International Law for the Post–Cold War Era.* A Joint Research Project of the ASIL (Washington, D.C.) and the Institute of State and Law (Moscow). Edited by Lori Fisler Damrosch, Gennady M. Danilenko, and Rein Mullerson, 93–139. Boulder, CO: Westview Press, 1995.

Muravchik, Joshua. *The Imperative of American Leadership: A Challenge to Neo-Isolationism.* Washington, D.C.: AEI Press, 1996.

Murphy, John F. "Force and Arms." In *The United Nations and International Law,* edited by Christopher C. Joyner, 97–130. Oxford: Clarendon Press, 1997.

———. "International Crimes." In *The United Nations and International Law,* edited by Christopher C. Joyner, 362–381. Oxford: Clarendon Press, 1997.

Nathan, James A., and James K. Oliver. *American Foreign Policy and the American Political System.* 3rd ed. Baltimore, MD: Johns Hopkins University Press, 1994.

Natsios, Andrew S. *U.S. Foreign Policy and the Four Horsemen of the Apocalypse: Humanitarian Relief in Complex Emergencies.* Westport, CT: Praeger/Center for Strategic and International Affairs, 1997.

Neier, Aryeh. *War Crimes: Brutality, Genocide, Terror, and the Struggle for Justice.* New York: Times Books, 1998.

New Republic (editorial). "Accomplices to Genocide." 7 August 1995, 7.

———(editorial). "Going to Ground." 19 April 1999, www.thenewrepublic.com.

New York Times (editorial). "At Least Slow the Slaughter." 14 October 1992, E16.

———. "Full Text of the Presidential Debate, Part 3." 4 October 2000, www.nytimes.com (accessed 6 October 2000).

Nye, Joseph S. Jr. "Redefining the National Interest." *Foreign Affairs* 78 (July/August 1999): 22–35.

O'Connor, Mike. "Bosnia Economy Still at Mercy of Political Leaders." *New York Times,* 22 November 1998, 3.

O'Hanlon, Michael. *Saving Lives with Force: Military Criteria for Humanitarian Intervention.* Washington, D.C.: Brookings Institution, 1997.

Organization for Economic Cooperation and Development. *Towards a New Global Age: Challenges and Opportunities; Policy Report.* Paris: OECD, 1997.

Oudraat, Chantel de Jonge. *Intervention in Internal Conflicts: Legal and Political Conundrums.* Working Papers, Global Policy Program, No. 15. Washington, D.C.: Carnegie Endowment for International Peace, August 2000.

Owen, David. *Balkan Odyssey.* San Diego: Harcourt Brace, 1995.

Page, Benjamin L., and Jason Barabas. "Foreign Policy Gaps between Citizens and Leaders." *International Studies Quarterly* 44 (September 2000): 339–364.

Parker, Geoffrey. "Early Modern Europe." In *The Laws of War: Constraints on Warfare in the Western World,* edited by Michael Howard, George J. Andreopoulos, and Mark R. Shulman, 40–58. New Haven: Yale University Press, 1994.

Paust, Jordan J., M. Cherif Bassiouni, Sharon A. Williams, Michael Scharf, Jimmy Gurule, and Bruce Zagaris. *International Criminal Law: Cases and Materials.* Durham, NC: Carolina Academic Press, 1996.

Petraeus, David. "Military Influence and the Post-Vietnam Use of Force." *Armed Forces and Society* 15 (summer 1989): 489–505.

Pfaff, William. *The Wrath of Nations: Civilization and the Furies of Nationalism.* New York: Touchstone Books, 1993.

———. "Land War in Kosovo?" *New York Review of Books* 46 (6 May 1999): 20–21.

Philpott, Daniel. "On the Cusp of Sovereignty: Lessons from the Sixteenth Century." In *Sovereignty at the Crossroads?* Edited by Luis E. Lugo, 37–62. Lanham, MD: Rowman & Littlefield, 1996.

Pirnie, Bruce R., and William E. Simons. *Soldiers for Peace: An Operational Typology.* Prepared for the Office of the Secretary of Defense. Santa Monica, CA: Rand, 1996.

———. *Soldiers for Peace: Critical Operational Issues.* Prepared for the Office of the Secretary of Defense. Santa Monica, CA: Rand, 1996.

Posen, Barry R., and Andrew L. Ross. "Competing Visions for U.S. Grand Strategy." In *America's Strategic Choices,* edited by Michael E. Brown, Owen R. Cote, Jr., Sean M. Lynn-Jones, and Steven E. Miller, 1–49. Cambridge, MA: MIT Press, 1997.

Powell, Colin L. "Why Generals Get Nervous." *New York Times,* 8 October 1992, A35.

Powell, Colin, with Joseph E. Persico. *My American Journey.* New York: Random House, 1995.

Prunier, Gerard. *The Rwanda Crisis: History of a Genocide.* New York: Columbia University Press, 1997.

———. "The Great Lakes Crisis." *Current History* 96 (May 1997): 193–199.

Radin, Max. "Justice at Nuremberg." *Foreign Affairs* 24 (April 1946): 369–384.

Ramsey, Paul. *The Just War.* Lanham, MD: University Press of America, 1983.

Reich, Walter. "Unbelievable Horrors That Some Want to Deny." *Philadelphia Inquirer,* 16 April 2000, D7.

Reisman, W. Michael, and Chris T. Antoniou, eds. *The Laws of War: A Comprehensive Collection of Primary Documents on International Laws Governing Armed Conflict.* New York: Vintage Books, 1994.

Rieff, David. *Slaughterhouse: Bosnia and the Failure of the West.* New York: Simon & Schuster, 1995.

———. "The Humanitarian Trap." *World Policy Journal* 12 (winter 1995–96): 1–11.

———. "Camped Out." *New Republic,* 25 November 1996, 26–28.

Riemer, Neal, ed. *Protection against Genocide: Mission Impossible?* Westport, CT: Praeger, 2000.

Roberts, Adam. "From San Francisco to Sarajevo." *Survival* 37 (winter 1995–96): 7–28.

———. *Humanitarian Action in War.* Aldelphi Paper 305. London: Oxford University Press for the IISS, 1996.

———. "NATO's 'Humanitarian War' over Kosovo." *Survival* 41 (autumn 1999): 102–123.

Rodman, Peter W. "The Fallout from Kosovo." *Foreign Affairs* 78 (July/August 1999): 45–51.

Rohde, David. *End Game: The Betrayal and Fall of Srebrenica, Europe's Worst Massacre since World War II.* New York: Farrar, Strauss & Giroux, 1997.

———. "Kosovo Seething." *Foreign Affairs* 79 (May/June 2000): 65–79.

———. "Jury in New York Orders Bosnian Serb to Pay Billions." *New York Times,* 26 September 2000, www.nytimes.com (accessed 6 October 2000).

Rosenau, James N. *Turbulence in World Politics: A Theory of Change and Continuity.* Princeton: Princeton University Press, 1990.

———. *Along the Domestic Foreign Frontier: Exploring Governance in a Turbulent World.* Cambridge: Cambridge University Press, 1997.

Rothchild, Donald, and David A. Lake. "Continuing Fear: The Management of Transnational Ethnic Conflict." In *The International Spread of Ethnic Conflict: Fear, Diffusion, and Escalation,* edited by David A. Lake and Donald Rothchild, 203–226. Princeton: Princeton University Press, 1998.

Rothgeb, John M. Jr. *Defining Power: Influence and Force in the Contemporary International System.* New York: St. Martin's Press, 1993.

Rubin, Trudy. "Gen. Powell's Perplexing Policy." *Philadelphia Inquirer,* 22 September 1995, A23.

Rudasingwa, Dr. Theogene, Ambassador of Rwanda to the United States. *Genocide and Crimes against Humanity: Early Warning and Prevention.* At the United States Holocaust Memorial Museum, Washington, D.C., 9 December 1998.

Safire, William. "General Shilly-Shali." *New York Times,* 21 April 1994, A19.

Schabas, William. *Special Report: The Genocide Convention at Fifty.* 7 January 1999, www.usip.org (accessed 25 June 2000).

————. *Genocide in International Law.* Cambridge: Cambridge University Press, 2000.

Scheffer, David J. "International Judicial Intervention." *Foreign Policy* 102 (spring 1996): 34–51.

————, U.S. Ambassador-at-Large for War Crimes Issues. "The United States: Measures to Prevent Genocide and Other Atrocities." Address at the Conference on "Genocide and Crimes against Humanity: Early Warning and Prevention." The Holocaust Memorial Museum, Washington, D.C., 10 December 1998.

Scherrer, Christian P. "Preventing Genocide: The Role of the International Community." Prevent Genocide International, www.preventgenocide.org (accessed 1 April 2000).

Schlesinger, Arthur Jr. "Back to the Womb? Isolationism's Renewed Threat." *Foreign Affairs* 74 (July/August 1995): 2–8.

Schmidt, Markus. "Treaty-Based Human Rights Complaints Procedures in the UN: Remedy or Mirage for Victims of Human Rights Violations?" *Human Rights* 2 (spring 1998): 13–18.

Schmitt, Eric, and Michael R. Gordon. "British Pressing Allies to Deploy Ground Troops." *New York Times,* 18 May 1999, A1, A8.

Scully, Gerald W. "Dept. of Gee, Now That You Mention It: Genocide Is Bad for the Economy." *New York Times,* 14 December 1997, sec. 4, p. 7.

Seiple, Chris. *The U.S. Military/NGO Relationship in Humanitarian Interventions.* Carlisle Barracks, PA: Peacekeeping Institute; Center for Strategic Leadership, U.S. Army War College, 1996.

Sells, Michael A. *The Bridge Betrayed: Religion and Genocide in Bosnia.* Berkeley: University of California Press, 1996.

Sharp, Jane M. O. "Dayton Report Card." *International Security* 22 (winter 1997/98): 101–137.

Shultz, George P. "Terrorism and the Modern World." Address before the Park Avenue Synagogue in New York City, 25 October 1984. *Department of State Bulletin* 84 (December 1984): 14–17.

————. *Turmoil and Triumph: My Years as Secretary of State.* New York: Charles Scribner's Sons, 1993.

Silber, Laura, and Allan Little. *Yugoslavia: Death of a Nation.* New York: Penguin Books, 1997.

Simon, Douglas W. "The Evolution of the International System and Its Impact on Protection against Genocide." In *Protection against Genocide: Mission Impossible?,* edited by Neal Riemer, 17–39. Westport, CT: Praeger, 2000.

Simon, Thomas W. "Grading Harms: Giving Genocide Its Due." Paper presented at the International Symposium on Contemporary Forms of Genocide, University of Nebraska-Lincoln, 15–16 April 1996.

Singer, Max, and Aaron Wildavsky. *The Real World Order: Zones of Peace/Zone of Turmoil.* Chatham, NJ: Chatham House, 1993.

Slomanson, William R. *Fundamental Perspectives on International Law.* St. Paul, MN: West, 1990.

Smith, Bradley F. *The Road to Nuremberg.* New York: Basic Books, 1981.

Smith, Michael J. *Realism from Weber to Kissinger.* Baton Rouge: Louisiana State University Press, 1986.

Smith, Roger W. "Human Destructiveness and Politics: The Twentieth Century as an Age of Genocide." In *Genocide and the Modern Age: Etiology and Case Studies of Mass Death,* edited by Isidor Wallimann and Michael N. Dobkowski, 21–39. Syracuse, NY: Syracuse University Press, 2000.

Sohn, Louis B., and Thomas Buergenthal. *International Protection of Human Rights.* Indianapolis, IN: Bobbs-Merrill, 1973.

Stanley Foundation. "Problems and Prospects for Humanitarian Intervention." Report of the Thirty-Fifth United Nations of the Next Decade Conference, Vail, Colorado, 11–16 June 2000.

Steel, Ronald. *Temptations of a Superpower.* Cambridge, MA: Harvard University Press, 1995.

Stevenson, Charles A. "The Evolving Clinton Doctrine on the Use of Force." *Armed Forces and Society* 22 (summer 1996): 511–535.

Stiglitz, Joseph E., and Lyn Squire. "International Development: Is It Possible?" *Foreign Policy* 110 (spring 1998): 138–151.

Stimson, Henry L., and McGeorge Bundy. *On Active Service in Peace and War.* New York: Harper & Brothers, 1947.

Stimson, Henry L. "The Nuremberg Trial: Landmark in Law." *Foreign Affairs* 25 (January 1947): 179–189.

Stone, John. "Air-Power, Land-Power and the Challenge of Ethnic Conflict." *Civil Wars* 2 (autumn 1999): 26–42.

Stremlau, John. *People in Peril: Human Rights, Humanitarian Action, and Preventing Deadly Conflict.* Report to the Carnegie Commission on Preventing Deadly Conflict, May 1998. New York: Carnegie Corporation, 1998.

Strozier, Charles B., and Michael Flynn, eds. *Genocide, War, and Human Survival.* Lanham, MD: Rowman & Littlefield, 1996.

Summers, Colonel Harry G. Jr. *On Strategy: A Critical Analysis of the Vietnam War.* New York: Dell, 1984.

———. *On Strategy II: A Critical Analysis of the Gulf War.* New York: Dell, 1992.

Sutton, Robert I. "Managing Organizational Death." In *Readings in Organizational Decline,* edited by Kim S. Cameron, Robert I. Sutton, and David A. Whetten, 381–396. Cambridge, MA: Ballinger, 1988.

Tal, Uriel. "On the Study of the Holocaust and Genocide." In *The Nazi Holocaust.* Vol. 1: *Perspectives on the Holocaust,* edited by Michael R. Marrus, 179–224. Westport, CT: Meckler, 1989.

Talentino, Andrea Kathryn. "Bosnia," and "Rwanda." In *The Costs of Conflict: Prevention and Cure in the Global Arena*, edited by Michael E. Brown and Richard N. Rosecrance, 25–52, 53–73. Lanham, MD: Rowman & Littlefield, 1999.

Taras, Raymond C., and Rajat Ganguly. *Understanding Ethnic Conflict: The International Dimension*. New York: Longman, 1998.

Taylor, Telford. *Nuremberg and Vietnam: An American Tragedy*. New York: New York Times, 1970.

———. *The Anatomy of the Nuremberg Trials*. New York: Alfred A Knopf, 1992.

Taylor, William J. Jr., and David H. Petaeus. "The Legacy of Vietnam for the U.S. Military." In *Democracy, Strategy, and Vietnam: Implications for American Policymaking*, edited by George K. Osborn, Asa A. Clark IV, Daniel J. Kaufman, and Douglas E. Lute, 249–268. Lexington, MD: Lexington Books, 1987.

Thompson, Mark. "Generals for Hire." *Time*, 15 January 1996, 34–36.

Totten, Samuel, and William S. Parsons. "Introduction." In *Century of Genocide: Eyewitness Accounts and Critical Views*, edited by Samuel Totten, William S. Parsons, and Israel W. Charney, xxi–xxxiv. New York: Garland Publishing, 1997.

Trueheart, Charles. "Journalists Take Aim at Policymakers: In Europe and U.S., Media Mirror Mood." *Washington Post*, 21 July 1995, A27.

Truman, Harry S. "Message to Congress Transmitting First Annual Report on U.S. Participation in the United Nations, 5 February 1947." In *Public Papers of the Presidents: Harry S. Truman, 1947*, 121–122. Washington, D.C.: U.S. Government Printing Office, 1963.

Tucker, Neely. "Nations Are Accused of Downplaying Massacre in Rwanda." *Philadelphia Inquirer*, 1 April 1999, A12.

United Nations. *The United Nations and Human Rights, 1945–1995*. UN Blue Books Series, vol. 7. New York: Department of Public Information, 1995.

———. *The United Nations and Rwanda, 1993–1996*. UN Blue Books Series, vol. 10. New York: Department of Public Information, 1996.

———. *The Blue Helmets: A Review of United Nations Peace-keeping*. 3rd ed. New York: Department of Public Information, 1996.

———. "Kofi Annan Emphasizes Commitment to Enabling UN Never Again to Fail in Protecting Civilian Population from Genocide or Mass Slaughter." Press Release, SG/SM/7263/AFR/196 (16 December 1999).

———. *Report of the Panel on United Nations Peace Operations* (Brahimi Report), 17 August 2000, www.un.org (accessed 1 September 2000).

UN Commission on Human Rights. *Resolution 1995/89 "Situation of Human Rights in the Republic of Bosnia and Herzegovina, the Republic of Croatia and the Federal Republic of Yugoslavia (Serbia and Montenegro)*," 8 March 1995.

UNHCR. *The State of the World's Refugees, 1997–98: A Humanitarian Agenda*. Oxford: Oxford University Press, 1997.

UN Security Council. *Final Report of the Commission of Experts Established Pursuant to Security Council Resolution 780 (1992)*. UN Document S/1994/674, 27 May 1994.

Urquhart, Brian. "For a UN Volunteer Military Force." *New York Review of Books* 40 (10 June 1993): 3–4.

———. "In the Name of Humanity." *New York Review of Books* 47 (27 April 2000): 19–22.

———. "Some Thoughts on Sierra Leone." *New York Review of Books* 47 (15 June 2000): 20.

U.S. Department of State. "Erasing History: Ethnic Cleansing in Kosovo." (May 1999):

Vaccaro, J. Matthew. "The Politics of Genocide: Peacekeeping and Disaster Relief in Rwanda." In *UN Peacekeeping, American Policy, and the Uncivil Wars of the 1990s,* edited by William J. Durch, 367–407. New York: St. Martin's Press, 1996.

Vayrynen, Raimo. "Introduction," and "Norms, Compliance, and Enforcement in Global Governance." In *Globalization and Global Governance,* edited by Raimo Vayrynen, xi–xiv, 25–46. Lanham, MD: Rowman & Littlefield, 1999.

Vrazo, Fawn. "Milosevic, Four Aides Indicted." *Philadelphia Inquirer,* 28 May 1999, A1.

Wallimann, Isidor, and Michael N. Dobkowski, eds. *Genocide and the Modern Age: Etiology and Case Studies of Mass Death.* Syracuse, NY: Syracuse University Press, 2000.

Walzer, Michael. *Just and Unjust Wars: A Moral Argument with Historical Illustrations.* 2nd ed. New York: Basic Books, 1992.

———. *Thick and Thin: Moral Argument at Home and Abroad.* Notre Dame, IN: University of Notre Dame Press, 1994.

———. "The Politics of Rescue." *Social Research* 62 (spring 1995): 53–66.

———. *On Toleration.* New Haven: Yale University Press, 1997.

———. "Kosovo." *Dissent* (summer 1999): 5–7.

Warkentin, Craig, and Karen Mingst. "International Institutions, the State, and Global Civil Society in the Age of the World Wide Web." *Global Governance* 6 (April–June 2000): 237–257.

Warner, Mary Beth. "Echoes of an Ugly Past, Heard in a Troubled Present." *Philadelphia Inquirer,* 10 May 1998, H1–H2.

Wasserstein, Bernard. *Britain and the Jews of Europe, 1939–1945.* Oxford: Clarendon Press, 1979.

Waters, Malcolm. *Globalization.* London: Routledge, 1995.

Wedgwood, Ruth. "Fiddling in Rome: America and the International Criminal Court." *Foreign Affairs* 77 (November/December 1998): 20–24.

Weinberger, Caspar W. "The Uses of Military Power." *Defense* (January 1985): 2–11.

Weiner, Myron. "Security, Stability, and International Migration." *International Security* 17 (winter 1992–93): 91–126.

Weiss, Thomas G., and Cindy Collins. *Humanitarian Challenges and Intervention: World Politics and the Dilemmas of Help.* Boulder, CO: Westview Press, 1996.

Weiss, Thomas G. *Military-Civilian Interactions: Intervening in Humanitarian Crises.* Lanham, MD: Rowman & Littlefield, 1999.

White House. *Presidential Directive Decision 25: The Clinton Administration's Policy on Reforming Multilateral Peace Operations,* May 1994.

———. *A National Security Strategy for a New Century.* (1997): www.whitehouse.gov.

Whitney, Craig R., and Eric Schmitt. "NATO Had Signs Its Strategy Would Fail Kosovars." *New York Times,* 1 April 1999, A1, A12.

Whitney, Craig R. "Confident in Their Bombs, Allies Still Plan for Winter." *New York Times,* 5 May 1999, A9.

Wiesel, Elie. "Some Words for Children of Survivors: A Message to the Second Generation." In *The Holocaust Forty Years After,* edited by Marcia Littell, Richard Libowitz, and Evelyn Bodek Rosen, 7–17. Lewiston, NY: Edwin Mellen Press, 1989.

Williams, Michael C. *Civil-Military Relations and Peacekeeping.* Adelphi Paper 321. Oxford: Oxford University Press/International Institute for Strategic Studies, 1998.

Winter, Roger. "Never Again—Again." Web page of the U.S. Committee for Refugees, www.refugees.org (February 1999).

Wippman, David. "Can an International Criminal Court Prevent and Punish Genocide?" In *Protection against Genocide: Mission Impossible?,* edited by Neal Riemer, 85–104. Westport, CT: Praeger, 2000.

Wittkopf, Eugene. "What Americans Really Think about Foreign Policy." *Washington Quarterly* 19 (summer 1996): 91–106.

Woodward, Bob. *The Commanders.* New York: Simon & Schuster, 1991.

———. *The Choice.* New York: Simon & Schuster, 1996.

Woodward, Susan. L. *Balkan Tragedy: Chaos and Dissolution after the Cold War.* Washington: Brookings Institution, 1995.

World Bank. *Global Economic Prospects and the Developing Countries, 1997.* Washington: World Bank, 1997.

Wyman, David S. *The Abandonment of the Jews: America and the Holocaust, 1941–1945.* New York: New Press, 1998.

Yacoubian, George S. Jr. "Reconciling the Causation of Genocide: A Theoretical Perspective on the Armenian Tragedy." Paper presented at the International Symposium on Contemporary Forms of Genocide, University of Nebraska-Lincoln, 15–16 April 1996.

Zartman, I.W. *Collapsed States.* Boulder, CO: Lynne Reinner, 1995.

Zimmermann, Warren. "The Last Ambassador: A Memoir of the Collapse of Yugoslavia." *Foreign Affairs* 74 (March/April 1996): 2–20.

———. *Origins of a Catastrophe: Yugoslavia and Its Destroyers—America's Last Ambassador Tells What Happened and Why.* New York: Times Books, 1996.

———. "Milosevic's Final Solution." *New York Review of Books* 46 (10 June 1999): 41–43.

Index